The House of My Friends

In memoriam: Bob and Beryl Rendell

The House of
My Friends

Memories and Reflections

Eric James

continuum
LONDON • NEW YORK

Continuum

The Tower Building	15 East 26th Street
11 York Road	New York
London SE1 7NX	NY 10010

www.continuumbooks.com

First published 2003

British Library Cataloguing-in-Publication Data
A catalogue record for this book is available from the British Library.

ISBN 08264–7062–9 (hardback)

Typeset by RefineCatch Limited
Printed and bound by
MPG Books Ltd, Bodmin, Cornwall

Contents

Introduction

I have called my book *The House of My Friends* for several reasons. Friend-ship has always been of huge importance to me: the subject of friendship and the friends themselves.

I have also wanted this collection to form a kind of autobiography: covering the fifty years of my ordained ministry, which I celebrated at Michaelmas 2002.

Several of the chapters are biographical studies of very different people whom I have so loved and admired that I have felt them to be my friends: though some of them were dead long before I was born.

'The house of my friends' has also a very particular meaning. When, as Director of the charity Christian Action, I agreed to work alongside the Archbishop's Commission on Urban Priority Areas – which produced the report 'Faith in the City' – I tried, unsuccessfully, to find an empty vicarage to live in within inner London. The cost of accommodation would otherwise have been prohibitive. Eventually, one of the members of the Christian Action Council and his wife bought a house in Ken-nington, inner South London, in which I have lived now for over twenty years. Alas, my benefactors are both now dead, but I shall never forget their generosity and friendship. They have enabled my ministry to others; and I still think of where I live as literally 'The house of my friends'.

But there is another more painful meaning to the title. It comes from a verse in the book of the prophet Zechariah:

And one shall say unto him, What are these wounds in thine hands? Then he shall answer, Those with which I was wounded in the house of my friends. (13.6)

I am thankful for my fifty years of ordained ministry; but they have not been 'all smiles'. And I didn't expect them to be – in the steps of him who walked the Way of the Cross.

But what I wasn't prepared for was – at the beginning of 1970 – the experience of betrayal *within the Church*; within the 'house of my friends', and at a high level. The details do not matter now. It's important to remember always that there is a cost to telling the truth. It is significant that the words 'the house of my friends' are the words of a prophet; and if you're sometimes called to be a prophet you must not expect to remain one of the crowd, or to retain all your friends.

I should also record what happened when I delivered the Eric Abbott Memorial Lecture on 'Spirituality, Shakespeare and Royalty' in Westminster Abbey in 1998. The BBC asked for a copy of the lecture before it was delivered. They promised to keep it under embargo until it had been delivered. Their promise was broken, and my house was besieged by the media *before* I had delivered the lecture, all of them maintaining I was going to say – as a Chaplain to H.M. the Queen – that I believe in an elected monarchy. That is not what I was going to say, as those who read the lecture (now Chapter 12 of this book) will see.

After the lecture, I was asked to answer my accusers on BBC's *Newsnight*. Jeremy Paxman began, 'You have said in Westminster Abbey this evening that you believe in an elected monarchy.' 'Show me where I have said that in my manuscript,' I replied. But it was no good. The media were determined to maintain I had said what I did *not* say. An elected monarchy was 'news': what I actually said was not news! Yes. There is a cost to telling the truth.

But, in the end, 'The House of My Friends' is not simply in this world – as my final chapter 'The spiritual care of the elderly' makes clear. The great preacher and Dean of St Paul's, John Donne, speaks of 'that house, where there shall be no darkness nor dazzling, but one equal light; no noise nor silence, but one equal music; no fears nor hopes, but one equal possession; no ends nor beginnings, but one equal eternity; in the habitations of thy majesty and thy glory, world without end'.

Yes. 'Bring us, O Lord God, at our last awakening into the house and gate of heaven . . .'

Eric James
27 March 2003

1 The house of my friends

If anyone were to ask me, 'What's the most important thing in life for you?' I think I would probably have to answer in a single word: 'Friends'. Of course, some friends are more important than others; but quite a number are *very* important to me. And if someone were to say to me, 'But, as a priest, isn't God more important to you than any of your friends?', I'd have to say that God is 'above all, and through all, and in all'; and it's in and through my friends that I think I have learnt, and still do learn, most about God, and receive most from him.

Eric Abbott, the Dean of King's College, London, where I was a student, later Dean of Westminster, who was one of my closest friends till he died, and who of all people taught me most about friendship, said to me when I was at King's: 'Most people find the One through the one: you must find the One through the many.' It was a very didactic statement to make to an impressionable student in his early twenties, and I'm not sure whether it's right to be so directive, but it was made in love, meaning, I think, 'You will only be happy if you look upon life in this way'. That Eric was right I have no doubt, and simply for the reason he states, friendship is hugely important for me. Eric said to me on one occasion:

> God gives us love. Something to love
>   He lends us; but, when love is grown
> To ripeness, that on which it throve
>   Falls off, and love is left alone.

I was going through a painful time around then, and I pressed Eric to say where the verse came from. 'Don't know, boy,' he said, characteristically. It was years later that I discovered it in a poem 'To J.S.' by Tennyson. 'J.S.' was James Spedding (1808–81), and I discovered it when I was staying with a descendant of his, John Fryer-Spedding, in the very house where James Spedding had been born – Mirehouse, near Bassenthwaite, in the Lake District. It is through friendship primarily that I have found and still do find the One. And for that reason I never cease to be astonished that there are so few books written directly on the subject of 'Friendship'.

There was a marvellous book, *The Friendship of Christ*, written by Canon Charles Smyth during the Second World War, when he was Dean of Corpus Christi College, Cambridge. It was a book as much about human friendship in general as about the friendship of Christ. It was a wartime book in every way (occasioned, I suspect, by the pain of the parting of friends in wartime) and has been out of print for twenty years.

Incidentally, I echo the sentiments Charles Smyth expressed in the Foreword to his book. 'The analysis of human friendship has not been altogether easy or congenial,' he wrote.

> *Secretum meum mihi*: one does not choose to wear one's heart upon one's sleeve: and, for any man whose friends mean as much to him as mine have meant to me, the analysis of friendship on the basis of his own experience is a sort of morbid anatomy. A man may bring himself to write a memoir of someone he has loved – his mother, his wife, his friend – and the quality of his love will be implicit on every page: but it is a very different matter to ask him to write in cold blood, not about the person he has loved, but about his affection for that person.

The time has come to make up that which is lacking now that Charles Smyth's book is not available to us. If I live, I'd like to write a book about friendship which builds on Charles Smyth's pioneer work. All I shall do now is to sketch out the rough plan of what such a book might be, and to shade and colour just a part of the sketch, leaving it manifestly unfinished.

The first chapter of such a book should undoubtedly concern definitions, not because I would want to arrive at a neat definition of friendship (I doubt whether that's possible) but because I think a great deal of damage has been done by people who have been too precise in their definitions of friendship.

C.S. Lewis, who knew the love literature of antiquity and the Middle Ages as well as any other modern scholar, and who could write English with a persuasive simplicity and disarming felicity, wrote in 1960 a book full of marvellous insights called *The Four Loves* – having in mind Affection, Friendship, Eros and Charity.

In a characteristic passage, Lewis wrote:

> Friendship has least commerce with our nerves; there is nothing throaty about it; nothing that quickens the pulse or turns you red and pale. Lovers are always talking to each other about their love; friends hardly ever about their friendship. Lovers are normally face to face: absorbed in each other; friends, side by side, absorbed in some common interest. Above all, Eros, while it lasts, is necessarily between two only.

Fine writing, undoubtedly. There's only one thing wrong with it: much of it simply doesn't tally with experience – by which I mean, of course, *my* experience! I think Lewis probably feared the erotic, and thought there was something so wild and dangerous about it – which is, of course, true – that it must be strictly confined, and battened down under hatches. He feared it getting mixed up with friendship, and therefore rather desperately tried to exclude the erotic – much as the Swedish theologian Anders Nygren, in 1932, in an influential study of Christian Love called *Agape and Eros* had tried to keep the erotic entirely separate from the self-giving Love of God. I would want to say that if God is 'above all and through all and in all' he is above the erotic *and* works in and through the erotic, as well as in and through distilled self-giving. Not only is there no need, but it can also do great harm, entirely to separate friendship from the erotic. In my first chapter, therefore, I would probably, with Lewis, distinguish Affection, Friendship, Eros and Charity; but I would certainly not divide them.

I am not a man with a huge command of the Classics, but I'd want to have a chapter that comes to grips with Plato and Aristotle on friendship, not least in the Nichomachean Ethics, and move on to Cicero, to his *De*

3

Amicitia, because I think it is quite important to observe people valuing and evaluating something like friendship *outside* the Christian tradition as well as within it. The God who is 'above all and through all and in all' works in a world much larger than the Church, and his working in friendship, the world over, is one of his chief evidences. And it would be only after I had looked at friendship in the ancient Classical world that I would want to move on to the Bible.

In the Old Testament there are enigmatic aphoristic proverbs on friendship, and purple passages like David's lament over Jonathan; the record of that friendship of David and Jonathan is clearly one of the greatest stories of friendship in all literature. But it is when you steep yourself in the Gospels, in the friendships of Jesus, and particularly in the Fourth Gospel, that you know you have been led near to the heart of friendship. Jesus called Lazarus 'our friend', and then there were his two sisters: 'Now Jesus loved Martha, and her sister and Lazarus.' Peter called himself the friend of Jesus, and there was also, of course, the 'beloved disciple'. Jesus himself chooses to call his relationship to his disciples one of friendship: 'I have called you friends . . .', which makes all his life with his disciples a kind of commentary on the nature of friendship. 'Ye are my friends,' he says, 'if . . .' 'Greater love hath no man than this, that he lay down his life for his friends . . .' So the Cross itself is to be seen as the supreme example of friendship.

There is a good deal also in St Paul on friendship – from his personal experience. Really, there is a *book* to be written, not simply a chapter, on 'The Bible and Friendship'.

It would not be long in any book that I wrote before I came to one of my heroes where friendship is concerned, Aelred of Rievaulx, whose book *Spiritual Friendship* is undoubtedly one of the great Christian Classics, yet eminently readable. It is a kind of Christianized version of Cicero's *De Amicitia*.

Aelred was born into the family of a Saxon priest at Hexham, and spent much of his early years at the court of King David of Scotland. He became Abbot of Rievaulx in 1147, and undoubtedly had a genius for friendship.

I have a special affection for Aelred, not least because Walter Daniel, a monk of Rievaulx for seventeen years, who wrote the life of Aelred, makes it clear that Aelred used particularly to love some of the monks at Wardon

Abbey in Bedfordshire – only a few stones of which remain – now 'Old Warden' in the Diocese of St Albans. As a Canon of St Albans Abbey – which Aelred would also have visited – I used to imagine Aelred calling at Wardon – at least once a year, we are told – making it, for instance, his last port of call before he crossed the Channel on his way to Rome or Clairvaux, where he met St Bernard.

At the beginning of Aelred's *Spiritual Friendship* there is a charming dialogue between Aelred and Ivo, one of the monks at Wardon. Aelred begins:

> Here we are, you and I, and I hope a third, Christ, is in our midst. There is no one now to disturb us. There is no one to break in upon our friendly chat, no man's prattle or noise of any kind will creep into this pleasant solitude. Come now, beloved, open your heart, and pour into these friendly ears whatsoever you will, and let us accept gracefully the boon of this place, time and leisure.

Ivo, in the course of their dialogue, says:

> Would that your Lordship would grant me this favour: that, as often as you visit your sons here, I may be permitted, at least once, to have you all to myself, and to disclose to you the deep feelings of my heart without disturbance.

Ivo, in fact, died before Aelred could take up his pen to write the second part of *Spiritual Friendship*, so he begins it with a tribute to Ivo.

What supremely distinguished Aelred from other writers is a daring phrase in which he changes what St John had written, 'God is Love', into 'God is friendship'; and he adds: 'He who abides in friendship abides in God, and God in him.'

A very important chapter on Christian friendship should be given the title 'Shakespeare and friendship'. Again, I have a rather personal attachment to Shakespeare. For the seven years of the Second World War, 1939 to 1946, from the age of 14 to 21, I worked on Bankside on the South Bank of the Thames, at a riverside wharf, near to where Shakespeare's plays were first produced and he himself acted, at the Rose and Globe

Theatres. In those years I found myself thinking of Shakespeare not simply as a famous playwright, nor as a figure of history, but as a man who might pop out at any moment from Rose Alley and the adjacent Bear Garden into Bankside. I came to read him not as so many do at school, but more as a sort of local writer, indeed, a local inhabitant – as a man who wrote from the experience of his own relationships, not least his own friendships.

A few hundred yards along Bankside was Southwark Cathedral – in Shakespeare's time, St Saviour's Church, the former priory church of St Mary Overie. During those war years I learnt the organ there. Later, from 1966 to 1973, I was a Residentiary Canon of the Cathedral, and lived close by. In the centre of the chancel of the Cathedral is the tombstone of Edmund Shakespeare, William's actor brother. William had paid for the expensive funeral of Edmund 'with a forenoon knell of the great bell of St Saviour's'. The funeral was probably arranged for the morning, rather than the customary afternoon service, so that William's fellow actors could attend on that bitterly cold day, when children played, and men and women promenaded, on the frozen Thames.

St Saviour's might almost have been called the actors' church. Both Philip Henlowe, the owner of the Rose, and his son-in-law, the actor and producer Edward Alleyn, were vestrymen there. Shakespeare's fellow actor, Augustine Phillips, lived along Bankside, and brought three of his children to be baptized there. A later member of Shakespeare's company, Lawrence Fletcher, was buried there, as, in time to come, John Fletcher and Philip Massinger would be, principal dramatists for the company called the King's Men. They were all Shakespeare's friends.

We do not know how often Shakespeare worshipped at St Saviour's. That he did worship there, and often, can hardly be doubted. There is no evidence he ever violated the legal requirements of attendance upon the services of the Church of England, and the lack of evidence to the contrary creates the strongest possibility that he was a regular attendant at the worship of the Established Church. (A parish church like the one at Southwark had a system of passing out metal tokens to each member of the parish, which he or she had to deliver up at the communion table on Sunday or face severe consequences. If any adult male taxpayer did not go to church regularly his politics were immediately suspect.) Though his father was a Catholic, Shakespeare and his children were baptized and buried in the Church of England, and it is highly unlikely that so well known a theatrical figure as he was would have been able to contravene the compulsory attendance requirements without attracting the notice of the anti-theatrical London officials.

To say that Shakespeare was a 'conforming member of the Church of England' is, of course, to say little about his personal religion. It is, to my mind, as false to try and prove that Shakespeare was an orthodox member of the Established Church as it is to prove that he was not. What we can say with some certainty is that Shakespeare was steeped in the Bible and the services of the Church, and would have listened to sermon upon sermon. The very works of Shakespeare are bound to be the record, to some extent, of what Shakespeare believed, in response to the dialogue between his sensitive self and, for instance, the Genevan Bible – the 'new English Bible' which had been published shortly before he was born.

What Shakespeare wrote has often illuminated for me the great and central truths of the Christian faith, not least, as I say, the truths of Christian friendship. What Shakespeare believed about friendship is, of course, scattered about the whole corpus of his writings. In Sonnet 64 he articulates the anxiety of every friend: that 'Time will come and take my love away'. Even while he *has* his friend that anxious thought is 'as a death'. He weeps 'to *have* that which he fears to lose' (emphasis added). But Shakespeare describes the threat of Time as no one else has described it. In this Sonnet, a thousand years of stone crumble before our eyes. The very sound and rhythm of the seashore and the destruction of the coast suggest the ravages of Time. The pomp and dignity of state, of position and riches – and their destruction – speak of the transience of even the strongest friendship:

> When I have seen by Time's fell hand defac'd
> The rich-proud cost of outworn buried age;
> When sometimes lofty towers I see down-raz'd,
> And brass eternal slave to mortal rage;
> When I have seen the hungry ocean gain
> Advantage of the kingdom of the shore,
> And the firm soil win of the watery main,
> Increasing store with loss, and loss with store;

> When I have seen such interchange of state,
> Or state itself confounded to decay;
> Ruin hath taught me thus to ruminate –
> That Time will come and take my love away.
>   This thought is as a death, which cannot choose
>   But weep to have that which it fears to lose.

It is the anxiety at the heart of friendship of which Shakespeare here speaks. And in *Romeo and Juliet*, *Troilus and Cressida* and *Othello*, Shakespeare spells out, in each play, a different way in which love is destroyed. In *Romeo and Juliet*, Romeo voices his fears:

> O blessed, blessed night! I am afeard
> Being in night, all this is but a dream,
> Too flattering sweet to be substantial.

In *Troilus and Cressida* there is the same fear:

> The end crowns all;
> And that old common arbitrator, Time,
> Will one day end it.
> What's past and what's to come is strew'd with husks
> and formless ruin of oblivion.

In *Othello* the fear becomes reality another way: love has moved Desdemona to a defiance of her father otherwise inconceivable. She says:

> If I do vow a friendship, I'll perform it
>   To the last article.

Love has caused Othello to renounce what he calls his 'free unhoused condition' which he would not otherwise have given up 'for the sea's worth'. On the surface, it looks as though their mutual love is destroyed by Iago's treachery. But at a deeper level the essential traitor is within Othello himself. Othello speaks true when he says to Desdemona 'When I love thee not chaos is come again.' But he fashions his devotion into a kind of abstract and idealized order and perfection – of 'content so *absolute*' – so that his love for Desdemona is more a revelation of his own need than of a real and actual knowledge of her.

When two people not yet accustomed to each other suddenly seem again total strangers we may be sure there was some unreality in their loving. Desdemona is in part an image of Othello's own creating which is at the mercy of his secret fears and suspicions. The perfection of love which he would assert and enjoy is part of his soul's desire and vision, but has little to do with the 'real' Desdemona. So what at first looks like generous love turns out to be full of self-regard. The extent of Othello's disillusionment and his dedication to revenge are both the outcome of his compulsive love of self, disguised as love itself. Desdemona is scarcely a person to Othello. She becomes the symbol of all that corrupts the world of his ideal. He escapes from reality by way of self-dramatization; from what looks like love he descends to more and more self-love, and thence to self-hate and ruin.

Othello, contemplating the spectacle of himself, is overcome with the pathos of it. In the very lines which for some people are the height of pathos and the perfection of noble tragedy, others maintain – and I have come to agree with them – Othello is indulging in histrionic self-pity:

> Oh now, for ever
> Farewell, the Tranquil mind; farewell Content;
> Farewell the plumed Troops, and the big Wars
> That make Ambition, Virtue! Oh farewell,
> Farewell the neighing Steed, and the shrill Trump,
> The spirit-stirring Drum, th' ear-piercing Fife,
> The Royal Banner, and all Quality,
> Pride, Pomp and Circumstance of glorious War:
> And O you mortal Engines, whose rude throats
> Th' immortal Jove's dread Clamours counterfeit.
> Farewell: Othello's Occupation's gone.

Even Othello's famous last words are so dramatic as to have some unreality to them:

I kissed thee ere I killed thee . . .

Yet one cannot but be moved by his words:

> Speak of me as I am; nothing extenuate,
> Nor set down aught in malice: then you must speak
> Of one that loved not wisely but too well.

In all these tragedies Shakespeare was nevertheless pointing us to 'a more excellent way' – a way in which love is *not* at the mercy of time, the destroyer.

I cannot believe that when he wrote Sonnet 116 Shakespeare did not have in mind St Paul's great hymn of love in I Corinthians 13. In his plays, human love is 'Time's fool', but the love of which he writes in Sonnet 116 is more than human: 'It is the star to every wandering bark'; the guiding Star, fixed and immutable, by which we uncertain navigators may safely direct our course; a bright transcendent Star that can shine upon – within – our darkness. In the end, it is to this divine Love, this divine Light, we have to offer ourselves, our souls and bodies, and all our relationships, again and again; and then, please God, our relationships may reveal something of that Light and Love.

> Let me not to the marriage of true minds
> Admit impediments. Love is not love
> Which alters when it alteration finds,
> Or bends with the remover to remove:
> O, no! it is an ever-fixed mark,
> That looks on tempests and is never shaken;
> It is the star to every wandering bark,
> Whose worth's unknown, although his height be taken.
> Love's not Time's fool, though rosy lips and cheeks
> Within his bending sickle's compass come:
> Love alters not with his brief hours and weeks
> But bears it out even to the edge of doom.
>   If this be error, and upon me prov'd,
>   I never writ, nor no man ever lov'd.

Shakespeare, I have no doubt, had mused often and long upon St Paul's words: 'Now remaineth faith, hope, and love, these three. And the greatest of these is love' – the love of God, supremely revealed in the triumphant suffering of Jesus Christ, our lord; which love may redeem, strengthen and indwell all our relationships, all our friendships, making them not simply human but divine.

Thirty years before Shakespeare, the French essayist Montaigne was born, and I would want to say something about his superb essay on friendship. I wish I could say to you – particularly as Preacher of Gray's Inn – that there would also be a chapter on Francis Bacon. He was, of course, Earl of Verulam (St Albans) where I am still an Honorary Canon. He was one of the great men of Gray's Inn. Shakespeare lived from 1564–1616. Bacon was almost his contemporary. Born three years before him, he died ten years after him. But his essay 'Of Friendship and Followers' says little to me of the heart of what I mean by friendship. 'There is little friendship in the world,' he writes, 'and least of all between equals.' I like his remark that 'Talk is but a tinkling cymbal where there is little love' and, of course, that 'Friendship re-doubleth joys and cutteth griefs in half.' I've no doubt Bacon was a friendly person – he erected a memorial, a summer-house, in the Walks of Gray's Inn to the memory of his friend Jeremy Beltenham. He dedicated his book *Arguments of Law*, when Solicitor-General, 'to my lovinge friends and fellowes the Readers Ancients Alter-Barristers and Students of Graies Inn' and ended the book by signing himself 'Your loving friend and fellow, Francis Bacon'.

There is to be found more of depth and quality in Bacon's near con-temporary, Jeremy Taylor; born 13 years before Bacon died, he lived until 1667. His *Discourse on the Nature and Offices of Friendship*, which he wrote ten years before he died, really makes you think about friendship. 'Some friendships are made by nature;' he writes, 'some by contract; some by interest; and some by souls.'

> Treat thy friend nobly, love to be with him, do to him all the worthiness of love and fair endearment, according to thy capacity and his . . . Give him gifts and upbraid him not, and refuse not his kindnesses, and be sure never to despise the smallness or impropriety of them.

If for Jeremy Taylor friendship is 'the marriage of souls', so also marriage is 'the queen of friendships'.

Over 300 years have passed since he penned that phrase. Any book written today would need to have some discussion not only of heterosexual marriage and friendship but of life-long commitment to homosexual friendship, male and female; and of the place not simply of the erotic in friendship but also of the place of the physical and of the forgoing of the physical. That there is some element of physical attraction in almost every friendship is undeniable. If we take the friendships of Aelred and of Shakespeare seriously we cannot avoid the subject of homosexuality and friendship as well as of marriage and friendship.

Aelred was not afraid of 'special friendships' in the monastery, which, later, François de Sales and Vincent de Paul were to forbid altogether. *There* is another important subject.

In the chapters on Christian friendship I should want to give a very special place to Forbes Robinson (uncle of Bishop John Robinson) whose *Letters to Friends* – first published for private circulation only in 1916, after his death – I began to re-edit when I was a Chaplain at Cambridge; indeed, that task was the first occasion of my meeting with John Robinson, then Dean of Clare, in 1957. (Michael Manktelow took over and completed the task when I left Cambridge and went to Camberwell, and the book was published under the title *Disciple of Love*.)

Forbes Robinson wrote in one of his letters: 'Love for one person, if it be true love, leads you at once to God, for "God is Love". I do not know what that means, but I do know that the little meaning I can see in it explains everything: "As we love, God is there: we see God, we are in God."'

No one more or better than Forbes Robinson has written of the relation of prayer to friendship: 'To influence you must love: to love you must pray.' He even wrote, as a Cambridge chaplain: 'When I desire to see the truth come home to any man, I say to myself: If I have him here he will spend half an hour with me. Instead, I will spend that half an hour in prayer for him.'

Forbes would often spend a couple of hours in intercession for his friends, yet the basis of his friendship was often also to some degree physical. He numbered a water-polo Blue, a rugby international and the first man to run three miles in under fifteen minutes, amongst his undergraduate friends. This interweaving of the physical and the spiritual could not nowadays be ignored.

There are other great writers on friendship – notably Kahlil Gibran – whom my book would need to include. And I would want a chapter on great friendships, like that of Boswell and Johnson. The friendship between Dietrich Bonhoeffer and his biographer Eberhardt Bethge would certainly find a place. Can anyone ignore the creative power of the friendship of Benjamin Britten and Peter Pears? But I think it is significant that the most profound and penetrating descriptions of friendship are probably to be found in fiction. I think of the novels of E.M. Forster; of Lennie and George in Steinbeck's *Of Mice and Men*; of John Hilliard and David Barton in Susan Hill's *Strange Meeting*; of the novels of Herman Hesse; of L.P. Hartley's story of childhood friendship *The Shrimp and the Anemone*; of Vladimir and Estragon in *Waiting for Godot*; and so on.

Forster is in many ways the apostle of friendship, yet, to use his own words, he is 'cynical in a very tender way'. In *The Longest Journey* Ansell says to Rickie:

> 'I should say you've been fortunate in your friends.'
> 'Oh – that !' said Rickie.
> But he was not cynical – or cynical in a very tender way. He was thinking of the irony of friendship – so strong it is, and so fragile. We fly together, like straws in an eddy, to part in the open stream. Nature has no use for us; she has cut her stuff differently. Dutiful sons, loving husbands, responsible fathers – these are what she wants, and if we are friends it must be in our spare time. Abraham and Sarai were sorrowful, yet their seed became as the sand of the sea, and distracts the politics of Europe at the moment. But a few verses of poetry is all that survives of David and Jonathan.
> 'I wish we were labelled,' said Rickie. He wished that all the confidence and mutual knowledge that is born in such a place as Cambridge could be organised. People went down into the world saying, 'We know and like each other; we shan't forget.' But they did forget, for man is so made that he cannot remember long without a symbol; he wished there was a society, a kind of friendship office, where the marriage of true minds could be registered.

'Why labels?'
'To know each other again.'

There is one subject which, alas, I could not omit in any realistic book on friendship. At the head of the chapter I would put the text from Zechariah that I mentioned in the Introduction and from which I have taken the title of this chapter and book.

> And one shall say unto him, What are these wounds in thine hands? Then he shall answer, Those with which I was wounded in the house of my friends. (Zechariah 13.6)

Our Lord's words to Judas, 'Friend, wherefore art thou come?', form one of the most poignant and painful phrases in all the Scriptures – indeed, in all literature. The betrayal of friends and friendship – we have encountered it already in *Othello* – is an inescapable subject where human beings are concerned. But our Lord teaches us, as no one else can teach us, how to handle that betrayal; or, if we ourselves are the betrayers (and *Othello* teaches us that the subject and object of betrayal are not always easily distinguished), how he will deal with us.

I think it is significant that one of the finest oblique descriptions of human friendship is told in the story of Mole, Rat, Badger and Toad in *The Wind in the Willows*. Who can forget that description of dawn on the riverbank? In the silence of the growing daylight, as Nature is flushed with colour, Rat turns and whispers to Mole; his eyes, we are told, 'shining with unutterable love'. The description of the friendship as between *animals* makes it possible to describe it at all. But Rat, Badger, Toad and Mole, we all know, are *not* animals. They are us!

The end of my book – and the end of this chapter – will, of course, have to be about the End of Friendship; if it ends, or if it has some eternal quality, which, if 'God is friendship', I would maintain it has. Again, it wouldn't be easy to put what I would want to say into words. And the device that was used nearly eighty years ago was used by another to no less brilliant effect twenty years later, in *The House at Pooh Corner*. I quote:

They walked on, thinking of This and That, and by-and-by they came to an enchanted place on the very top of the forest called Galleons Lap, which is sixty-something trees in a circle; and Christopher Robin knew that it was enchanted because nobody had ever been able to count whether it was sixty-three or sixty-four, not even when he tied a piece of string round each tree after he had counted it. Being enchanted, the floor was not like the floor of the Forest, gorse and bracken and heather, but close-set grass, quiet and smooth and green. It was the only place in the Forest where you could sit down carelessly, without getting up again almost at once and looking for somewhere else. Sitting there they could see the whole world spread out until it reached the sky, and whatever there was all the world over was with them in Galleons Lap.

Suddenly Christopher Robin, who was still looking at the world with his chin in his hands, called out 'Pooh!'

'Yes?' said Pooh.

'When I'm – when . . . Pooh!'

'Yes, Christopher Robin?'

'I'm not going, to do Nothing any more.'

'Never again?'

'Well, not so much. They don't let you.'

Pooh waited for him to go on, but he was silent again.

'Yes, Christopher Robin?' said Pooh helpfully.

'Pooh, when I'm – *you* know – when I'm *not* doing Nothing, will you come up here sometimes?'

'Just Me?'

'Yes, Pooh.'

'Will you be here too?'

'Yes, Pooh, I will be, really, I *promise* I will be, Pooh.'

'That's good,' said Pooh.

'Pooh, *promise* you won't forget about me, ever. Not even when I'm a hundred.'

Pooh thought for a little while. 'How old shall *I* be then?'

'Ninety-nine.'

Pooh nodded. 'I promise,' he said.

Still with his eyes on the world, Christopher Robin put out a hand and felt for Pooh's paw.

'Pooh,' said Christopher Robin earnestly, 'if – if I'm not quite . . .' he stopped and tried again. 'Pooh, *whatever* happens . . . you *will* understand, won't you?'

'Understand what?'

'Oh nothing.' He laughed and jumped to his feet. 'Come on!'

'Where?' said Pooh.

'Anywhere,' said Christopher Robin.

So they went off together. But wherever they go, and whatever happens to them on the way, in that enchanted place on the top of the Forest a little boy and his Bear will always be playing.

Some say that is unforgivable sentimentality; some that both Kenneth Grahame and A.A. Milne represent something infantile, immature, a wistful search for Innocence, an escape from *un*friendly reality.

I am persuaded that even the friendship of, say, Bonhoeffer and Bethge would not survive the psychological hatchet these days, if that hatchet were placed in some hands.

I am also persuaded that where the great mysteries of life are concerned – like friendship – we human beings will always be lost for words; we shall always need imagery like an Enchanted Place.

The rest is silence.

2 A working faith

When I began to reflect afresh on the subject 'A working faith' – I immediately hit a kind of underwater rock in the sea of faith, which could best be encapsulated in a text from St Paul: 'What hast thou that thou didst not receive?' (1 Cor. 4.7a). The more I reflected, the more it became clear how much my life and faith have been shaped by what I have *received*: by circumstances over which I have had little or no control; and, because that's true, I suspect, for most of us, I want to dwell on that point for much of what I have to say to you.

My parents – whom, you'll not be surprised to hear, I did not choose! – were born in Camden Town, between King's Cross and St Pancras. They got on a little – so they got out – of London, and I was thus born in Chadwell Heath, in the private housing that was part of Dagenham, ten miles east of London. I was the youngest of four children. We were all sent to the Methodist Sunday School, which I shall always remember gratefully, but that corrugated-iron Methodist Chapel closed down, so I became a choirboy at the local Anglican Church. And if anyone asks me, 'Why are you an Anglican?' my first answer must be, 'Because the Methodist Church closed down.'

At a very early age (five or six), my mother taught me my first notes on the piano, and, before I was ten, my aunt, the organist at a nearby Presbyterian church, began to teach me the organ. Both these beginnings in music opened a door on a world of mystery, of which the high priests were people like Johann Sebastian Bach. My 'working faith' had its roots and origins, therefore, in family, Sunday School, choir and music.

When I passed the Eleven-Plus, as it was then called, I went to the new local grammar school for the 133,000 people of the Dagenham housing estate – Dagenham County High, later to be the seat of learning of

Dudley Moore. The school conveniently began its life in 1936, when I was eleven. I didn't do very well at school – at home, I remember being called 'the dunce of the family'. My brother was undoubtedly the scholar – he gained a First Class BD at London University – but at school I did quite well at Music, English and Religious Knowledge. And another world of mystery was opened for me, the world of poetry. I remember one afternoon, when Mr Sheppard, our English Master, read Rupert Brooke's 'The Great Lover', I wanted the world to stop, the poem was so beautiful:

> These I have loved:
> White plates and cups, clean-gleaming,
> Ringed with blue lines . . .

Beauty, made through words, had become – without effort from me – a part of my 'working faith'.

But school, in the centre of Dagenham, with the huge Ford works within sight of its classrooms, began to add another dimension to my faith. My father was a valuer and assessor; we lived, as I've said, in private housing, and, politically, my father was Conservative. It was clear that my parents were embarrassed by some of my Dagenham schoolfriends, and I became acutely aware of class divisions, instinctively knowing they were wrong. That verse from St Paul says it all: 'What hast thou that thou didst not receive?'

In 1939, war broke out. Our organist and choirmaster suddenly had to leave us, and on the first Sunday of the War I took over – at fourteen. The horror of war had already communicated itself to me, particularly through my mother. One Saturday afternoon in 1936 my father was twiddling the knobs of his home-made wireless set and found a foreign station. I remember the terrifying sound of the boots of the Nazi soldiers on the cobbles of the Rhineland, as they marched in to occupy it, and the sound of their voices as they sang in unison. But most of all I remember the terror on my mother's face, and in her voice, as she asked my father, 'Is it war?' Well, it was – three years later. But the War gave me a whole series of strange gifts that affected my 'working faith'.

Just before the War, our local vicar received two refugees into his vicarage. One was a Jewish boy of my own age, Hans Kisch, who had arrived from Vienna. He had only two suitcases with him – all his clothes and possessions were in one, and the other was full of silk ties from his father's silk-tie shop in the Piccadilly of Vienna. Hans and I, in due course, sold those ties as Hans' only capital. His father and mother never appeared. Hans was often, therefore, a sad lad; but my friendship with him was my first experience of passionate friendship: of the kind of friendship which you live for, and live on. Friendship became central for the rest of my life to my 'working faith': the possibility of friendship and the realization of it.

The other refugee our vicar invited into his home was a German pastor, Heinz Helmut Arnold, and his Danish wife. Pastor Arnold had been released from a German concentration camp. He was suffering from the frostbite he had received whilst working in the quarries outside the camp. His hands were raw, and had to be bandaged afresh each evening. He was a gentle, quiet, saintly person. I learnt from him about 'man's inhumanity to man', but I also learnt from his example how to respond to it. He never spoke an angry or vengeful word. He was the first person to speak to me of the German theologian and martyr for his faith, Dietrich Bonhoeffer.

On some Saturday afternoons, Pastor Arnold would go up to London to join other Christian refugees at Holy Trinity Church, Kingsway, where they would meet with Bishop George Bell, then Bishop of Chichester, whom Pastor Arnold regarded as both his father-in-God and the man who had saved him from Hitler. I learnt from that relationship something about the possibility of Christian action which I have never forgotten.

When the War came, as I said, I was fourteen. My father decided to take me away from school, and wanted me to go into a railway signal box. I resisted, and found myself a job with a Norwegian shipping firm in the City – until Norway was invaded in April 1940. I moved then to a riverside wharf on the Thames, where I was an office boy. In September 1940, on the morning after a night of air-raids, I watched the wharves we owned on the north side of the Thames, by London Bridge, burning to the ground. We still had one wharf left, on the South Bank, on the site of what is now the new Globe Theatre, immediately opposite St Paul's Cathedral.

Before I recount what working at that wharf meant to me, I must mention several other 'gifts' I received. Hans Kisch suddenly had to leave London at the outbreak of the War, and went eventually to America. I never saw him again, and I learnt – as many did in the War – the pain of the parting of friends. But soon, a soldier, John Rowe, was billeted on our vicarage. He was an ordinand who had begun to train for ordination at Leeds University, through the Community of the Resurrection, and we immediately became friends. I had a birthday and a Christmas present from John every year from 1939 until he died an untimely death in 1970 at the age of fifty. I was godfather to his first-born son. In the War, John became a Captain in the Royal Marines. After the War, he gained a Double First in Classics at Leeds. He was for a time Vice-Principal of Wells Theological College. I never had a greater friend. He taught me about worship, about theology, and about writers like Charles Williams. I made my first Confession to his parish priest near his home in Nottingham.

John accompanied me when, in 1940, I went – with great trepidation – to Southwark Cathedral, to be interviewed by the organist Dr E.T. Cook for the job of Deputy Organist. I did not get it! I had not revealed in my application that I was only 15. But Dr Cook said he would like me to be one of his pupils. He had himself been Deputy Organist at Worcester Cathedral, when Elgar would often come into the organ loft. When Edgar Tom Cook taught me the Elgar Organ Sonata, I knew I was close to Elgar himself. Southwark Cathedral was only a few hundred yards along the river from the wharf where I worked. I could practise and have my lessons there at lunchtime and in the evenings. When the Cathedral was bombed I went on learning the organ in Guy's Hospital Chapel.

But what did that riverside wharf teach me? As people were called up, I became, in spite of my youth, more and more the manager of the place: ensuring that the barges were quickly loaded and unloaded, looking after the dock labourers, relating to the four owners of the wharf, and dealing with the queue of haulage contractors, who from eight in the morning till five in the evening came to collect and deliver goods: dried fruit, mica, machinery, wine, tins of soup or spam or corned beef, peanut butter – you name it! Most of the haulage contractors in those days still used horse-drawn vehicles. I often lunched in the crane box with the men, and I came to know some of the homes of those who lived nearby, in Bermondsey, Southwark and Lambeth. Often at night they and their families spent hours in shelters – in the London Underground, for instance. Several of them were bombed out, losing all they possessed. Their language was rich; their sexual adventures were an education; their humour (not least in adversity) was indomitable. In those War years at the wharf I learnt a lot about my fellow human beings, and I came to despise class-based snobbery.

On 10 May 1941, John Rowe and I celebrated his twenty-second birthday by going to the Queen's Hall to hear Elgar's *The Dream of Gerontius*, sung by the Royal Choral Society, conducted by the then Dr Malcolm Sargent. It moved me beyond words. It was my first hearing of it, but I remembered unforgettable phrases: 'Learn that the Flame of the Everlasting Love doth burn ere it transform.' John had to get back quickly to his barracks in Sloane Square. I went straight home. As soon as I reached home the siren sounded. Queen's Hall was destroyed that night, and much else in London. *The Dream of Gerontius* made me think of the life beyond this, as also did the fact that several of my friends in my church choir – and some with whom I had worked – lost their lives. The War, and *Gerontius*, forced me to think of 'matters of life and death'. 'Praise to the Holiest in the Height', from *Gerontius*, is still at the heart of my 'working faith'.

In 1944, Cuthbert Bardsley, later Bishop of Coventry, came to South-wark Cathedral as Provost. He came up into the organ-loft one day while I was practising, before he'd been installed. So began a friendship which influenced my life greatly. He became my friend and confessor.

As mentioned earlier, my time at Bankside confronted me with Shake-speare, and Shakespeare confronted me with the mysteries of time, of love, and of the royalty of human nature. But it was not only Shakespeare whose writings fed me in those War years. I still treasure the first editions of T.S. Eliot's *Four Quartets*, which I bought in a City bookshop, one by one, as they came out: *East Coker* in September 1940; *Burnt Norton* in February 1941; *The Dry Salvages* in September 1941; and *Little Gidding* in 1942. The 'creed' of my 'working faith' is still, in part, what Eliot writes in *Little Gidding*:

> With the drawing of this Love and the Voice of this Calling
> We shall not cease from exploration
> And the end of all our exploring
> Will be to arrive where we started
> And know the place for the first time.

In 1945, Cuthbert Bardsley introduced me to Canon Eric Abbott, who had just become Dean of King's College, London. In September that year I began night school at King's, in order to gain the qualifications that would enable me to begin training for ordination. That 'matriculation' involved about ten subjects, including Hebrew, Latin and New Testament Greek. Eric Abbott himself taught me my Greek alphabet; and I soon knew that in Eric I had another marvellous friend, and a friend for life. My decision to be ordained had not really been a specific 'decision' to pursue that calling. Priesthood had gradually become part of me – it simply enabled me to be more fully and more truly myself.

Work in London during the War had afforded me various opportunities for what I will call 'oblique preparation' for ordination. I often used to go and hear Dr Donald Soper speaking, on a Wednesday lunchtime, on Tower Hill. I took every opportunity to hear William Temple, who became Archbishop of Canterbury in 1942. When he died suddenly, in 1944, I heard the news at 8 o'clock on my wharf office radio – and burst into tears. 'Was he a friend of yours?' asked the wharf foreman, standing alongside me. 'I felt he was,' I replied.

At the end of the War, the music of Southwark Cathedral soon became some of the best in London. The young Kathleen Ferrier sang there in Bach's *St Matthew Passion*. Bach's *St John Passion*, Brahms' *Requiem* and *The Dream of Gerontius* were all in the repertoire of the Cathedral Special Choir – and, as I've suggested, contributed to my 'working faith'.

I began a Preliminary Year at King's in 1946, and began the course for the London BD in 1947. I cannot say that the theological lectures at King's did much to shape my faith. The London BD Course then seemed a world away from the world's problems and from the world in which I had worked. It never, for instance, addressed the question of nuclear war, though Hiroshima had been destroyed as recently as 1945. It was people like Reinhold Niebuhr, at a conference of the Student Christian Movement in Edinburgh, who did more to shape my theological faith. Eric Abbott profoundly influenced the personal spirituality of us all.

I got a great deal out of doing a Prize Essay on the Jacobean preacher and poet John Donne. And, before I was ordained, I spent several weeks on Iona, preceded by some weeks with George Macleod, the leader of the Iona Community, and a score of delinquent youths, on Mull. I also went on a course in Sheffield run by Canon Ted Wickham and the Sheffield Industrial Mission. These experiences spoke eloquently to me, and helped to fashion a faith related to work and life.

At Eric Abbott's direction, I was ordained in 1951 to St Stephen's, Rochester Row, in Westminster – opposite his house, which was part of the King's College Theological Hostel. It was then one of the most notable parishes in England. George Reindorp, later Bishop of Guildford and of Salisbury, had transformed it from an empty shell into a thriving church with a large staff. He was a gifted preacher and broadcaster. He quickly despatched me to a speech trainer 'to have my Cockney accent removed'! (I never knew I had one!)

The north of the parish of 10,000 was admirals, generals, MPs, civil servants. The south, in large part, comprised huge blocks of council flats built to rehouse those who had previously lived in slums. There were several major hospitals within the parish. Visiting day after day the houses and the hospitals; preaching regularly to a large congregation (sermons had to be submitted for detailed criticism to the vicar!); working with a gifted team and congregation: this was as shaping an experience as one could have hoped for in one's first years of ordained ministry.

When my four years as a curate were coming to an end, Eric Abbott suggested I went next as Chaplain to Hong Kong Cathedral. It was all fixed up when the Dean's young son died, causing the Dean to postpone a fresh appointment. It was then fixed that I should go to Lincoln Theological College as Chaplain, but that, too, fell through. I went to stay at St Mary's Abbey, West Malling, waiting – like Mr Micawber – for 'something to turn up'. While I was there, Simon Phipps, Chaplain of Trinity College, Cambridge, later Bishop of Lincoln, came there looking for a second chaplain to work with him. The Abbess suggested me! I could not think what I had to give Trinity – never having been to Cambridge or to a public school, from which most Cambridge undergraduates then came – but there was no other job seemingly on offer. 'What hast thou that thou didst not receive?'

In fact, my time at Trinity hugely shaped the rest of my life. There were about a thousand undergraduates and research students to get to know; 300 or so freshmen each year, and 300 leaving. I saw them individually, at half-hour intervals, and was surprised and delighted that so many wanted to return to talk over at greater depth a variety of questions – about their past, present and future. Many of those undergraduates became friends for life. But there were also a hundred distinguished Fellows of the College whom one would sit next to each day at lunch and dinner. I received more than I can say from sitting next to, say, John Polkinghorne one evening, and discussing the origins of the universe with him; the next night discussing the works of George Meredith with G.M. Trevelyan; the next, the atomic bomb with Otto Frisch – who had made the bomb possible, but who was deeply unhappy at how what had been developed at Los Alamos had been handled. My time at Trinity was 'an education', and certainly widened and deepened my 'working faith'. The first person I had to a meal in my rooms was Dr Billy Graham, who was conducting a mission to the University at the time.

After four years of this heady brew, I returned to South London to be Vicar of the inner-city parish of St George's, Camberwell. The parish had been the College Mission of Trinity since the 1880s, and part of my brief was to do what I could to enable Trinity men to learn about the inner-city. I had a lot to learn myself! The church was built in 1824 to seat 1400. The congregation on a Sunday was about a hundred. As soon as I began to take weddings and baptisms I realized what a massive housing problem there was in London. My faith could not be content with proclaiming an infant a child of God and then leaving it to the mercy of ghastly housing, or to the huge hostel for the homeless on the borders of the parish. I was soon into the minutiae of faith and politics.

The gap between the Prayer Book – the only liturgy then – and the people of the parish (not least the young, in the large youth club we had formed) turned me quickly into an enthusiast for renewal and reform. I had returned to South London with the new Bishop of Southwark, Mervyn Stockwood, who had been Vicar of the University Church in Cambridge, and with the new Bishop of Woolwich, John Robinson, who had been Dean of Clare College, Cambridge. I had been close to both of them. Part of my brief from Bishop Mervyn was to help inaugurate a pioneer form of training for ordination by night school and at weekends – the Southwark Ordination Course. We soon linked up with the Roman Catholic Seminary for Worker Priests at Pontigny in France. That, too, shaped my 'working faith'.

The South London 'brew' was hardly less heady than Cambridge. It was soon called 'South Bank Religion', but it involved more than South London. The Bishop of Woolwich became notorious nationally, first as the 'Lady Chatterley' bishop – defending D.H. Lawrence's novel success-fully in the law courts; but, secondly, through his bestseller, *Honest to God*, which I had read for him in manuscript. Four years back in South London convinced me that the renewal of the Church locally needed to be sup-ported nationally, so I became full-time head of the movement 'Parish and People.' From that movement came both organizational reform in the Church and renewal of its liturgy and spirituality.

After two years stumping the country in the cause of reform and renewal I was made a Canon of Southwark Cathedral, with a brief to address the problems of the inner urban areas of the diocese, mostly the riverside areas. All went well until 1972; then, suddenly, I had to confront a matter that involved both personalities and principles, and that caused me – with great reluctance, and pain – to resign from the Diocese of Southwark. In relation to a working faith, let me say that Eric Abbott had once said to me, when I was a student: 'You're a romantic, and unless you have a high doctrine of corruption you will not survive'; after which he added: 'corruption in Church and state.' Well, at that time I encountered corruption in the Church – near the top. But of that I will say no more.

In fact, the 'curse' of that time became a blessing, for two reasons. I decided that for the health of my 'working faith' I needed to look at a larger world. I took six months sabbatical between jobs and visited Nigeria, Uganda, Zambia, South Africa, Australia, New Zealand, Fiji, Vanuatu, the Solomon Islands, New Guinea, Singapore, Hong Kong, India and Sri Lanka. I regard those six months as a hugely important strengthening of my 'working faith'. Robert Runcie, whom I had known in Cambridge, was very kind to me on my return from abroad and asked me to be Canon Missioner of St Albans, the diocese of which he was then bishop, having special regard to the new towns in the diocese, and to places like Luton and Watford; and to helping people in the more rural areas understand the realities of the urban situation.

When, in 1978, I was asked to be Preacher to Gray's Inn, Robert Runcie encouraged me to combine it with my St Albans' canonry; and when, in 1979, I was asked also to be Director of the charity Christian

Action (founded in Oxford just after the War), Robert Runcie gave me again the same generous advice.

In due course I became full-time Director of Christian Action, and it was in that capacity I was able to play a major part in initiating what was called 'Faith in the City'. It was in May 1981, shortly after the Brixton Riots, that I received a postcard from Robert Runcie, then Archbishop of Canterbury, from Santiago de Compostella, Spain: 'Bought a *Times* today and saw Clifford Longley on Inner Cities – it calls for a substantial letter from you . . .' I did as I was told and wrote the letter – published on 27 May 1981 – in which I suggested the immediate appointment of an Archbishop's Commission on the inner-city and the urban priority areas. In due course the Archbishop appointed such a Commission. We spent two years at work on the Report, which, in his biography of Robert Runcie, Adrian Hastings concluded was 'The most important venture of his whole archiepiscopate, the enterprise in which he affected the most people, was most attacked and most justified, the venture for which he is in the long run likely to be most remembered.' I would claim 'Faith in the City' to be part of my 'working faith'.

It was in 1986 that Archbishop Trevor Huddleston surprised me by asking me to write his biography. For nearly ten years, subsequently, Bishop Trevor and I met every six weeks to talk together, and I followed in his footsteps in South Africa, Tanzania and in the Indian Ocean. Then I had a stroke, confining me to hospital, and it became clear that I could not do all the work on that biography that remained to be done. But the privilege of studying the life of someone like Trevor Huddleston – in no academic way – is something that is bound to shape very considerably one's 'working faith'.

I was Preacher to Gray's Inn for nineteen years, and if you should want to understand my working faith in greater detail you could do worse than delve into the half-dozen books of sermons I have had published since I began at Gray's Inn; for I saw my task as not only a Preacher but also a Pastor – a kind of industrial chaplain to the judges and barristers of the Inn, working out from a pulpit not least what judgement and justice, both personal and social, should mean in our national and international society today.

Here I might draw to a close, aware that I have told you only a fraction of what has shaped my 'working faith'; but I have decided there is one more aspect of that faith which I ought briefly to include. When I was 65, I told the then Treasurer of Gray's Inn (also then my 'boss') that on the forthcoming Sunday I should be 'coming out' on TV as a 'gay' priest, and if he wanted to sack me, so be it. He smiled and said, 'What's new, Eric? We value you for what you are.' I said, 'Well, thank you; but if I'd told you that I was "gay" when you were considering my appointment, I suspect you would not have appointed me.' 'Yes,' he said, reflectively, 'that's probably true.' 'Well,' I said, 'does that have anything to say about a just society?' – which, presumably, should be of particular concern to an Inn of Court.

The sexuality of each one of us is surely a major ingredient of our 'working faith', but especially when at the very centre of our faith is the Incarnation, the Word made Flesh. I am thankful not least to those gay priests who have helped me to fashion and sustain my 'working faith' as someone who is gay – people like Eric Abbott, Cuthbert Bardsley, Harry Williams (my Dean of Chapel at Trinity College, Cambridge) and others. I have felt it a particular responsibility to do all I could to sustain in the faith my gay friends, and no one can be a pastor and confessor and think that only the unmarried can understand from within what it is to be homosexual.

Sexuality is a very important part of what I think of when I reflect on that phrase of St Paul: 'What hast thou that thou didst not receive?' To be more precise, my homosexuality is an important part of what I think of when I consider what I have received from God. It is for the Church today to decide whether it believes homosexuality is a gift from God – as much a gift as heterosexuality is a gift from God, as much a gift as heterosexuality is to others – or whether it is a perversion that comes from . . . well, if not from God, where does it come from?

'What hast thou that thou didst not receive?' is fundamental to my working faith.

3 Eric Symes Abbott: a portrait

When in July 1983 the then Dean of King's, Richard Harries, entered the Great West Door of the Abbey for the Memorial Service to his predecessor, Eric Symes Abbott, he was in the company of someone attending in an official capacity who had never been privileged to know Eric personally. Astonished at the sudden sight of so great a concourse of people gathered for a Memorial Service, Richard Harries' companion exclaimed; 'But what had he *got*?'

It would need a full-scale biography adequately to answer that question. In the nature of the case, a single chapter can only be 'notes towards' an answer. The material was originally delivered as a lecture, that I was honoured to give on the first anniversary of the death of one whom so many loved and revered in the several offices to which he was called in the course of more than fifty years of ordained ministry, ending finally as Dean of Westminster Abbey.

To portray Eric Abbott is an awesome task, constrained by specific limits. The letters and postcards, for instance, which he so diligently wrote, day after day, year after year, may perhaps be published some day, but, as yet, it has been impossible to consult them all. Furthermore, Eric himself imposed upon any future biographer another limitation. Some time before his death, he deliberately destroyed almost all his sermons and other writings – in 'seventeen black sacks'. He announced the fact with a grim yet sardonic assertiveness. He regarded all he destroyed as 'ephemera'. Whether this destruction was the product of a wise and considered judgement or a conscious or subconscious act of self-rejection – indeed, of self-destruction – in, say, a sudden or lasting mood of depression, and whether it was something done towards the end of his life which he would not have done in earlier years, is impossible to say. The world tends to pay too much attention to people's 'last words' – and acts; but although Dr Johnson said that the approach of death may 'concentrate the mind wonderfully' – and he himself tried to destroy much of his life's work of writing before he died – it may also disturb and derange it. Yet in this seemingly negative action one may also hear an echo of Eric himself saying with positive conviction, 'I have finished my course. My ministry has been essentially a living ministry: of a living person to the living. I do not want what I wrote to be given a significance beyond my life which I do not believe it should be given.' And all who knew Eric will have some understanding of what he meant. Eric was not really a writer, except of letters, and those were essentially to a particular person for a particular moment. He was a master of the spoken word. And though the memory of his inimitable inflexions and intonations lingers on, the spoken word is essentially evanescent. 'Incarnation is limitation' Eric used to say. And the creative acceptance of limitation was part of his 'gospel'. So, accepting the limitations of a single chapter, and of this chapter and author in particular, let me attempt one man's answer, one friend's answer, to the question: 'Eric Symes Abbott: what had he *got*?' (or, as he would have said: '*What* had he got?').

Let me begin at the beginning. Eric did not destroy all his papers, and what he so deliberately preserved is thus given a singular significance.

One packet of letters, for instance, Eric kept most carefully. It contains the letters his mother wrote to him, and he to her, when he was but nine years old and his mother was away at the Lincolnshire coast looking after his ailing father, shortly to die of the angina and heart failure which would eventually cause Eric's own death.

One poignant postcard, in verse, from his mother, reads:

> If wishes were wings
> To you I would fly
> But wishes are not –
> 'Have patience' I cry;
> 'Some day before long
> Wishes all will come true
> And miles no more sever
> Daddy, Mother, and you.'

Another letter from his mother reads:

> I heard a little boy tell his Daddy this morning that he had caught
> some shrimps. I wished I could hear my little boy's voice.
> I saw some children bathing and swimming in the pool this morning.
> I wished I was looking at my children.
> I saw some boys and girls with school bags over their shoulders this
> morning, and I wished I could see my boys and my girl . . .
> Oh dear! I should so like to be able to put my arms right round you
> now, my little Eric, and hug you up – but the arms are not long
> enough to reach you. Never mind, the love is big enough to know
> how right things will be some day.

In January 1912, when Eric was not yet 6, he had written:

> My dear Mother,
>   I hope your headache is very much better, for we cannot have you
> poorly.
> With much love from
Little Eric

Eric also preserved a remarkable 'Story of the Little White Rose', which he
had written when he was six and a half. It is countersigned by his mother:
'I certify this to be Eric's unaided work.'

One of the few sermons Eric kept was the first he ever wrote – in
'pothooks' – as a schoolboy.

> St Luke. Chap. 5. part of v. 11. They forsook all and followed him.
> To those three men it meant a great deal to give up all, and without
> going to say, 'Farewell', to father, mother and relations, follow the
> Lord. Yet I am sure that in after years they did not regret that they
> had done this thing. From this text we, too, must learn to give up all
> and follow God. We must learn to give either money, time, or work,
> to God's cause. In this time of war, funds are God's cause, because
> the money they receive is used to help the right. But all the time,
> while we hear of victories great or small, of huge captures by the

Allies of men, guns, and food, we must not forget the work that the Son of God, just before he ascended, gave us to do. His command was, 'Go ye into all the world and preach the Gospel to every creature.' We, too, must make, or help to make, huge captures of men for God, whose 'yoke presseth but to ease'. It was our Saviour's command and by saving you can put a penny per week in the missionary box, thus helping to bring about the convertion [*sic*] of the world . . .

Eric's grandfather on his father's side had been a schoolmaster. His father, who died in 1916 when Eric was nearly 10, was headmaster at the time of Dunkirk Primary School, Nottingham. His mother, when she met Eric's father, was a teacher. Eric's brother Wilfred, who died in 1936 of tuberculosis – attributable to privations as a prisoner-of-war in 1918 – was also a teacher. So, too, was Eric's sister Doris.

Eric made clear to his friends that the bond between him and his mother, not least after the sickness and death of his father, was almost unbearably close. And thus it was to be until his mother died – also of heart failure, but with some form of muscular dystrophy as well – in 1931, when Eric was nearly 25.

It was certainly a very vulnerable Eric who went from Clarendon Street Preparatory School, as Dame Agnes Mellor Scholar, to Nottingham High School. And the child was father to the man.

To the end of his life Eric always retained a special regard and affection for Nottingham High School. Kenneth Adam, erstwhile Director of BBC Television Services and Eric's contemporary, prophesied with much modesty that Eric would be the most famous of the school prefects of his generation. That that was so, Eric would have said, was due not least to the influence of Katherine Whitehorn's father, Alan, who went from Nottingham High School to be Classics Master at Marlborough. Besides teaching him Classics, Alan Whitehorn – with whom Eric kept in touch all his life – opened for him the doors of poetry and literature. Alan once said that he would consider his life fulfilled, and the time come to retire, if he had taught a bishop. To have taught Eric Symes Abbott, Dean of Westminster – a bishop to so many bishops – was surely, as Eric again would have said, 'enough'.

There must have been much relief as well as rejoicing in the heart of Eric's mother when she heard that her Head Boy son had won a scholarship to Jesus College, Cambridge. His fellow Nottinghamians at Cambridge were not a little surprised when they learnt that Eric had quickly joined the College Boat Club. (I now proudly possess the rudder of the Second Lent Boat which Eric, weighing 9 stone 3 pounds, coxed in 1927.) He was proud ever after that he was awarded a Trial Cap the next year. John Du Boulay Lance has written that 'at that time, though Jesus Boat Club was famous for its rowing, it was infamous for its behaviour; but although Eric did not join in the "booze-ups", he was very popular and highly respected for his principles'. Eric read Classics at Cambridge and got a First in Part I. But perhaps it was 'messing about in boats' – it often is – that caused him to get only a Second in Part II. Or was it that he was busy over too many things, including the Presidency of the Student Christian Movement in the University? At all events, in 1928 he crossed Jesus Lane to Westcott House, to be under perhaps the greatest single influence in his life: B.K. Cunningham.

I also now possess Eric's own copy of Bishop John Moorman's *B.K. Cunningham: A Memoir*, with Eric's pencilled markings and underlinings on many of its pages. Within it, Eric had placed a printed copy of the sermon he preached in Leeds Parish Church on 26 September 1944, at the Memorial Service to B.K.

'He is the man who stepped in at that formative time in our life as no other could have done,' Eric said. But what is extraordinary is that so much of the sermon might have been written, word for word, about Eric himself. Boldly in that sermon, as if he were anticipating and consciously countering the criticism that he and others were simply imitators of B.K., he takes as his text 'Be ye imitators of me, as I am also of Christ.' He agrees that Paul was bold to use the words – bold, but absolutely right! He says,

> 'When we look at this saying of Paul on its human side in the experience of the Church, we surely find that if a man is a great man, he will have disciples, and if his greatness is that of faith working by love, he will have the devotion of those disciples, and in that devotion they will imitate the master, sometimes consciously, more

often unconsciously: they will catch his accents, they will reproduce that way in which their master had expressed the truth, the words and phrases which were 'moving and ravishing' to him will be moving and ravishing to them; moreover, having seen the master at work, and especially among people, in that peculiar form of work which we call pastoral, they will imitate him again, asking themselves instinctively when doubts arise concerning the right action or the right attitude to a problem – What would *he* do?

But the end of the sermon is as important as the beginning: 'What more do I recall,' he asks,

> without which this poor tribute to the 'best-loved man in the Church of England' (as he has been called) will be more incomplete even than it is? He exalted personal relationships, he respected the self-respect of other men, he gave us our freedom – and asked us to do the same for the people whom we should serve. He gave us our freedom – how dangerous this was! How bad it was for the weaker men – and who shall say that he was not among the weaker men? But who *in the end* would choose not to have had that freedom with which B.K. left us free, if it was truly understood *in the end*?

It interests me that preaching at Eric's Requiem at King's College, I should have quoted, in ignorance, just that passage from Bishop King's *Spiritual Letters* which Eric in his sermon at B.K.'s Memorial Service quoted as the words by which he said B.K. ordered *his* life.

> It will want heaps of talk . . . mountains of talk – with individuals: and you will have to be worn out and done for, and broken-hearted and miserable and not understood and deceived, before you begin to get the right sort of relation which is absolutely necessary for the students' sake *now*, and to enable them to know what to do when they go out, be ordained and preach and give meditations; and get them to see that you are heart and soul in earnest to bring them one and all not to yourself but to the mind of Christ. Then they will love you, and you will soon be entangled in hopeless love for them, and

you will be broken-hearted again, and suffer miseries, and then the life will begin again!

Be *patient* and *wise* and *work with others*. Do not be tempted to break away, but lead all on together, or as many as will . . .

. . . Only by breaking your heart into pieces over and over again can you hope to make them begin to think of believing that there is such a thing as love. Don't mind, be miserable, but don't stop loving them. You will never regret all the misery you go through: and it is not lost, no, not one bit of it. Not one drop of heart's blood that falls from a love-broken heart ever gets lost: angels look after it if men don't, and it bears fruit.

In 1950, Eric wrote me a letter in which he said: 'My own *real* breakdown, which lasted several months and had a strong emotional content, occurred at Westcott House.' The letter continues:

There is too much love within us, and no expression of it is fully satisfying. The longing for Heaven *is* the longing for the perfection of Love given and received, and the longing for Love is the longing for death. Yet we *can't* have that death for the wrong reason. We easily confuse the longing for Love and the longing for escape and Lethe, and so God makes some at any rate of the great lovers go on living.

Eric was writing then from his own experience, his own painful experience; and he was being then to me before my ordination what B.K. had been to him before his.

Eric was ordained in St Paul's Cathedral in 1930, to serve at St John's, Smith Square, Westminster, under 'Wooders', as Eric always called the gruff C.S. Woodward, later Bishop of Bristol. Eric rarely spoke of his actual ordination service, but often – and significantly – he recalled and retailed how on the night of his ordination, when he went to bed and drew back the curtains and looked out across the river from his 'digs' on the Embankment near Ponsonby Place, he saw, flashing in neon lights on the Brewery the opposite side of the Thames, the words 'Take Courage'.

When Eric was in hospital, many years later, he despatched me to search for something he needed in his Vincent Square home, and in the search I came across the manuscripts of the stories he composed for his Scout Troop at St John's. Perhaps the example of the *Stories told to Scamps* his vicar had published had had their influence. But Eric's stories were uniquely his own. I was then curate at St Stephen's, Rochester Row – by then combined with St John's – in the early fifties, and there were still many who well remembered the curate of St John's who had been such a loving pastor to them twenty years before.

Eric was at St John's for barely two years; but to be Chaplain of King's, thus beginning his long association with the College, and to move to the Theological Hostel in Vincent Square, seemed an obvious step to all. For the next 25 years Eric was to give almost all his time – and almost all of himself – to those he was helping to prepare for ordination. In the summer of 1934, 22 undergraduates drawn from various faculties helped Eric run a camp for nearly 200 unemployed, mostly in their early twenties. He repeated the enterprise in the long vacations of the years that remained to him of his four years at King's. Those four years – including two in which he was also Chaplain to Lincoln's Inn – quickly passed. And at only 30, in 1936, Eric was made Warden of Lincoln Theological College – the *Scholae Cancellarii*, as he preferred to call it. But those he had prepared for Confirmation at St John's, and the staff both there and at King's, together with those whom he had come to know at the Hostel in Vincent Square, were in his Intercession Book for the rest of his life.

When Eric was first Warden of Bishop's Hostel, the Bishop of Lincoln was Nugent Hicks, whose wife was known to the 'boys' at the Hostel – and not only to them – as 'the Lincolnshire Handicap'. Eric inherited at Lincoln from Leslie Owen a staff of academic and personal distinction: Michael Ramsey, Hugh Ashdown and Bryan Bentley. Eric Mascall soon succeeded Michael Ramsey, and, shortly afterwards, Christopher Evans and George Simms arrived. J.H. Shrawley as Chancellor added his weight to the theological teaching.

Lincoln under Eric was not a school of the prophets, nor, indeed, of future bishops. Eric was clear that his primary purpose there was to prepare well-trained parish priests.

On Trinity Sunday in 1943, in the midst of the Second World War – which had, of course, a profound effect upon the life of the College – Eric broadcast from the Chapel of the *Scholae Cancellarii* an address on the ministry. The next year he wrote a letter on the diaconate which in future years he would always send to those who were being ordained. Both the address and the letter were printed, and, brief as they were, there is little doubt that in both of them Eric succeeded in expressing the heart of what he believed about diaconate and priesthood, not simply in 1944 but for the rest of his life. In the letter he writes:

> When we are priests let us still go on being deacons and let us deacon our priesthood to men. Do we think that they care a straw whether we have a sacrificing priesthood? All the immense meaning of our priesthood which derives from the meaning of who Jesus Christ is, and what He has done, has got to be ministered to them by our continuing humility-in-diaconate. But some priests say: 'I am a priest', and they leave the diaconate behind; it falls away from them as a discarded thing, when it is meant to be still their power of contact, because God's tool is the priest's humility, of which in the realm of Holy Order the diaconate is sacramental . . . I am not saying that the diaconate is greater than the priesthood! But I am saying that there is constant need for men in Holy Orders to recover the humility of Christ in their dealings with men, and to bring the Sacrifice close to men through the foot-washing . . . 'I am among you as he that serveth'.

At Lincoln, in 1940, Eric became Canon Abbott: a title by which he was to be known throughout the Church of England for twenty years; but as Canon and Prebend of *Sanctae Crucis* Eric characteristically treated his stall as more calling than status.

In 1945, Eric returned to King's and to London, to wrestle with the minute particulars of as complex a university institution as one could imagine. He was Dean of the whole College, whilst in charge of the Theological Faculty and Warden of the Hostel in Vincent Square.

It was when he was Dean of King's that I myself first came to know Eric. I want now therefore to write more personally concerning what it meant for one person to be a student under Eric.

When I first met Eric he was 40 and I was 21. I was still working at a riverside wharf on the south bank of the Thames. I had left school in

Dagenham at 14, when the Second World War broke out, and had been working at the wharf for seven years. Cuthbert Bardsley, then Provost of Southwark Cathedral, where I learnt the organ in my lunch hours, had put me in touch with King's and with Eric when I passed my selection board for ordination. In those days it was necessary to matriculate before one could begin training for ordination at King's or at most other theological colleges; but King's had a course of evening classes and a preliminary year for this purpose. It was for me a daunting prospect that I had to matriculate in Geography, Mathematics, Roman History, English, Latin and New Testament Greek, when my formal education had come to such an abrupt end so many years before; and the thought of learning Latin and New Testament Greek 'from scratch' was particularly intimidating.

Characteristically, Eric had decided to take the New Testament Greek evening class himself. He held it in the Dean's Room on C Corridor. Half a dozen of us sat round his large table whilst he walked round it, and us, in academic gown, with his mortar-board in his hand.

He began at the beginning, with, of course, the alphabet. At first, I was utterly embarrassed and tongue-tied in these unfamiliar academic surroundings and in the presence of this forbiddingly immaculate man. (Eric was always immaculate – to a fault – till almost his last hours.) But I was soon aware of his uncanny influence and attraction. Every word from him counted. He looked at one directly from his open round face. He had the look of a young owl – even if that owl were noted as much for its love as its wisdom. There was a twinkle in his eye and a touch of humour that helped one to relax.

The very first evening, when he made us copy out the Greek alphabet and went round to see what each of us had written, he paused when he came to me, bent down to look over my shoulder, and, with a smile when he saw that I had given a dot to an iota, whispered quietly, 'Dot not!'; and, as he said the words, to give each of them emphasis and in mock rebuke, he touched me gently on the head, twice, with the tip of his mortar-board.

I doubt whether Eric ever had any idea of the significance of that touch. It diminished the distance between us and conveyed the assurance of friendship. Indeed, it was for me the beginning of a friendship that lasted nearly forty years. There was a discipline and detachment to the touch, yet it was also intoxicating and the lighting of a fire. Much of my confidence that I could eventually climb what then seemed the Matterhorn of matriculation – with Eric as my guide – stemmed from that evening.

What soon became clear was that Eric – a marvellous and memorable teacher of New Testament Greek – was using the opportunity the evening class provided for several other purposes. There were few possibilities of general, let alone private, conversation with him at this stage; but in the few comments he made, he revealed how much he had already observed and knew about one. I felt he had seen me 'under the fig tree'. At home, I was regarded as the dunce of the family – which was in part why I had been taken away from school at 14. Eric immediately, in merely a class for beginners in New Testament Greek, made me feel my ideas were valuable, indeed that *I* was valuable. You soon felt that the class, and King's itself, was to him above all a school of Christian friendship.

When the preliminary year ended, and some of my fellow students went off to other colleges to pursue their studies, I was bereaved at the break-up of the fellowship I had experienced. I blurted out to Eric what I felt. He wrote one of his long letters to me – the first of many. It contained seminal phrases I could ponder for hours, indeed for years: 'Love must enlarge *and* contract.'

It is difficult for me now to imagine training for ordination without Eric, for I depended so much on his counsel. There seemed then, as there still seems now, a 'great gulf fixed' between the Church, the world of theological studies, and the riverside world where I had worked. I was often dismayed beyond words at it. Eric bore the brunt of my impatience and rebellion. In one of his first letters to me, he wrote:

> Fr Benson, the founder of Cowley, was fond of pointing out how much of the Passion of our Lord throughout his life was derived from the willingly-accepted *limitation* inherent in the *Incarnation*. The difference between a patient and an impatient person (giving them both their due and thinking the best of both) is, to my mind, that the patient one *at his best* has entered more deeply than the impatient into the necessary limitations of a ministry based on *kenosis* . . .

Later that year he wrote to me:

We *must* know Our Lord in the body of His humiliation if we are to know Him in the body of His Glory. And we are forced into a realism about Church-members which is absolutely 'Beauty and the Beast': you *must* embrace the ugly beast before it turns into the 'glorious body' of the Prince.

There is a personal crisis in the course of the training of many students, but I think that is bound to be particularly so in the case of theological students. It is crucial how that crisis is handled. B.K., we have already observed, took care of Eric in his crisis. When mine occurred, I simply left a note addressed to the Dean, saying I had decided to finish at King's, and leaving it purposely ambiguous whether I meant to bring to an end more than my theological training. Immediately Eric got a message to me, inviting me to lunch that weekend at the Hostel in Vincent Square and to a talk afterwards. I accepted, but I was undoubtedly near to breakdown. I felt sick and faint as I sat next to Eric at High Table – socially, lunch in a university hall of residence was then to me an entirely unaccustomed and intimidating experience. After the meal, Eric took me through to coffee in his house, and with only a few questions, reached the heart of the matter. No psychiatrist or counsellor ever got so far so fast – not with me. And I am still working at that largely intuitive diagnosis Eric made. I have never been able to fault it. This was the first major and intimate conversation I had had with Eric, but I was aware from that moment that, to put it simply – and difficult as it was to believe – Eric loved me. He said as much when he ended his letters. But the form of those letters was often: 'I should like you to read . . . so-and-so.' He was feeding my mind as well as my heart, and feeding it with material that was not part of the normal literature of the course. Edward King, Forbes Robinson, P.T. Forsyth, R.C. Moberly, Reinhold Niebuhr, Charles Williams, the Abbé de Tourville, Julia de Beausobre. I had only to raise a heartfelt question (for example: 'Shouldn't a Christian be up and doing, reforming? Is it really more Christian to be passive?') and he would respond with a thought-provoking letter.

No one can be either active or passive all the time. Over our activity, as over our passivity, broods the activity, ceaseless and creative, of

God himself. Judging our activity and passivity, and redeeming it, is the Passion of Christ, His greatest Action. All our activity is rendered temporal only; i.e. is robbed of its 'eternity', unless it is offered to God in love and by His love is given an eternal quality. Whether to be active now, or passive now, whether to be silent now or to speak, is a matter of choice, a matter of faith, and therefore a matter of risk. Even the reformer is not reforming *all* the time! He brings the old out of his treasure as well as the new. The thing is to be supple in our Lord's hand, to ask to be used, to be watchful, and then – here goes! – and behold, you are active or passive, as the case may be, and as faith requires, and then, whatever the visible outcome, you thank God for using you.

It was clear that in some of his letters – especially when he wrote of love itself – Eric, as I have suggested earlier, was sharing his own problems as well as dealing with mine. And what was manifest was that he was striving to display the particularity of love to those who needed it at a particular time whilst also, at much personal cost, endeavouring to show forth the equality of love for all.

Near the end of my time at King's, in 1951, Eric suggested we holidayed together in Cambridge. That time together opened my eyes to the size of Eric's burden. Each day he would sit at a desk – on holiday – writing letters and postcards from 9.30 until just before lunchtime, when we would have a short walk; and again he would write for some time in the afternoon or early evening. I would sit beside him, writing or reading, to give him some company; observing this routine of birthday and wedding anniversary cards, letters of loving care for other students and former students, and the more weighty letters of direction and advice that would influence the future of the Church of England. He would make detailed preparations, for instance, for the King's College annual Staff Party; but I was alarmed, the day before we returned to London, at the fearful state of anxiety the thought of returning to term and to all that lay ahead produced in him.

Yet we had much fun, too, on holiday. The then Bishop of Ely preached an appallingly dull sermon on the Epiphany to an all but empty and ice-cold Cathedral. During the sermon, a puckish Eric peeped through the tracery of the choir stalls and whispered, 'Boy, you could do better than this!' Eric – of Jesus College – adored introducing me to Cambridge, giving me, with his pink Leander scarf about his neck, my first glimpse of the Cam, of Trinity Great Court, and of the 'unforgettable, unforgotten' delights of Madingley and Grantchester. Other memorable holidays in, for instance, Aldeburgh and Anglesey were to follow.

On the eve of my ordination, Eric wrote:

> You know how much I love you and how deeply interconnected our lives have become under God's Providence. But the point is that my love and that of all your friends must now be engaged in helping you to turn your life Godwards, that tomorrow morning you may give yourself to Him wholly, and then He will give you back to the Church, to the world, and us, as one who is His first and foremost, and ours for His sake.

Loving like that – not just me, but so many at King's, and not only at King's – was more than a 'problem' for Eric. 'Five years at King's', he wrote 'have now very nearly killed me – I mean that . . . Isolation *is* great, even when one is surrounded by great love, and the only final Comforter is the Holy Ghost. It *does* hurt *sometimes*, you know, to be unmarried.'

Eric seemed to speak more and more of Death, more than thirty years before his death. He wrote:

> 'Time will come and take my love away' says the Shakespeare Sonnet, and 'This thought is as a death, which cannot choose but weep to have that which it fears to lose'. How great an advance it is then, when we learn not to fear that loss; and this, I think is something of what you mean by your quest of changelessness. Or put it thus: Is my weak will nevertheless strong enough to say to God and mean it 'Thou Alone Sufficest me'? Unless we get to that point, even our precious love and friendship here will only feed the fear of loss.

Thirty years on, it is clear to me that the curse of Eric's loneliness was in part redeemed by the blessing of the friendship it drove him to seek from and to give to others. It will have played some part in his insistence when he came to King's that the three-year course for ordinands should be extended to a fourth year in a college in the country where relationships could be modelled on the intimacy he had experienced at Westcott and at Lincoln. It will also have played some part in his refusal to delegate his responsibilities to those to whom he had given pastoral care of that Fourth-Year College at Warminster. (For each fortnight of term, on Friday afternoons, he would journey to Warminster, returning to London late Saturday.) It undoubtedly drove him to drive his body beyond all reason. Dr Geoffrey Hale – Eric's physician and the doctor to most of the students at Vincent Square for many years, who retired to Rye – has written a most remarkable account of Eric's medical history. It was in 1950 that Eric was first warned that his work must be 'pared down'. In 1951 he wrote from the White Hart Hotel in Lincoln that Steep Hill had 'defeated him' and given him heart pain. Characteristically, he wrote that he would not be able to see Dr Hale until 9.30 p.m. on the day that Dr Hale suggested an appointment. The heart symptoms had, in fact, begun in 1947. Eric was admitted to the Westminster Hospital with a coronary in January 1952, but when released was soon overworking again, with signs of angina following. He was advised to take a half-day off midweek, a rest every afternoon and a day off at weekends. 'But,' writes Dr Hale, 'I doubt if his conscience allowed him to take this advice.'

It may well be that Eric's election in 1956 as Warden of Keble College, Oxford, saved his life, for apart from a little angina on exertion he was in relatively good health for a decade until 1963.

When the history of the training of the clergy of the Church of England comes to be written, there can be no shadow of doubt that Eric Abbott will have within it one of the highest places of honour. In the number alone of clergy for whose training he was directly responsible, at Lincoln and King's, he is without equal. As a personal pastor, friend and mentor – and especially as a teacher of prayer – the same is true. Perhaps Eric is vulnerable to criticism at one particular point; that he continued uncritically the tradition of Edward King and B.K. with the very different candidates who came to King's. B.K. Cunningham himself, as long ago as 1926, had written, 'Times are changing, and the sacrificial, the prophetic and the pastoral interpretations of priesthood cannot be longer held apart.' B.K. was aware that he had been directly responsible for the training of 'English gentlemen in Holy Orders', and that what were now required were as much parochial prophets as pastors and priests. Eric was not very good on prophecy. He was exceptionally good on pastoral priests. But he once said to me, rather angrily, in a negative moment, 'I have been asked at King's to make silk purses out of sows' ears.' I knew what he meant – there were few 'sows' ears' at Westcott. But I was not very happy with the remark; and it was not simply that this arrogant schoolboy from Dagenham was unhappy to be labelled, by implication, a 'sow's ear' – by the son of a Nottingham Primary School Headmaster (albeit a most beloved friend). It was that I believed then, and still do, that in the end the future of the Church depends on the ordination of 'sows' ears' – so-called.

It is sometimes difficult for those who knew Eric primarily at Lincoln or King's to realize that when he left King's he still had over a third of his life to live: just over three years at Keble, fifteen at the Abbey, and nine years in retirement. The fact is worthy of mention, because Eric was a person who never stopped growing, and very considerable changes took place in him after 1956, when he left King's.

Eric was elected Warden of Keble when the College was entering upon a new phase of its life as a full college of the University. He went to Oxford 'somewhat grimly'; but, in the event, he was relieved that his primary responsibility was no longer solely theological students.

And when, in 1959, he returned to Westminster, there can be little doubt that the climax of his tenure of the Deanery was the celebration of the 900th anniversary of the founding of the Abbey, beginning on Innocents' Day, 28 December 1965, with the great Inaugural Service, with its profoundly human theme of 'One People', which sought to relate the Abbey to the needs and aspirations of the modern world.

The Abbey, to Eric's delight, brought him in touch with men and women of the world, and of the world over. He had spoken in his Installation Sermon on St Andrew's Day, 1959 – when he preached on the text 'Sir, we would see Jesus' – of his vision of the Abbey as a great church in which all questing men and women, irrespective of faith and race, would 'see Jesus'. More and more Eric saw himself as one of those in quest.

I remember myself coming to the Abbey to the Thanksgiving Service to mark the Independence of Nigeria. Eric had been Dean of Westminster only a year, and I wondered what he would make of the occasion. I need not have wondered. He took for his text: 'Brethren, ye have been called unto liberty, only use not liberty for an occasion of the flesh, but by love serve one another.' 'Three words,' he began, 'to sum up this brief sermon: Independence: Dependence: Interdependence.' I fancied I had heard the theme from his lips before, and the manner, but it was no longer an ecclesiastical theme but something that concerned the whole of humanity.

At the Abbey, 'craftsman's art and music's measure' meant much to Eric, as did literature and drama: not though as abstractions, but, as always, through people – like Malcolm Sargent and Sybil Thorndike.

In his address at the Memorial Service to Eric, the Archbishop of Canterbury described him as a 'much loved pastor to the Royal Family'. Eric prepared three Royal princesses for their weddings at Westminster and officiated at many another Royal occasion; and there is no doubt that this sphere of his pastoral ministry gave him a particular satisfaction. Significantly, amongst the few letters he preserved are a number from members of the Royal Family.

Not all Eric's friends who visited him were equally positive in their reaction to the galaxy of signed royal photographs with which he was pleased to surround himself, not least because not all recognized the profound theology of royalty Eric brought to this aspect of his ministry.

I remember how moved he was when in 1968 I went with him to see Ian McKellen as Richard II. He kept on repeating afterwards Richard's great words:

> I live with bread like you, feel want,
> Taste grief, need friends . . .

It is not too much to say that that sentence summed up much of Eric's attitude to royalty. He literally 'had compassion on them'. I remember also at the time discussing with him John Danby's study of *King Lear: Shakespeare's Doctrine of Nature*. Eric was much taken with Danby's words: 'In the state it is the king in every man who submits to the king on the throne.' The apparent paradox of such an equality entailing such a real subordination excited Eric, as paradoxes were often wont to do. For him, royalty still said something moral and mystical about man – every man can be and should be and *is* a king. But Eric was also aware, in as down to earth a manner as could be, that the public's concentration on royalty gave him as Dean of Westminster pastoral and evangelical opportunities that were very considerable and that it would be a dereliction of duty to ignore.

For the last ten years of his time at the Abbey, Eric was plagued with ill health. In March 1963 he had a lung infection, and in September of the same year he was admitted to the Westminster Hospital with the first signs of the cerebrovascular disorder that was from then on to threaten his working life.

His doctors tried to insist that he had a midweek break and cut down his correspondence by a third. Eric was by then aware – but did not like others to be aware – of his slight speech problem, his tiring right hand when he wrote, and a drag in his left leg. He continued not to take his heart problems very seriously, trusting to his chest pain to check him if he did too much. But he had an underlying fear of a major stroke, with the concomitant fear of not being able to do his job to the standard he believed it should be done, of having no one to whom he could turn for day-to-day nursing care if he became paralysed, and of not having enough money to support himself if he had to retire before he was pensionable. Even in 1964, he began to realize that if he did too much he became less efficient. Yet this was before the exertions of the 'Non-gentenary Year'.

It was such anxieties that made Eric look for a cottage where he could go midweek and escape from the work that came to him almost hourly when he was in residence. In 1965 he bought Bramble Cottage, at Chiddingfold, which, with its garden, was to be a place of special delight to him to the end of his days.

During the great celebrations of the 900th anniversary – when hardly a day passed without some special service – Eric was often afraid that, dragging the load of his vestments, he might collapse in procession. He was particularly anxious at services at which the then Archbishop of Canterbury, Dr Ramsey, was present. Dr Ramsey seemed quite unable to steer a straight course up the aisle, and Eric was afraid that one day there would be a collision, with disastrous consequences! Eric turned down at that time all suggestions about using a stick or having a helping hand. And it has to be said that until the very last in most things, with most people, Eric was almost impossible to help. (Even after, say, tea together, he would never let me carry a tray of dishes into the kitchen. He simply had to do it himself.)

In March 1966, Dr Hale went to visit Eric and found that by mid-morning he had already dealt with eighty letters. Returning from a holiday in Greece in April 1967 he was confronted by several hundred letters. Not surprisingly, he was soon in the Middlesex Hospital, for a month, where, mercifully, it was discovered that the slight blood-vessel clots were occurring in the brain stem, not in the cerebrum, which accounted for the fact that his concentration and mental activity were unimpaired. In July 1970, Eric was again admitted to the Middlesex. Of course, between his times in hospital he was always now on anti-coagulant and sedative pills, as well as receiving regular physiotherapy, yet the pain from his heart was never far away. 'But above all, the heart must bear the longest part,' Eric would often say, with a mixture of sigh and smile.

So, reluctantly, he retired, in 1974 – full of honours: a Freeman of the City of Westminster; a Doctor of Divinity of London University; knighted in 1966, he was created on retirement an extra Chaplain to the Queen.

Eric was delighted to have a home again in Vincent Square – he wouldn't have wished to be anywhere else – and he was grateful that a generous friend had made it possible for him to have the flat and keep his cottage at Chiddingfold, to which he went, as he would say, 'religiously' each week.

Eric was in some ways incapable of retirement. For several years he went on preaching for his friends. He took a special pleasure in the meetings of the Fellowship of St Faith where he would teach people to pray as only he could. He continued to be a 'friend of the soul' to probably as many penitents as almost any other spiritual director in the land; and his great company of friends, men and women, lay and ordained, still sought a space in his diary. So his days were almost as full as they had ever been.

People who had been to Eric for confession over many years noticed changes in him, not least in what he said to them. He was more relaxed; he seemed to be allowing himself a looser rein; but it was also as though gradually he was being released from some of the anxiety and fear that lay behind some of his control. He was better at allowing people to do things for him, like drive him to his cottage or even prepare meals for him. In earlier years there was something of the ascetic about him; now he knew there was no need to invent or impose disciplines; life itself imposed 'enough and to spare'.

I have left till last one hugely important aspect of Eric's life. When I was a young priest, Eric had written to me, 'Most people find the One through the one: you must find the One through the many.' I realized that Eric was again talking from his own experience and that it had not been an easy path to tread. He would often, for instance, quote the text, 'He saved others; himself he cannot save' as though it was a principle of existence he had proved to be only too true.

Sometimes people who speak of 'finding the One through the many' are avoiding total commitment to any one person – not because of vocation but because, for one reason and another, they are afraid of, or incapable of, sharing the centre of themselves with anybody. Perhaps at the time Eric wrote to me that may to some extent have been true of him – though all the time he was looking after theological students he had ample vocational reasons for seeking to find 'the One through the many'. But just before Eric left King's, he met – at Easter 1955 – John Robson. That meeting was the beginning of a friendship which lasted all Eric's remaining years. For nearly thirty years John and Eric holidayed together. Hardly a week went by when they did not see each other; hardly a day when they were not in touch with each other – through John's years at Huddersfield, and as Chaplain of Christ's Hospital, and, later, as Chaplain of Wellington College. Nothing in Eric's life changed him more, I am persuaded, than the loving care he allowed himself to receive from John.

It was John who, in December 1981, when Eric, in intensive care in hospital at Worcester, desperately wanted to get back to London, drove him through the winter snow and shared Christmas with him at the Westminster Hospital. John then helped settle a reluctant Eric into his new home at Haslemere, and sat with him there in his darkest days, and was with him in the many faints and collapses that lay ahead.

On Eric's 77th birthday, 26 May 1983, he was delighted that the then Dean of Westminster, and his wife Lilian, and the Surveyor of the Fabric found time to visit him at Haslemere. But it was clear that the end was near, and within a few days John had begun the final vigil of several nights and days with Eric at the Royal Surrey County Hospital in Guildford. It was John who was there to hear Eric's strong 'Amen' to the Chaplain's final prayers, and to hear Eric say, near his end, 'I am very peaceful . . . very happy.'

It was John who, in the early hours of 6 June 1983, watching the tell-tale screen that was monitoring Eric's heartbeats, saw the pattern become more and more irregular and intermittent, until the beat failed and the fluorescent green line on the scanner suddenly became straight and continuous. 'Is that how it ends?' John asked the ward sister.

We sang at Eric's Memorial Service, because he so loved it, that hymn ascribed to Thomas à Kempis with the lines:

> O how glorious and resplendent,
> Fragile body, shalt thou be . . .

There is reason to believe that Eric's body was, paradoxically, tougher than he sometimes imagined it to be. But Eric's self-knowledge was very considerable. I can remember often singing with him another hymn that he greatly loved: Isaac Watts' 'There is a land of pure delight where saints immortal reign'. One verse he always remarked upon was:

> But timorous Mortals start and shrink
> To cross this narrow Sea,
> And linger shivering on the Brink,
> And fear to launch away.

Eric, from almost his first to his last breath, knew himself to be a 'timorous Mortal'. His vulnerability was, perhaps, his best gift – that is why he so needed his scarlet cassock and his other protections and controls. *And that is why he could be so sensitive and sympathetic to the vulnerability of others – of all sorts and conditions.*

Eric's mother had written, when he was but a lad: 'Never mind, the love is big enough to know how right things will be some day.' We believe, in faith, that, for Eric, through Christ, the 'some day' is no longer *not yet* but *now.*

4 A celebration of 150 years: St Stephen's, Rochester Row, Westminster

I have one obvious qualification for writing for this celebration: age, which can take me back into more of the years of the life of St Stephen's than many could manage. As someone said to me with acid accuracy, 'Who else is there *left* to give it?' It's true: I had personal knowledge of and affection for many of the clergy who served here, and indeed for many of the laity. But as I reflected on my own nearly fifty years' experience of ordained ministry – which began at St Stephen's and for which I shall never cease to be thankful – I gradually gained the confidence that I might be equipped, through my particular experience, to hear something of what the Spirit was saying to St Stephen's at a critical time in its history.

Though I do not wish to dwell exclusively on the past, I will allow myself just a single reference to what I will call 'the Dickens connection' with St Stephen's. You will find it in the very first paragraph of his *Sketches by Boz*, which could not be more pertinent to my theme, for it is entitled, 'Our Parish'. He writes:

> How much is conveyed in those two short words – 'The Parish'! And with how many tales of distress and misery, of broken fortune and ruined hopes, too often of unrelieved wretchedness and successful knavery, are they associated! A poor man, with small earnings and a large family, just manages to live on from hand to mouth, and to procure food from day to day; he has barely sufficient to satisfy the present cravings of nature, and can take no heed of the future. His taxes are in arrear, quarter-day passes by, another quarter-day

arrives: he can procure no more quarter for himself and is summoned by – the parish. His goods are distrained, his children are crying with cold and hunger, and the very bed on which his sick wife is lying, is dragged from beneath her. What can he do? To whom is he to apply for relief? To private charity? To benevolent individuals? Certainly not – there is his parish. There are the parish vestry, the parish infirmary, the parish surgeon, the parish officers, the parish beadle. Excellent institutions, and gentle, kind-hearted men. The woman dies – she is buried by the parish. The children have no protector – they are taken care of by the parish. The man first neglects, and afterwards cannot obtain, work – he is relieved by the parish; and when distress and drunkenness have done their work upon him, he is maintained, a harmless babbling idiot, in the parish asylum.

We can be sure that those who, one hundred and fifty years ago, celebrated the consecration of St Stephen's both delighted in Dickens' obvious caricature of the parish of his day and yet recognized the truth that lay at the heart of it.

What is undeniably obvious – so obvious that to state it could seem merely a 'glimpse of the obvious' – is the immense change in Westminster in general, and in this parish in particular, since Dickens first put Rochester Row into the mind of Angela Burdett-Coutts (who was later, in 1871, to be made a baroness). There is a note to a letter from Dickens of 14 September 1852 to Miss Coutts in the published edition of their letters, which records that, 'Adjoining the Church was Miss Coutts' school for boys, girls and infants, with which were connected Guilds, Working and Friendly Societies, Bible Classes, and a soup kitchen that in the course of a few years served over 70,000 dinners to the indigent of this poor district.' One is left with the paradoxical question: would we even have known St Stephen's today were it not for the poor of yesterday – of 1850 – *and* were it not for the rich, in the person of Angela Burdett-Coutts?

It is, of course, the change from that extreme Victorian poverty to our relative affluence today which is the first and most obvious change as one looks back to the beginnings of St Stephen's. But, as I've said, I do not intend to detain you in Victorian Westminster. I want to move immediately forward to the parish as George Reindorp received it, when, in 1946, he left the navy for what was undoubtedly then a very run-down St Stephen's.

There are a revealing couple of paragraphs in F.R. Barry's auto-biography *Period of My Life* that beautifully portray part of the present St Stephen's parish, which was, in those pre-war years, within the parish of St John's Smith Square, of which the then Canon Barry had been Rector from 1933–41:

> Once across Horseferry Road, you were in a different world altogether. A few years before there had been a disastrous flood, when the Thames had come right over the Millbank area and ruined many of the poorer dwellings, with a great deal of suffering and loss. In this disaster, the then Vicar, Woodward, had been the hero, challenging principalities and powers to make good the loss and provide new homes for his people. This led to intensive rehousing; and, to the existing LCC estate, had been added a Westminster City estate (the high Lutyens chessboards) in and around Page Street.
>
> In these two estates alone there was a population numbering somewhere about 8,000 which was the field for our parochial ministry as then generally understood. Many of them were in low-paid occupations and some were living below the poverty line. There was no national insurance then, and the Church had to function as the relieving officer, raising all the money it could in Smith Square in order to disburse it in Page Street. Beyond that, of course, there was the familiar programme of visiting, clubs, countless organisations, a large Church school (infant and junior), and all the apparatus of a 'poor' parish. Woodward left it brilliantly organised and it was a breathless task to keep up its pace.

That part of the parish as Barry had known it was, of course, within the parish to which George Reindorp was instituted and which, like Wood-ward, he brilliantly organized – combined with the St Stephen's parish north of Regency Street and south of Victoria Street.

But now I must ask the painful question, even more pertinent now than my first question concerning Victorian Westminster: with George

Reindorp having departed the parish in 1957 to be Provost of Southwark, who or what has caused most change to St Stephen's parish since the Reindorp era?

When I came to St Stephen's in 1951 it was already, in popular estimation, a very 'successful' church, though the word 'success', in the light of the Cross of Christ, is the most difficult word to handle in the whole Christian vocabulary. Let us say, St Stephen's was as *seemingly* successful then as in any of its 150 years. Its large staff gathered large congregations and its vicar had, without question, huge gifts as preacher, pastor, leader and administrator, which, later, he would continue to employ as Bishop of Guildford and then Salisbury.

I have carefully said, '*seemingly* successful', for, as Disraeli once said, 'The Church of England has not lost the great cities; it has never had them', and the success of George Reindorp in no way countered that assertion. Indeed, the very success of the Reindorp regime at St Stephen's, which was undeniably mainly with the middle- and upper-classes and often with people who came from beyond the borders of the parish – from Dolphin Square, Chelsea and St Thomas's Hospital across the Thames – was sometimes in danger of fostering the illusion that it had faced and answered the charge of Disraeli.

George Reindorp, it needs to be said, had been trained in the mid-thirties, at Westcott House, Cambridge, under the doyen of theological college principals, Canon B.K. Cunningham, who had written the following revealing paragraph in a volume of essays entitled *The Future of the Church of England*, published in 1926:

> . . . the influence of the Church of England has been largely due to what may fairly be called the culture of her clergy. For many generations previous to the Great War, its Ministry had been drawn almost exclusively from the Public Schools and older Universities. These men may have been neither trained preachers nor expert priests, but they were pre-eminently 'English gentlemen in Holy Orders'. Now it is easy to sneer at this, and the inadequacy of the description may be granted, yet beyond question there is something singularly effective in the quality of a 'gentleman', and nowhere is that quality more surely discerned and responded to than by the

poorest classes in our big towns or by the 'native' in the foreign field, whether it be China, India or Melanesia. A sense of humour rooted in a sense of proportion, a quickness of sympathy, a resolute refusal to take personal offence, and an innate courtesy which, as Bishop Francis Paget has defined it, consists in respect for the self-respect of others, are among those gifts of leadership which belong to the public school tradition. When *noblesse oblige* is combined with personal devotion to our Lord and love of mankind for His sake, the resultant grace of character has, to a large extent, made up for the deficiency in professional training or in theological learning. In the ministry of the Church of England . . . 'personality' has counted, and the past methods of 'training', more amateur than even our present theological colleges, did succeed in some measure in bringing the man, enriched by all that England had given him, into closer fellowship with God through devout study of the New Testament and sent him forth to visit God's children that were scattered abroad. Life in touch with Him Who is Life passing into other lives in the daily pastoral visitation has been the crowning glory of our Ministry. After all, was not that the supreme way of the Incarnate Son of God?

I do not myself know a more dangerous and, indeed, dismaying passage in the recorded history of the Church of England of this last century than that passage, written by, as I've said, one of George Reindorp's chief mentors, but, of course, not only of George Reindorp. Simply to read it fills me with foreboding. What place does it allow in the ordained ministry for Peter the Fisherman?

To read that passage might prepare one to find that George Reindorp had little sympathy with or understanding of Disraeli's dictum. But, in fact, he was, thank God, well aware of how St Stephen's was failing to have much effect on the rehoused slums that formed the bulk of the population around Millbank and the south of the parish; and it was George Reindorp who took the first steps towards the building of a church which would be local to Millbank – St John's, Causton Street – and which would be built largely with the monies received from the War Damage to St John's Smith Square, hence the name of the new church: St John's. It is, however, hugely significant that St John's, only opened in 1958, was to be closed in 1976.

Yet by building St John's, St Stephen's had at least recognized that the localities of Millbank and Page Street provided the Church with intractable problems, even if it seemed not to recognize just *how* intractable those problems had proved, for a century at least – and not only in Westminster but in cities like Sheffield . . . and, indeed, Paris. The problem of what is sometimes called 'the priest and the proletariat' was, and is, a problem not to be solved simply by building new churches.

Building St John's church, Causton Street, even if it was an initiative that failed, should not fill anyone with great guilt; it was at least something attempted in local ministry and something done. But let me now repeat the question that we need to confront: who or what has caused most change to St Stephen's parish *since* the Reindorp era?

I have spent much time pondering that question and have surprised myself with what I now believe to be the unavoidable answer. Whatever one's politics, there is no escaping the answer that one woman – not an ecclesiastic, but a woman who, though no longer living in this country, is a Dame of the British Empire – is chiefly responsible for the greatest change to this parish since George Reindorp: Dame Shirley Porter. Hailing from a family of asylum seekers, of Polish-Jewish extraction, in the late nineteenth century, her father the founder of Tesco's and her husband its chairman, Lady Porter was responsible, in the late 1980s, for the conversion of public housing in Westminster into private housing, on a vast scale. When I was here in the early fifties, St Stephen's still had a huge council flat population. That population has largely disappeared from this part of Westminster, as it has from other parts. Dame Shirley's action may have been right or wrong – that is not my point in writing. My simple point is that it has undeniably changed the face of this parish, reducing the population to less than half of what it was in my day.

I must, however, make another point. I can find no record of St Stephen's or any other church in Westminster, or group of churches such as a Deanery, making any comment publicly on this major social change. And such silence is surely of great significance. The prophet Isaiah, for instance, would not have kept silent on such a change. That silence may, indeed, betoken a weakness in theology, but not only theology. Too often such incarnational subjects as housing have been omitted from the life, thought and action of the Church – as Basil Jellicoe, the founder of the St

Pancras Housing Society, was wont to remind the Church. (The 12-year-old Trevor Huddleston heard Fr Jellicoe preaching on 'Housing and the Gospel' in All Saints', Margaret Street, and later remembered what he had heard when he was confronted by Johannesburg's housing.)

But I repeat, I do not want to debate what should or should not have happened, what should or should not have been said. It is for me primarily to underline this chief change to the parish of St Stephen's. It has meant, of course, a considerable change in the class structure of St Stephen's – the parish and the congregation. But it has meant more. Bill Davidson, who was here longer than any recent vicar – eighteen years from 1965 to 1983 – wrote a courageous article entitled: 'Abandoned on Friday'. That is how he often felt, he said, when so many of his parishioners departed at weekends to their second homes in the country. If that was true in Bill's time, how much more is it true now, when so much more of the parish has become Westminster *pieds-à-terre* since the Porter Policy triumphed?

I am bound to treat the subject of 'Who is here at weekends?' as of considerable importance, because it raises acutely other important questions. 'What is the Church?' 'What is St Stephen's?' 'What loyalty does it evoke and command and what should it evoke and command?' 'What kind of church does St Stephen's want to be?' 'What cost of discipleship do those who belong to it think it now appropriate to pay?'

I must underline some other effects of what I have called the 'Porter Policy'.

When I was at St Stephen's, the Tower Youth Club and the Quest Club were very important parts of the life of the Church. They met on Sunday nights and on one or two week nights. The Youth Club fed the Church as the youth grew up. It fed the servers' guild – the Brotherhood of St Stephen – and the choir. 'Where have all the flowers gone?' – the young of the families of Westminster. I have loved seeing the children in church when I have visited recently but, alas, they are bound to be only from those families the Porter Policy has allowed to remain in Westminster.

Another important part of St Stephen's in my day was the Old People's Club. I read with great interest the vicar's report that 'among the longer-term residents who live here, one in four of the older people live on their own . . . Visiting one large estate in the south of the parish, members of the congregation found that a large number of older residents had no or minimal social contact, while one in ten had not been out in the previous week.' I am aware of the good work of the Drop-in Centre in Vauxhall Bridge Road; but, again, there is reason to think that many of the elderly of the parish have in fact moved away, for economic reasons, since the Porter Policy began to bite.

In my day, weddings and funerals were frequent. Now they are relatively few. It is obvious that not many now can afford to begin married life in Westminster.

But it is, of course, not only the Porter Policy which has caused such a seismic change in the structure of St Stephen's. When I was involved, the hospitals dominated the parish. Doctors and nurses bulked large in the congregation. They came from St Thomas's – with one of the nurses' homes in the parish; the Westminster Hospital; the Grosvenor Hospital; the Gordon Hospital; the Westminster Children's Hospital and the British Empire Nursing Home. All – all of them – have moved away or closed. Each curate visited a ward of forty beds in the Gordon Hospital on a Friday, and probably returned there to patients during the week. At least once a week we told stories to the children in the wards of the Children's Hospital. But it was the doctors and nurses, whose contribution to the shape and the life of St Stephen's was considerable, whose absence now is so marked and so missed.

Of course, the schools are still going, and I greatly admire the part the vicar and members of the congregation play in them. Burdett-Coutts was able to be, in my time, almost exclusively a parish school. You met the parents living in the parish at the gates of the school each day.

Incidentally, I can never forget the gentle rebuke of Miss Blowers, the marvellous headmistress of Burdett-Coutts, when one morning I had used the teacher's rostrum as a rowing boat to row some imagined young disciples across the lake of Galilee. 'You enjoyed your lesson this morning, didn't you?' Miss Blowers said to me, as she waylaid me outside the classroom at the end of the lesson. 'Yes, I did,' I said, enthusiastically. 'I don't think the teachers in the classrooms next door greatly enjoyed themselves,' she said tartly, and walked away.

The huge decline in the population of the parish and the removal of the hospitals meant that a smaller staff was plainly appropriate. St Stephen's was no longer such an obvious training parish for junior clergy; and the clergy house, built to house a large staff and opened in 1962, was soon redundant. But what seems not to have been evaluated by the diocese is the great difference in the job and role of a parish priest when the team of full-time staff is decimated.

We are nearly up to date: that is to say we are nearly ready to confront the facts of St Stephen's today and to face the question of the future. But, first, let me recount a recent incident in my experience. It's curious, I find, how often seemingly random incidents convey a kind of coincidental but relevant message.

A few weeks ago, I was invited to a flat in Ashley Gardens, to the ninetieth birthday of the widow of a Gray's Inn QC. Our hosts were the nephew and niece of the chief guest, who loved their aged aunt as much as we all did. I was intrigued to enter an Ashley Gardens block of flats that I had not entered for over forty years. I said to the nephew, 'And who was your predecessor in this flat?' He smiled an embarrassed smile. 'I don't know whether I should tell you,' he said, but then immediately blurted out: 'I'm afraid it had become a very expensive brothel – used, we gathered, by very "top people"!!' I said, 'Didn't the people on other floors know?' 'Oh, no,' he replied, 'Ashley Gardens is now a very anonymous area.' I thought, that might be merciful! But it wouldn't make the work of a parish priest any easier.

It put me in mind of another very great change in the parish since my day. Then, all you did was 'knock, and it would be opened unto you'. Now, you have to phone first. Indeed, in my day, you could often stand outside and shout up from the street, 'Mrs Buxey, are you in?' 'Yes,' she would reply, 'come on up.' Not of course, even then, in Ashley Gardens!

There is, in fact, another cautionary tale that I should like to tell before we face the facts of today: another story from the past. It happened just after I was ordained deacon, in 1951. There was a meeting of the deanery clergy one morning and, before it, a Celebration of the Holy Communion in the Chapel of Mary Sumner House, in Tufton Street; and the Archbishop of Canterbury, Geoffrey Fisher, had consented to walk over Lambeth Bridge and be the celebrant. He asked me to serve him. After the service, he asked me to sit next to him at breakfast. He had been Bishop of London and knew all the clergy. He said to me quietly, and to my utter surprise, 'You know, James, this isn't really a deanery. It's a collection of individualists, and every church is a separate show. There's Canon Smythe of St Margaret's. There's P.T.R. Kirk of St Peter's, Eaton Square. There's Brewis of St James's, Piccadilly. There's Ross of St Matthew's. There's Jock Henderson of St Paul's, Knightsbridge. There's George Reindorp. They're probably here this morning only because I'm here. They don't believe in a deanery. They're individuals proud of their own separate shows.' I was astonished that the Archbishop should speak so freely to me, so few days after my ordination. But he was largely right! And my question is: has this changed? Is the Church of England in Westminster still a 'pick-'n'-mix' affair? Each parish, maybe each priest, maybe each person in the pew, rooting for their 'own show'? And is this what the Church was meant to be? Is this 'Congregational Church' what the Church of England should be? This is not, of course, a simple question; nor is it patent of a simple answer.

When I started putting together the material for this chapter, the first thing I asked for was the Electoral Roll Officer's Report for the year. I was told that the roll totals 157 people; 64 of them resident within the parish; 65 non-resident but within walking distance; 28 non-resident and beyond walking distance. Those figures are a help, but they raise as many questions as they solve. How realistic is it today to think of St Stephen's as a 'parish' church, of a geographical locality? What commitment to the locality does the congregation feel? What local commitment can it realistically ask and expect to exercise? Do those who live or work within the bounds of the parish – people who live in, say, Marsham Court or Morland Buildings or Willow Place – feel it is their parish church? 'For anything to be real, it must be local,' wrote Chesterton. In what sense is St Stephen's now local to people – and to whom? Some would say, 'Frankly, in Central London, the parochial system has collapsed and is best forgotten.' But does the diocese – the bishop and the archdeacons – believe that? Or, more important, do they recognize and acknowledge that?

There are, I fear, several other inescapable questions. We have not yet mentioned St Stephen's Church as a building. Maintenance and repair work is a costly business. Nor have we mentioned the kind of worship that it offers within. And there's another subject, which you will not be surprised I should like to illustrate with an anecdote: the subject of communication.

When I was a curate, I was privileged to prepare Clem Mitford for confirmation. He was in his twenties. He lived, significantly, not in the parish but in Chelsea. He was an intelligent Etonian who had refused to be confirmed at an earlier age. In due course he was to become the 5th Baron Redesdale. Alas, he was to die young. Clem had come to St Stephen's rather typically – that's to say, casually. He'd just dropped in one day to see what was going on. He found that St Stephen's suited him, and he asked me if there were any old people he could visit. There were. Clem had a heart of gold. He also owned a chain of launderettes, and he spent most of his working life running it. As a result, he knew quite a lot about 'communication'. And he said to me one day, 'You know, whatever else we do at St Stephen's, we must run it like the best-run launderette. The world must know where it is, what it's for, and when it's open.' 'He, being dead, yet speaketh.' Where it is. What it's for. When it's open.

Of course, St Stephen's is not simply a launderette. You don't have an expensive spire on a launderette. A launderette doesn't have a building designed by Benjamin Ferrey, a pupil of Pugin. And it's worth reminding ourselves that the inspiration for this chapter was the 150th anniversary of the consecration of a particular building.

Clem Mitford had to decide where there were too few, and too many, launderettes. The radical question is, of course, whether there are too many churches in Westminster now. Is St Stephen's still needed? Who would miss it? Equally important, who should ask that question – and see that it is answered?

The people of St Stephen's have been generous in their giving, but, if the monies from St John's had not come along through the 'providential accident' of war, would St Stephen's have survived? These are questions which are surely appropriately asked, and faced, at a significant anniversary such as that celebrated by St Stephens. But we must not forget that, within the parish, St Mary's, Vincent Square, St Andrew's, Ashley Place, and St John's, Smith Square, have all already been closed – and within living memory, just! It's appropriate and important to ask how much a church costs – not just the building – and how many churches we need and can afford.

When Clem Mitford was running his launderettes, there was a review at the Royal Court Theatre with a super song, 'I found fulfilment at the launderette'. If people found fulfilment at St Stephen's, that could literally be beyond price.

At this point, I believe it is appropriate that I should refresh you with a poem, rather than an anecdote. It's called, 'In Search of a Round Table'.

> Concerning the why and how and what and who
> of ministry,
> One image keeps surfacing:
> A table that is round.
>
> It will take some sawing
> to be roundtabled,
> some redefining
> and redesigning.
> Some redoing and rebirthing
> of narrowlong Churching
> can painful be
> for people and tables.
> It would mean no daising
> and throning,
> for but one king is there,
> and he was a footwasher –
> at table, no less.
>
> And what of narrowlong ministers
> when they confront
> a roundtable people,
> after years of working up the table
> to finally sit at its head,
> only to discover
> that the table has been turned round?
>
> They must be loved into roundness,
> for God has called a People;
> not 'them and us'.
> 'Them and us
> are unable
> to gather round,

for at a roundtable,
there are no sides
and All are invited
to wholeness and to food.

At one time
our narrowlong Churches
were built to resemble the Cross,
but it does no good
for buildings to do so,
if lives do not.

Roundtabling means
no preferred seating,
no first and last,
no betters and no corners
for the 'least of these'.
Roundtabling means
being with,
a part of,
together, and one.
It means room for the Spirit
and gifts
and disturbing profound peace for all.

We can no longer prepare for the past.
We will and must and are called
to be Church,
and if He calls for other than roundtable
we are bound to follow.

Leaving the sawdust
and chips, designs and redesigns
behind,
in search of and in the presence of
the Kingdom
that is His and not ours.

I have included that poem here – significantly, written by a Canadian, Chuck Lathrop – because it directs us inescapably to the heart of the matter.

When we have done considering the parochial system, locality, buildings, social change, money, Dame Shirley, and so on, and so on . . . I believe that, to honour its heritage, we have, paradoxically, to forget where St Stephen's started, over 150 years ago, the 'Shape of the Church' then; we have to forget where it had got to in 1950; and ask instead, 'What does it mean to be Christ's Church in Westminster today?'

I am not, of course, simply suggesting we forget 2000 years of Christian history and tradition. I, who have received so much from the liturgy and worship of the Church, and the music and art of the centuries, could not do that. But the Christian who has been the most profound guide to *me* in my ministry has been Dietrich Bonhoeffer, who died in 1945 in a Nazi concentration camp, aged only 39 – when George Reindorp was still in the navy.

In May 1944, Bonhoeffer wrote – from prison – to his godson, Dietrich Bethge, the infant son of his friend and future biographer, Eberhard Bethge. He wrote:

> By the time you have grown up, the church's form will have changed greatly. We are not yet out of the melting-pot, and any attempt to help the Church prematurely to a new expansion of its organisation will merely delay its conversion and purification. It is not for us to prophesy the day (though the day will come) when men will once more be called so to utter the word of God that the world will be changed and renewed by it. It will be a new language, perhaps quite non-religious, but liberating and redeeming – as was Jesus' language; it will shock people, and yet overcome them by its power; it will be the language of a new righteousness and truth, proclaiming God's peace with men and the coming of his kingdom. 'They shall fear and tremble because of all the good and all the prosperity I provide for it.' (Jer. 33.9) Till then the Christian cause will be a silent and hidden affair, but there will be those who pray and do right and wait for God's own time. May you be one of them, and may it be said of you one day, 'The path of the righteous is like the light of dawn, which shines brighter and brighter till full day.' (Prov 4.18)

Two months later, in July 1944, Bonhoeffer wrote in prison:

> I'm still discovering, right up to this moment, that it is only by living
> completely in this world that one learns to have faith. One must
> completely abandon any attempt to make something of oneself,
> whether it be a saint, or a converted sinner, or a churchman (a so-
> called priestly type!), a righteous man or an unrighteous one, a sick
> man or a healthy one. By this worldliness I mean living unreservedly
> in life's duties, problems, successes and failures, experiences and
> perplexities. In so doing we throw ourselves completely into the arms
> of God, taking seriously not our own sufferings, but those of God in
> the present world – watching with Christ in Gethsemane. That, I
> think, is faith; that is metanoia; and that is how one becomes a man
> and a Christian. How can success make us arrogant, or failure lead
> us astray, when we share in God's sufferings through a life of this
> kind?

Bonhoeffer wrote, on the eve of the Second World War, a small book
which he called *Life Together*. I do not believe St Stephen's could better
celebrate its rich heritage than by simply getting together and working out
together what it means as a church to share 'Life Together'. That may, of
course, mean facing, in terms of your life and witness in Westminster,
what Bonhoeffer, in another book, termed 'The Cost of Discipleship'.

With that in mind, my sober and sobering conviction is that *St
Stephen's has never faced a more challenging time in all its century and a half
of history than it does now*. Not that this means a complete break with St
Stephen's' past. Indeed, I want to end with some remarks about a very
traditional Christian and his devotion which has something to say to us
today – about today and the future – which is surprisingly in tune with
Bonhoeffer.

Shortly before St Stephen's' 150th anniversary, Lord Coggan died. He
had, of course, been Archbishop of York and Canterbury. He was 90 years
old and had been living in retirement for twenty years. He was a gifted
Hebrew scholar, a teacher, a pastor and an outstanding preacher. He was
never a charismatic figure, but he was always the most courteous of
men. His biographer, Margaret Pawley, wrote that:

Those who wish to draw close to an understanding of Donald Coggan can do no better than study the poem by Charles Hamilton Sorley which the Archbishop chose to be sung as an anthem when he was consecrated as Bishop of Bradford in York Minster in 1956, and when he was enthroned as Archbishop of York in 1961, and again when he was enthroned as Archbishop of Canterbury in 1974. The poem was clearly of huge importance to him.

The poet, Charles Sorley, was in fact a first cousin of the politician Rab Butler who, of course, lived within the parish of St Stephen's, at 3 Smith Square, from 1938–70. Rab wrote an essay about Sorley in a book which profiled some of his friends. Sorley had been killed in the First World War, in 1915, aged only twenty. John Masefield, then poet laureate, said that Sorley was 'the greatest poet lost in the War'.

Sorley's poem was set to music as an anthem by the Irish composer, Charles Wood, who became Professor of Music in Cambridge just after the First World War. The poem is only eight lines in length, but any poem which won the praise and approval of such a politician and man of affairs as Rab Butler, and of such an Archbishop as Donald Coggan, is worthy, surely, of our attention.

I want to end this chapter, then, with those eight lines of Sorley, because I believe they draw so many people together. I can hear Bonhoeffer saying them in his prison cell. I can hear Rab Butler and Donald Coggan saying them, and Archbishop John Chisholm – curate here from 1947 to 1951 – and George Reindorp, and Winnie Dale in her wheelchair, and Mabel Wilkins, and nameless thousands upon thousands who have passed through the doors of St Stephen's in its one hundred and fifty years:

> This sanctuary of my soul,
> Unwitting, I keep white and whole,
> Unlatched and lit – if thou shouldst care
>   to enter or to tarry there.
>
> With parted lips and outstretched hands
> And listening ear thy servant stands
> Call thou early – call thou late –
> To thy great service dedicate.

5 'Better to hear a good sermon twice than a bad sermon once'

When it was announced, in 1958, that Mervyn Stockwood was to be Bishop of Southwark, it was front-page news. When, later, it was stated that the preacher at his consecration was to be the Reverend F.A. Simpson, few outside Cambridge were any the wiser. But in Cambridge it was the talk of the university, for there Simpson was well known as one of the last eccentrics.

Before Mervyn Stockwood's return to Cambridge, in 1955, as Vicar of the University Church, Great St Mary's, Simpson had not preached for nearly ten years, after a memorable Remembrance Day sermon, published in pamphlet form as 'A *Last* Sermon'. When, therefore, he preached again at Great St Mary's at the invitation of the new vicar, the then Regius Professor of Divinity, John Burnaby, made so bold as to brandish the published sermon before Simpson, and to ask him how he could possibly preach again, having had published a sermon with such a title. 'Burnaby,' said Simpson dismissively, 'I am surprised *you* do not know the meaning of the indefinite article.'

Simpson had been made a Fellow of Trinity in 1911, having written the brilliant first volume of what was projected as a four-volume biography of Louis Napoleon, but only two volumes of it had seen the light of day by the time he died.

In early life Simpson had travelled a great deal in Europe, and had flown across the Channel in his own Gipsy Moth, but in later years he rarely ventured out of Cambridge, spending much of his time roaming the college gardens, armed with a formidable pair of secateurs. He was unmistakable out of doors, because of his blue-grey woollen scarf slung over one shoulder – in winter over a shabby raincoat; on his head, most days, winter and summer alike, an equally shabby cloth cap. He had developed an immediate liking for Mervyn Stockwood when he came to Great St Mary's. Simpson was a man of strong likes and dislikes, which were not always of long duration. He had also decided to like me when I went up to Trinity, as Chaplain, and on my first day in Cambridge he knocked on the door of my rooms, immediately entered, introduced himself without removing his cloth cap, and, with a shy writhing, holding an envelope well away from him, presented it to me. 'I am Simpson,' he said. 'You come, I understand, from a background from which none of our previous chaplains has come. Pray do me the kindness of keeping entirely to yourself the contents of this envelope.' He then stepped backward a few paces, crooked his arm in farewell, writhed again, arm extended, executed a few more lurching steps backward toward the door, and left the room as suddenly as he had entered it. The envelope contained a most generous cheque.

Simpson sometimes suggested it was for difficulties of belief that he had virtually ceased to preach. 'How can one believe in the divinity of Our Lord,' he would characteristically ask, 'when he was so unconscionably rude to His mother?' On the rare occasions that he preached, even in these later years, it was likely to be the same sermon, on the subject of the Good Samaritan; but it was a remarkable sermon, which many undergraduates made a point of hearing while they were up in Cambridge. On one occasion he preached this sermon on succeeding Sundays in the chapels of Corpus and King's. The then Dean of Corpus, Roland Walls, is unlikely to forget the occasion, for Simpson had asked him to read as the lesson the parable of the Good Samaritan, but the dean had read an entirely different passage. Simpson reminded the congregation continually of the dean's failing, throughout the sermon. 'If only the lesson I had asked to be read had in fact been read, you would now be able to recall . . .' The dean wrote immediately to apologize, but Simpson returned his letter on the grounds that it was 'insufficiently abject'.

The next week he spotted in King's some of the undergraduates who had heard him in Corpus, and prefaced his sermon with the words, 'I see some here today whom I saw in another place but a week ago. To them may I say: it is better to hear a good sermon twice than a bad sermon once.'

It was the Chaplain to Catholic Students in Cambridge, Monsignor

Alfred Gilbey, who was the chief cause of Simpson being invited to preach at Mervyn Stockwood's consecration. As a freshman, Gilbey had read his first essays to Simpson in 1920, and when, in 1932, he returned to Cambridge, to Fisher House (the Catholic Chaplaincy), he heard Simpson deliver before the University one of his best sermons for the Commemoration of Benefactors. For many years Gilbey entertained Simpson to dinner on his birthday. In 1958, just after the announcement of Mervyn Stockwood's appointment, the future bishop was included in the party, and the question arose at dinner whom he should invite to preach at his consecration. Gilbey light-heartedly suggested Simpson. Simpson made a 'swooning gesture of deprecation', Gilbey recounts, but the very next morning he received a note from Simpson signifying his willingness to accept the invitation.

Nothing of this was known immediately to others, and when Simpson received the invitation in writing, he brought it to my rooms (but by no means to mine alone). It was the same knock and immediate entry as at our first meeting, and he thrust the invitation straightaway into my hands. 'Please read that,' he said, and, lurching a few steps away, he looked out of the window, maintaining his restless movements while I read the letter, and saying, not so *sotto voce*: 'What *shall* I do? . . . dear Mervyn . . .' When I looked up, he said: 'Of course, I cannot possibly accept. I am far too old.' (He was by then 75.) 'Besides,' he added, 'I have not journeyed to London for twenty years and more.' I felt sure at that moment he was *going* to accept, and was apprehensive as to what that would mean for some of us around him.

The final decision was by no means immediate. Simpson would come in day after day, and with sighs and groans and writhings would go over and over the reasons for and against acceptance. 'Dear Mervyn has so greatly honoured me,' he would say, 'I *must* do what he has asked.' And just when you felt he had set his face steadfastly towards what sounded like some task of towering and tremendous dimensions, he would say he could not go through with it, and bewail his hideous dilemma, and often physically 'about face'.

The consecration was to take place in Southwark Cathedral, where the then Provost was George Reindorp, later Bishop of Guildford, then of Salisbury, who had been my own vicar when I was a curate. Crucial for

Simpson's acceptance became the question of the height of the pulpit desk. 'Eric,' he said one day, 'it would be an unspeakable kindness were you to enquire of the Provost what is the precise height of his pulpit desk.' I did so enquire, and at first it seemed that might be the end of the affair. Simpson was a tall man, and the desk, he declared, would be far too low for his manuscript. (I was somewhat puzzled by this, for he had never been known to use a note in a pulpit.) However, within a few days there was another great entrance. Simpson had had an inspiration. Would I now 'add kindness to kindness' and ascertain from the Provost how much it would cost, were Simpson to present to the Cathedral a pulpit desk that would worthily commemorate the occasion. The new pulpit desk with F.A.S. (Frederick Arthur Simpson), A.M.S. (Arthur Mervyn Stockwood) and G.E.R. (George Edmund Reindorp) suitably entwined in a scroll on the face of the pulpit desk was, at considerable cost, speedily designed, approved, and put into position – and made adjustable, to cover eventualities.

Simpson seemed at last to have accepted the invitation; and then came the weeks and months when he would come to my rooms and discuss and often declaim those sentences on which he was working.

It was only on the very eve of our journey to London for the consecration that Simpson preached to me the sermon in its entirety; and with good reason. Parts of the sermon he revealed that evening were to be addressed directly and personally to 'My dear Mervyn'. I ventured to remind him that, as well as Mervyn Stockwood, there would be another bishop consecrated at the service to whom he would also be preaching – William Frank Chadwick, to be consecrated Bishop of Barking. At this news, which was certainly not news to him, Simpson flew into a mock fury. Why had he not been told? It was far too late now, he said, for him to alter what he had prepared. (And he did *not* alter it.) 'Barking!' he exclaimed, with infinite pain and disdain; and 'Who is *this* Chadwick?' At the time, Owen Chadwick was Master of Selwyn College, and Henry, Owen's younger brother, was Dean of Queen's.

On the day before the consecration we set out together for Cambridge station in a taxi. I looked after the luggage. Simpson's much-labelled, ancient leather case was as heavy as its contents; but he was more concerned for the safe conduct of some bottles of vintage port, strung together as one package, which he was taking as a present for our host from the stock he had laid down in the college cellars many years before. At the station he insisted I should find him a carriage with blinds. I told him there were now few carriages with blinds. At this he began to wail and to writhe. 'With no blinds, I shall go blind,' he cried. 'Blind, I shall not be able to see my manuscript. There is now no point in my going. I shall return to the college. I am an old man. Why did I say I would make such a journey? If it were not for dear Mervyn . . .'

Just before the train departed, I managed to propel him into an empty compartment and get the luggage on to the rack. Simpson sat there for some time, crying and moaning. Suddenly he stopped his crying, stood up, and jumped on the seat, holding on to the rack with one hand, unlocking the case on the rack with the other, then feverishly feeling around within it – while the train was in motion. Eventually he pulled from within the case a woollen Swiss skiing cap, white with a red bobble, which he said was his nightcap. His face was now the very picture of joy as he exclaimed triumphantly, '*Now* I shall *see*!' – and promptly pulled the cap down over his eyes. He then retired to the corner of the compartment and sat by the window on the platform side. Mercifully, the train made few stops.

I was relieved to see George Reindorp waiting to welcome us at the gate of the Cathedral. He conducted Simpson to the pulpit for him to give his approval to the new pulpit desk and to test his voice. Simpson became very agitated at the thought of using a microphone. Never in his life had he had need of such a 'gadget', he said, nor did he believe he had need of one now. But he was considerably mollified when George Reindorp hastened to inform him that the testing of his voice had been recorded – he had declaimed aloud, from memory, most beautifully, it must be said, St Paul's great hymn of love from 1 Corinthians 13. The Provost sagely suggested that Simpson might perhaps like to hear the recording. He said immediately that he had never before heard the sound of his own voice, and would be delighted to do so. He was conducted to the vestry, where he sat, eyes closed, enraptured, and, as he listened, he murmured at intervals: 'Beautiful . . . beautiful . . . *most* beautiful.'

I took Simpson straight from the Cathedral to Westminster. Our host for the night, Tony Tremlett, the Vicar of St Stephen's, Rochester Row, had gone to much trouble to make him comfortable. However, on being shown a bedroom with twin beds, Simpson was taken aback. 'Two beds?' he anxiously enquired. 'I could not sleep if I were not to sleep alone.' Tremlett assured him that no one else would be occupying the second bed. 'Then,' asked Simpson sharply, 'why have two small beds in one room when there might be one large one?' And suddenly he stretched his length on top of one of the beds, to prove that he was a very tall man and that his feet would stick out of the twin beds. He then sprang off the bed and began to demonstrate how, if only the beds were pushed together, they might provide him with just the kind of bed that would give him a good night's sleep. 'One large bed,' he continued to mutter, 'would be infinitely better than two small beds.'

I decided to interrupt, to suggest it was time for the walk to which he had long looked forward as a part of his excursion to London. We walked therefore to Westminster Abbey, and stood outside the deanery, where Simpson had lived for a time as a student. He leant against the stone walls, and shed a few tears, and sighed for the passing of the years. He wanted then to walk in St James's Park. We made our way through Westminster Abbey, but when we reached Parliament Square, at its busiest time, he became impatient with the traffic, and protested that it would never stop if you simply waited. (I wasn't 'simply waiting'; I was anxiously endeavouring to get him to use the pedestrian crossing.) He plunged into the traffic with both arms held high above his head, loudly exhorting me to follow his example. Cursing bus and taxi drivers looked with a mixture of astonishment and contempt at the two clergymen who were causing them to take such hurried avoiding action.

We walked in the Park, and, after Simpson had dramatically prostrated himself in prayer in Westminster Cathedral, we returned to Vincent Square, where I helped him dress for dinner at Lambeth Palace. I delivered him in a taxi at Morton's Gate, and promised I would collect him at not too late an hour. When I did, it was clear that he had had a good evening. Archbishop Fisher and he had discovered that they were both up at Oxford at the same time and had found they had much to talk about together. I hovered in the background while Simpson took his leave of the archbishop and Mrs Fisher, and thanked them profusely for the generosity of their hospitality. 'And may I just say,' Simpson is averred to have said as a Parthian shot, 'had you offered me alcohol I would have refused it.'

Next morning, when I went to wake him, the bed showed all the signs of unbroken sleep. It was May Day morning, and there was reason to hope that nothing now would disturb Simpson's relative composure. But suddenly, as we took a taxi to the Cathedral, he became obsessed with the thought that the nervous demands of the day might mean he would need to relieve himself during the service. Could he perhaps, even at this late hour, be given a seat somewhat nearer the vestry, so that he might slip out before the sermon – and after? The Provost was – at least on the surface – all sweetness and light, and the request was readily granted. I sat next to Simpson, and told him he was to go to the pulpit only when I told him to do, and that I would lead him there, after the verger. I said he had only one thing to remember. Before the sermon, and during the singing of the creed, there was a score of consecrating bishops to be conducted from their seats in the sanctuary to seats under the pulpit, that they might the better hear his sermon. He must not therefore begin to preach until they were in position. It was no good. Simpson was not going to wait for anyone that day once he was in the pulpit – let alone twenty bishops. The bishops were therefore still in solemn procession when, unforgettably, he began:

> It was heavy tidings, my fathers and my brethren, that they brought to us in Cambridge last November. We had seen, in a little more than three years, our University Church of Great St Mary's raised up from the very earth to be all, or almost all, that such a church could be. And when with that work so recent, so manifestly important, so still precariously poised, they came to us saying, 'Knowest thou the Lord will take away thy prophet from thy head today?', it was as much as some of us could do at first to answer, 'Yea, I know it, hold ye your peace.'

The sermon contained a number of Simpson's most characteristic sentences. Having in his very first paragraph spoken directly to 'My dear Mervyn', he transparently excused himself before its end by saying: 'Since I have stumbled on this direct form of address . . .'! Of the 'pittances' of the clergy, he said, 'Remember that a man is almost forced to think too

71

much about money if he has really too little of it.' But perhaps the most memorable moment of the sermon came unexpectedly in a passage on the gift of preaching. 'But to you, my brother, I hesitate to say this,' he said, 'for to you has been given a measure of eloquence; a rare gift, a noble gift, although unharnessed it can be a dangerous gift. But harnessed, not shackled, it will be all the more valuable in your new office, since not many of that office possess it.' Several of Simpson's episcopal auditors, sitting exposed to view in seats immediately below him, were visibly discomfited.

If it was not Simpson's greatest sermon, or even a great sermon – the archbishop called it 'deplorable' – it was undoubtedly great oratory, probably the greatest most of those in the Cathedral that day had ever heard or were likely to hear.

Later, I collected a happy but exhausted Simpson from the George Inn, Southwark, where Monsignor Gilbey had entertained the new bishop and his preacher to lunch. Mercifully, the return journey to Cambridge was without incident. Simpson slept soundly most of the way.

I did not see a great deal of him in the ensuing days or, indeed, years, for within a few weeks I, too, was to leave Cambridge, to become Vicar of St George's, Camberwell, the Trinity College Mission in south London. I joined Mervyn Stockwood, John Robinson – who was to be Bishop of Woolwich – and others, on the South Bank of the Thames. I tried always to see Simpson when I returned to Cambridge once or twice a year in the years that remained to him. He continued his daily pruning expeditions to the gardens of the colleges, and to entertain to port – 'older than themselves', as he often claimed – undergraduates who had caught his eye or who were the younger brothers or sons of undergraduates he had known in Cambridge in earlier years. He continued also to try the patience of longsuffering college servants.

On the Feast of St Cecilia, 1973, Simpson celebrated his 90th birthday. When, in February 1974, three days before he died, I went up to Cambridge to preach again at evensong in Trinity, I was told that he had been taken into a nursing home and was not likely to have long to live. I went round to the home. He was a sorry sight, lying flat in a cot, with his woollen scarf now slung over its side, but his cloth cap half on, half off his head. We exchanged a few words, but he was mostly silent. Suddenly his thoughts seemed to clear. 'Eric,' he said, more as a statement that as a question, 'you are preaching in Chapel tonight.' I said I was. 'Some people,' he said slowly and ruminatively, 'object to being named *publicly* in prayer.' And then, after a pause, he added: 'I do not *myself* object to being remembered . . .' (he paused) '. . . publicly' (he paused again) '. . . in prayer.'

6 A view from the South Bank

If you visit almost any of the tiny congregations of the inner area of South London, you will find some people, probably the majority, believing that these are hard times for the Church, and that in 'the good old days' – in Fr Smith's time, or Mr Brown's (but *not* Bishop Robinson's!) – things were different. ''E got the galleries full', they will say. And you are left with the impression that if only someone did *something*, they would be full again. This sense of present failure over against past success is increased by the *seeming* success of parishes only a few miles away in the suburban area.

In this situation it is important that people should be faced with the facts of the last century or so, summed up succinctly, as mentioned earlier, in Bishop Winnington-Ingram's statement in his 1896 book *Work in Great Cities*: 'It is not that the Church of God has lost the great towns; it has never had them.'[1] (The bishop had good reason to know, for at the time he was bishop suffragan of Stepney.) The illusion of past success is a burden grievous to be borne, and there is encouragement not only in realizing you are not alone in your failure – you have a century of church-goers with you – but also in the fact that you may indeed be seeing the truth of the situation, and able therefore to come to grips with it, for the first time in a hundred years.

There have, of course, always been some who have seen the true state of affairs. 'Great towns will never be evangelised by the parochial system', wrote the young Newman in the *British Magazine* in 1836. 'The unstable multitude cannot be influenced and ruled except by uncommon means.'[2] In 1855 Lord Shaftesbury observed: 'The parochial system is, no doubt, a beautiful thing in theory, and is of great value in small rural districts; but in the large towns it is a mere shadow and a name.'[3] In 1872 the great Bishop of Manchester, James Fraser (of whom his biographer wrote 'He was a wonderfully liberal man, considering his cloth and his lawn sleeves'[4]), said to his clergy:

> The parochial system, as ordinarily conceived, admirably efficient in rural parishes and among limited population, where the pastor knows and is known by everyone committed to his charge, breaks down in the face of that huge mass of ignorance, poverty, and wretchedness by which it is often confronted in the thickly peopled areas of our manufacturing towns.[5]

In 1886 Walsham How, Bishop of Bedford (which then included the East End of London) said tersely, 'The Church is nowhere in East London',[6] and summed up the facts of the urban Church in an undeniable and inescapable manner:

> Churchmen should ask themselves how the very selfsame motives which in the East of London keep people from church, in the West bring them to church. The people of East London thought of religion as belonging to a wholly different class from themselves.[7]

The situation is documented by Charles Dickens in *Hard Times*, first published in 1854:

> Coketown did not come out of its own furnaces, in all respects like gold that had stood the fire. First, the perplexing mystery of the place was, Who belonged to the eighteen denominations? Because, whoever did, the labouring people did not. It was very strange to walk through the streets on a Sunday morning, and note how few of *them* the barbarous jangling of bells that was driving the sick and nervous mad, called away from their own quarter, from their own close rooms, from the corners of their own streets, where they lounged listlessly, gazing at all the Church and chapel going, as at a thing with which they had no manner of concern.[8]

This, certainly, was the situation in South London. In 1888 *The Record* published a supplement on 'South London: Its Religious Condition, its

Needs, and its Hopes'. In it, each of the parishes of the inner area is surveyed: 98 parishes, 238 clergy, and 800,000 people.

What South London will be eighty years hence, it is terrible to conceive. *Christianity is not in possession in South London . . .* It is extremely difficult for us to realise the fact thus bluntly stated. After all these centuries of Christian organisation, with a Church still established by law, with hundreds of churches and chapels and services, and an army of clergy and lay workers, we may easily be charged with sensational exaggeration for saying that in South London Christianity is not in possession. Yet that it is the simple truth anyone can see for himself. Without counting the parishes – unhappily they exist – where the Church is utterly swamped, and has become a nonentity through the misfortune or neglect of those in charge, there are dozens of parishes, especially in the first line, in which the clergy are working nobly and straining every nerve to make religion hold its proper position, when one and the same result is shown in each case. Great efforts put out, a moderate congregation formed, but the bulk of the people untouched. In other words, a state of things exists which, if the Church were simply organising Missions in a heathen land, would not be unhopeful, but would certainly not suggest to anybody that the Mission stage was over, and that the land had been won to the Cross. Moreover, it seems to us that much of the hopelessness which attends religious efforts in South London arises from the fact that we begin with an assumption which is imaginary, namely, that the parochial system has an actual as well as a theoretical existence there. We are as yet so very far, indeed, from having made the religious work in each parish commensurate with the area and population of the parish, that anything achieved, no matter how successfully, still leaves a great gap between the actual and the ideal parochial condition. If we would only be content to look facts in the face, and to accept things as we find them, there would be much less discouragement, and it would be a great deal fairer to the clergy. For no one who has not felt it knows the depression which comes from a responsibility which is absolutely beyond our powers to discharge, and the dull grief which comes from having to regard every effort

made or sacrifice encountered, not as something done, but as a little
less left undone. The clergy have trials enough, without breaking
their hearts.[9]

The writer makes it clear that the situation is no less true of the Free
Churches.

The Nonconformists are in still worse difficulties. Voluntaryism
cannot cope with a whole city of level poverty. The religious future of
South London seems to be dependent on the Church.

In 1860, in *The History of the Primitive Methodist Connexion*, there is
this plea:

Look at London, Portsmouth, Bristol, Plymouth, Liverpool,
Manchester, Birmingham, Leeds, Bradford, Newcastle-upon-Tyne,
and several other large towns and cities! How little has the
Connexion done for them compared with their pressing wants and
its powerful resources! Cannot the ecclesiastical system of the
community be made to work with as much efficiency there as in
smaller towns and villages?[10]

In 1885, the *British Weekly*, analysing the results of its own census of
worship in London, noted the figures of attendance at Salvation Army
meetings 'with amazement and keen disappointment'.[11] Professor Simey,
in his recent biography of Charles Booth, the Victorian merchant and
ship-owner, who made such a major contribution to the development of
British sociology, has this to say about Booth's Third Series of *Life and
Labour of the People in London*, entitled *Religious Influences*, published in
1902–3.

The picture which finally emerged of the religious influences at work
in London was a depressing one, though Booth did not so regard it
himself. He was generous in conceding that the motives of those who
laboured in this field were often of the highest order, but the results
of their work he described in terms of failure with a dispassionate

calm which was often more devastating to his readers than would have been a cry of lamentation. 'It is just because the effort is so great that the results are so disappointing' was a typical remark. Though his explorations of this unknown territory had held him entranced for years, he had found no evidence to support the claim that organised religion was in any degree effective as an agency for the improvement of the condition of the people, except, as he drily commented, in so far as those who did the work themselves benefited from so doing. He thought that Income Tax and Christianity were practically the preserve of the same classes: the mass of the people he believed to be beyond the reach of any denomination.

His analysis led him to the conclusion that the churches had adapted themselves to the class structure, rather than acted as a force transforming it. Each class had a church which catered for its needs, though most of the working-classes held aloof altogether. The Evangelical Churches which were most hospitable to them, and in which they felt most at home, were also those which strongly emphasised the doctrine that conversion implied a changed way of life, a dedication of oneself to higher living, and the admission of a sense of guilt. However, the ordinary working man did not feel inclined to give up the simple pleasures and sins to which he was accustomed, and so far as guilt was concerned, his political leaders were busy convincing him that he was more sinned against than sinning.

The overriding impression conveyed by the Inquiry was thus that somehow or other the churches had lost contact with the stream of events at the end of the nineteenth century; the doctrines they preached simply did not make sense to the mass of mankind. It could not be argued with any show of reason that this was due to mere apathy, for the response by working men to the appeal of socialist principles provided direct proof that a creed which seemed to be relevant to the problems of their daily lives could stir them to active support. He recorded the opinions of two of his informants that 'it is only as to trade unionism that the working-classes are keen', and that whilst there was a power in politics to stir the masses 'what impotence there seemed in the Gospel to do the same'.[12]

Whatever else this is, it is not the picture of 'the good old days'.

But, no matter how well documented your history of their church, no matter how unanswerable the facts of the Church's failure to make the great mass of the people churchgoers, the reaction of the majority of the tiny congregation of the inner-city church – most likely an elderly group – when you set all this before them, will be frank disbelief. 'But we remember . . .', they will protest. And then will come some anecdote of some occasion when the Church was packed to capacity. And their memories are not betraying them.

St George's, Camberwell (where I was myself vicar from 1959 to 1964) was built in 1824 to seat 1734 people. Less than half its seats were free. Here is Charles Booth's significant comment on the life of St George's just before the turn of the century:

St George's . . . is the parish entrusted to the Trinity Mission . . . The mission is the most remarkable of its kind, but, when compared with the high hopes that were entertained, there have been many disappointments, for it has neither received the support nor achieved the results looked for. It is mainly from children and young people that response is won, while work among adults, as usual, is apt to be successful only in so far as it is not undertaken upon definitely religious lines . . . In dealing with individuals there is much to inspire hope, but when a wider outlook is taken the glow fades, and, above all, the failure to reach men remains 'the disappointment' of this great undertaking. This is so although the clergy chosen have been very able men; although the parish has been well supplied with money; and although, while volunteer assistance from the College has fallen short alike of desires and of needs, this has still been forthcoming to an extent rarely equalled in other parishes. In spite of all disappointments, however, there is much that is striking about this attempt. Aims are kept high, and, although the mission has failed to stir the pulse of the neighbourhood, it has made itself respected, and has avoided all sensationalism in its methods. The parish, moreover, has all the usual organisations on a large scale; 1,800 children in its Sunday Schools; 300 in its Band of Hope; 400 older boys and girls in Bible-classes; various guilds with a total membership of some 500; as well as large clubs for girls, boys, lads, and adult men.[13]

These were the days when we did not have the great towns! But there is certainly something here to warrant people looking back on them as 'the good old days', for it is clear that in certain respects the Church has lost ground, and lost it heavily. Nevertheless, the significance of Booth's comment is not merely in the astonishing numbers, but in such phrases as 'mainly from children and young people', 'the failure to reach men', 'failed to stir the pulse of the neighbourhood'. And Booth has another comment to make on those who were attending the clubs of the Trinity Mission which is characteristic of what he has to say of many another group of people attached to the Church in those days: 'The principal difficulty is that the people who come are too respectable; corduroys are an infrequent sight.'

This comment of Booth's on the social structure of those associated with the Church is corroborated by C.F.G. Masterman, Fellow of Christ's College, Cambridge and later a Cabinet Minister, who lived for several years in one of the worst blocks of tenements in St George's Parish, using his rooms there as a base for social and political work in the neighbourhood. (He was a close friend of Scott Holland and Charles Gore.) At the beginning of the century Masterman wrote an essay on *The Religious Life of London*,[14] published by the *Daily News* and commenting on the *Daily News'* census of churchgoing in London, in which he wrote these revealing words:

> A poor borough may contain places of worship which attract well-to-do worshippers from a wide area. Southwark, for example, contains an Anglican and a Roman Catholic cathedral, as well as the great chapel made famous through the English-speaking world by the pastorate of Charles Spurgeon, whose enormous audience of 3,625 represents a similar cathedral gathering. In the poorest district of Lambeth, again, is the great church presided over by Mr F.B. Meyer, which draws a well-to-do and intelligent audience from all the southern suburbs. And on the other hand, such a statement altogether neglects the comfortable class of tradesmen and the

middle class who live in all the poorer boroughs, and provide perhaps the most ardent adherents of many flourishing religions. Any one intimate with such a district will know that it is this class in the main which contributes such worshippers as the churches and chapels are able to gather together in working-class districts. The places of worship line the main thoroughfares. Their frequenters are respectable, well-dressed men and women, the dwellers in those main thoroughfares and the better-class squares and streets that remain undestroyed. Investigate every place of worship down (say) Walworth Road from the 'Elephant' to Camberwell Green – the heart of a poor district. In all the varied centres of religion, whose buildings are thickly studded at close intervals, you will find no signs of obvious poverty. In the districts behind, in some obscure gathering of Primitive Methodists or Bible Christians, you may discover the class you are seeking. But in all central South London, the district with which I am most intimate, I have only seen the poor in bulk collected at two places of religious worship – Mr Meakin's great hall in Bermondsey, and St George's Roman Catholic Cathedral at Southwark – an object-lesson in (amongst other things) the wisdom of the permission of the late Archbishop of Canterbury for the use of incense 'for fumigatory purposes'. In London as a whole – apart from certain isolated and exceptional instances – I have no hesitation in asserting that it is the middle class which attend church and chapel, the working-classes and the poor who stay away.[15]

Masterman drives home his point:

The sight of the congregation of the Newington Tabernacle singing hymns on Sunday evening on the steps of the great edifice is a guarantee to the heedless stream which passes by that there are some who still believe in their religion. But work under the shadow of these cathedral gatherings in the humbler chapels is a depressing experience. The congregation slowly melts away, as the old faithful depart and the younger members are drawn to more obvious attractions. I know of few more depressing sights than the gathering of the few score dejected faithful scattered through buildings of size and pretension from which all the life has departed.[16]

The conclusion is clear. These were *not* the 'good old days', if by that is meant that in those days the working classes went to church. 'The Church of England offered working-class people no positive role in its life', wrote Fr Dolling, who worked for years in the slums of East London and Portsmouth.[17] That there were some full churches in the working-class areas there is no need to deny, or that the Church put out great efforts. But Masterman's conclusions are also undeniable:

> The new city race of workers is developing apart from the influences of religion. The spiritual world has vanished from their vision. The curtain of their horizon has descended round the life of toil which constitutes their immediate universe. Here and there, widely scattered, you may find a successful religious community of the poor; but these are mere isolated instances in an area of grey indifference. The energy, determination, and devotion put forth by adherents of all the religious bodies to convert some portion of this vast multitude, is one of the most noticeable displays of self-sacrificing effort to be found in modern England. Every expedient is essayed, from the guilds and fraternities, processions and banners of 'advanced' churches to the antics of 'Jumping Jack' or 'Salvation Joe' of a different school of Christianity. The wealthier members of the varied religions generously pour subscriptions and material gifts for the same arduous task. The best of the younger members of the Church of England undertake work amongst the poor, and certainly the standard of the clergy in the central districts where the churches are empty need not fear comparison with the standard in the outlying suburbs where the churches are crammed. If the works done in London today, one is inclined to assert, had been done in Sodom and Gomorrah, they would have repented in sackcloth and ashes.[18]

The works done in London were many and various. It is understandable, even at the level of self-interest, that church building should have seemed so important to the Victorians. The result of the activities of the

Church Building Commission from 1818 to 1856 was 600 new churches. According to the second report of the Ecclesiastical Commission in 1836 there were four parishes on the banks of the Thames with enough church-room for 8200 people and a population of 166,000. The building of a church often meant bringing into a district educated men and women, leadership, relief, social amenities and schools, morality and civilization, which might stave off what many feared: the triumph of the underworld. All men of good will who had the welfare of the working classes at heart wanted new churches, new chapels, new parishes, better-paid ministers, more ministers.[19]

The buildings went up, hundreds of them. Even so, the fact has to be faced that not enough of them went up if *all* the people were to be thought of as worshippers. Dr Owen Chadwick has written recently that

> Whitechapel, under its great evangelical vicar Champneys, was one of the best shepherded among slum parishes. In its eleven churches there was an average morning congregation of more than 500 persons. The churches were far from empty. But if every seat in all churches and chapels in Shoreditch had been occupied on a Sunday, more than eighty in every hundred inhabitants would have absented themselves from worship.[20]

There were not enough churches put up to cope with the population. The churches that were put up were not, in the main, filled. And certainly those that came to them were not, in the main, the working classes.

Most of the middle classes have now moved out to the suburbs of the great towns. The working classes are not now a 'huge mass of ignorance, poverty, and wretchedness'. The Welfare State has come, and the social and cultural position which the Church had at the turn of the century has now almost vanished. Since 1900 the population of the country has gone up by twelve million, whilst in the Church of England the number of ordained men has fallen by 5000. The mobile society has come. Whole areas have been renewed with what Berthold Brecht calls 'vertical recept-acles'. Yet in the heart of the great cities, and in London along the banks of the Thames, there remain huge areas of almost entirely working-class people. The Victorian churches are now almost empty, decaying, a financial burden to the tiny congregations and to the diocese. Whenever the churches are closed, as closed many of them must be, the tiny congregation almost invariably feels hurt beyond words.

As yet, no one has thought of any way to turn the working class into churchgoers. But now at last our failure is making us ask whether perhaps the attempt was right in the first place. Charles Masterman, prophet that he was, was asking the question sixty years ago:

> It is interesting to note how, in the discussion of remedies for the ineffectiveness of religion in modern England, almost all critics plunge straightway into the question of machinery . . . And each observer appears to hold that if that particular section of the machine in which he can detect a flaw could be repaired, or if a particularly up-to-date invention replaced some antiquated adjustment, the machinery of the Churches would once again grind out religious enthusiasm. With one it is the edifice. He deplores the cold, Gothic building, repellent to the poor. He would substitute large lighted halls of the remarkable and dignified style characteristic of the later nineteenth century, with plenty of carpets, paint and colour. With another it is the edifices themselves. Let the leaders of religion come into the streets, he holds, and the problem is solved. With one again it is the service, antiquated, unintelligible to the vulgar. Collect a band, he urges, sing the 'Holy City' and other moving modern melodies, weave into your prayers allusions to politics and incidents of the day. With another it is the sermon; the minister is too cold, or speaks with stammering tongue. Let us place a great preacher in every pulpit, and the masses will vehemently fight for entrance to our churches. Some advocate, some deprecate, the methods of the theatre. Some would abolish pews altogether, and let the men stand. Some see the inevitable advance of religion if pews are made more comfortable. Each one has convinced opinion as to what 'the poor' will come to – the large hall, the small mission, the street corner. Few seem to care to face the question what 'the poor' are to be offered when they come.[21]

One thing is certain now: the working classes (no longer, most of them, poor) will *never* come to join the tiny congregations in the Victorian buildings, to share in the imposed liturgy – 1662 or Series 2. The middle classes have moved away from the problem. Few of the hierarchy are yet fully seized of it, almost all of them still fondly imagining that some day the workers will come. But there are *some* in the Church who are content simply to live with the people of the inner-city areas, sharing and serving, together attempting to answer the problems which confront people, and the Church, in such areas; not only the material problems of housing and schooling but also of meaning and purpose. They offer, in the name of Christ, presence. Here is the hope of the Church. 'I am amongst you as one who serves.'

But is it not now high time for the Church to form a group to come to grips, on a fully ecumenical basis, with 'the missionary structure of the Church in the inner-city'? Theology and sociology would be its primary concerns. But I do not see these concerns as merely theoretical. We urgently need now an Urban Training Centre where theology can be 'dug' (to use F.D. Maurice's word) from the situation. We should have the experience of such seminal places as the Chicago Urban Training Center to be our guide. We should, of course, need money – it would be tragic if we have committed so much of our money to 'the system' that we had none left to give to experimental and exploratory work. But above all what is needed is Christians who by the 'minute particulars' of their commit-ment will make St Paul's 'We are members one of another' more than a platitude in terms of their association with those who live in the inner-city.

Notes

1 A.F. Winnington-Ingram *Work in Great Cities* (1896), p. 22; the bishop was quoting from a conversation between Archbishop Longley and Disraeli.

2 Cited by L.E. Elliot-Binns *The Early Evangelicals* (Lutterworth Press, 1953), p. 100, n. 1.

3 Cited by K.S. Inglis *Churches and the Working Classes in Victorian England* (Routledge & Kegan Paul, 1963), p. 25.

4 J. Arch *The Story of His Life* (1898), pp. 222–6.

5 Bishop's Charge (1872), pp. 76–7.

6 *Bishop Walsham How: A Memoir* (1898), p. 129.

7 Church Congress Report, 1880, pp. 94–5.

8   Charles Dickens *Hard Times* (1854), Chapter 5.
9   'South London: Its Religious Condition, its Needs and its Hopes'; a Survey published in *The Record* 6 January 1888.
10 J. Petty *The History of the Primitive Methodist Connexion* (1860), p. 447.
11 *British Weekly* 13 January 1888, p. 217.
12 T.S. and M.B. Simey *Charles Booth* (Clarendon Press, Oxford, 1960), pp. 149–50 (reprinted here by permission).
13 Charles Booth *Life and Labour of the People in London*, Third Series: *Religious Influences* (Vol. 6, 1902–3), pp. 28–9.
14 ed. R. Mudie-Smith (London, 1904).
15 C.F.G. Masterman *In Peril of Change* (London, 1905), pp. 268–9.
16 *Ibid.*, pp. 277–8.
17 R. Dolling *Ten Years in a Portsmouth Slum* (1896), p. 131.
18 C.F.G. Masterman *In Peril of Change*, pp. 271–2.
19 M.H. Port *Six Hundred New Churches* (SPCK, 1961).
20 Owen Chadwick *The Victorian Church* (A. & C. Black, 1966), p. 328.
21 C.F.G. Masterman, *In Peril of Change*, pp. 285–6.

For further reading: G. Kitson Clark *The Making of Victorian England* (Methuen, 1962); E.R. Wickham *Church and People in an Industrial City* (Lutterworth, 1957).

7 Lancelot Andrewes

Lancelot Andrewes has become my close friend. What I shall set before you is a very personal, indeed autobiographical approach to Lancelot Andrewes. And it's Andrewes the preacher whom I shall have most in mind. It so happens that at various points in my life, I'm happy to say, Andrewes has inescapably confronted me.

The beginnings

As I have suggested in earlier chapters, my time at a riverside wharf on the South Bank of the Thames, and, not least, my organ lessons at Southwark Cathedral during that period, drew me deeply into what I will call 'the world of Shakespeare'. That is, of course, a huge and wonderful world, which I've never ceased to be drawn into to this day. Lancelot Andrewes was one of Shakespeare's contemporaries – Andrewes was born nine years before him; he outlived him by ten years – and my going regularly to the Cathedral offered several reasons for being drawn also into Andrewes' world. Let me explain.

Winchester Palace

If, as I often did, you approached Southwark Cathedral from the West, along Clink Street, close to the river – where Clink Prison had been – a couple of hundred yards before you reached the Cathedral you would pass the remains of Winchester Palace (or Winchester House), where the Bishops of Winchester had had their residence for over 500 years. Lancelot Andrewes was the last bishop to live there. He was Bishop of Winchester from 1619 until his death seven years later. It was in 1814 that a fire revealed the rose window of the great hall of the Palace – a hexagon inset with 18 triangles. That window was not open to public view until the 'Blitz', when damage by fire to an adjacent warehouse exposed the window, which was only restored to its present state in 1972.

Organ lessons in Southwark

When I walked along Clink Street during the War, to my organ lesson, I would often think of Andrewes residing there until his death. Winchester Palace was my first 'meeting' with Andrewes, so to speak. But when I entered the Cathedral, very near to where the organ console then stood, in the south choir aisle, there was Andrewes' imposing tomb, he having been buried in his parish church. The tomb, which now stands between the south choir aisle and the sanctuary, was originally in the Bishop's Chapel, east of the retro-choir. The effigy of Andrewes on his tomb – in his Garter robes – is almost certainly contemporary with his death. The canopy to the tomb is the 1930 work of Sir Ninian Comper. His palace and his tomb both spoke to me of Andrewes.

T.S. Eliot and the *Four Quartets*

You will recall from earlier how, during my time on the riverside, I bought, one by one as they came out, T.S. Eliot's *Four Quartets*, each purchased from Alfred Wilson's bookshop in Gracechurch Street in the City. I had very little idea of the significance of Eliot; but I bought them, as though some guiding hand were at work. My intuition went far ahead of my understanding, I simply couldn't wait to buy them. They led me to Eliot's book of *Selected Essays 1917–1932*, which included an essay on Lancelot Andrewes that he had written in 1927 – a 'writer of genius' as Eliot called him. Eliot was, I suppose, my third meeting with Andrewes.

In consequence, I bought my first copy of Eliot's 'Journey of the Magi' in 1941, in a volume *The Waste Land and other Poems* published the year before. I bought it not least for 'Journey of the Magi', which Eliot had written in 1927, and which people seemed not to notice had inverted commas around its first five lines; these representing a quotation, lifted with hardly an emendation, from a sermon of Lancelot Andrewes.

Let me pause awhile on my autobiographical journey, and remind you of those five lines:

> 'A cold coming we had of it,
> Just the worst time of the year
> For a journey, and such a long journey;
> The ways deep and the weather sharp,
> The very dead of winter.'

Now let me quote part of the sermon from which those words came. Andrewes preached it before the King's Majesty – King James – on Christmas Day 1622, four years before Andrewes died, in his late sixties:

A cold coming they had of it
In this their coming, we consider, first, the distance of the place they came from. It was not hard by, as the shepherds – but a step to Bethlehem over the fields; this was riding many a hundred miles, and cost them many a day's journey. Secondly, we consider the way they came, if it be pleasant, or plain and easy; for if it be, it is so much the better. This was nothing pleasant, for through deserts, all the way waste and desolate. Nor secondly, easy neither; for over the rocks and crags of both Arabias, specially Petraea, their journey lay. Yet if safe – but it was not, but exceeding dangerous, as lying through the midst of the 'black tents of Kedar', a nation of thieves and cut-throats; to pass over the hills of robbers, infamous then, and infamous to this day. Last, we consider the time of their coming. It was no summer progress. A cold coming they had of it at this time of the year, just the worst time of the year to take a journey, and specially a long journey in. The ways deep, the weather sharp, the days short, the sun farthest off, in *solstitio brumali*, 'the very dead of winter'.

and came it cheerfully and quickly
And these difficulties they overcame, of a wearisome, irksome, troublesome, dangerous, unseasonable journey; and for all this they came. And came it cheerfully and quickly, as appeareth by the speed they made. It was but *vidimus, venimus* with them; 'they saw' and

'they came'; no sooner saw, but they set out presently. So as upon the first appearance of the star, as it might be last night; they knew it was Balaam's star; it called them away, they made ready straight to begin their journey this morning. A sign they were highly conceited of his birth, believed some great matter of it, that they took all these pains, made all this haste that they might be there to worship Him with all the possible speed they could. Sorry for nothing so much as that they could not be there soon enough, with the very first, to do it even this day, the day of his birth. All considered, there is more in *venimus* than shews at the first sight. It was not for nothing it was said in the first verse *ecce venerunt*; their coming had an *ecce* on it, it well deserves it.

and what should we have done

And we, what should we have done? Sure these men of the East shall rise in judgement against the men of the West, that is us, and their faith against ours in this point. With them it was but *vidimus, venimus*; with us it would have been but *veniemus* at most. Our fashion is to see and see again before we stir a foot, specially if it be to the worship of Christ. Come such a journey at such a time? No; but fairly have put it off to the spring of the year, till the days longer, and the ways fairer, and the weather warmer, till better travelling to Christ. Our Epiphany would sure have fallen in Easter week at the soonest.

Christ is no wild-cat

Nor it must not be through no desert, over no Petraea. If rugged or uneven the way, if the weather ill-disposed, if any never so little danger, it is enough to stay us. To Christ we cannot travel, but weather and way and all must be fair. If not, no journey, but sit still and see farther. As indeed, all our religion is rather *vidimus*, a contemplation, than *venimus*, a motion, or stirring to do ought. But when we do it, we must be allowed leisure. Ever *veniemus*, never *venimus*; ever coming, never come. We love to make no great haste. To other things perhaps; not to *adorare*, the place of the worship of God. Why should we? Christ is no wild-cat. What talk ye of 12 days?

And if it be 40 days hence, ye shall be sure to find His Mother and Him; she cannot be churched till then. What needs such haste? The truth is, we conceit Him and His birth but slenderly, and our haste is even thereafter. But if we be at that point, we must be out of this *venimus*. They like enough to leave us behind. Best get us a new Christmas in September; we are not like to come to Christ at this feast.

Southwark Cathedral in the Second World War

In the six years of the Second World War, incendiaries, high explosives and flying bombs took a terrible toll of Southwark. Most of the windows of the Cathedral were blown out. The organ was put out of action, so that, for a time, Dr Cook and I had to seek refuge in Guy's Hospital Chapel and its organ. At the end of the War, there remained a small but valiant congregation at the Cathedral, with, from 1944, a new and vigorous Provost, Cuthbert Bardsley, later to be Bishop of Coventry. I first remember him coming up the steps of the organ loft of the Cathedral – to which we had recently returned – to introduce himself. It was only days after his appointment, when he was still Rector of Woolwich.

Florence Higham

One of the people I met in the tiny remnant of a congregation at lunchtimes in the Cathedral was Dr Florence Higham. She clearly loved the Cathedral, and was to write a book about it called *Southwark Story*. She was a devout, very private person, an historian who wore her learning lightly, but loved to pass on to people like me her knowledge and love of the Cathedral. In 1952, she was to publish a small biography of Lancelot Andrewes. What she had to say taught me much about the *via media* of the Church of England as well as about Andrewes. She whetted my appetite not only for church history but for the history of England, and of both, at that time, I was appallingly ignorant.

Florence was my fourth meeting with Andrewes. She always had nuggets of knowledge to be found nowhere else. When, for instance, I said to her, one day, that in my lunch hours on Wednesdays I would often go to hear the Methodist preacher, Dr Donald Soper, standing on the wall outside the Tower of London and addressing the crowd, and that afterwards I would sometimes pop into the Toc H Church, All Hallows by the Tower, where 'Tubby' Clayton was the padre, she produced a gem like: 'Lancelot Andrewes, you know, was baptized in All Hallows.' And when I told her that I'd actually started work in 1939, not on the South Bank, but in Laurence Pountney Lane, off Cannon Street – until the destruction by bombs of our wharf on the north bank by London Bridge caused me to move to Bankside – Florence had another nugget to pass on: 'The Merchant Taylors purchased a house in the parish of St Laurence Pountney, where Andrewes lived, not far from Lower Thames Street. There he went to school, under the great schoolmaster Richard Mulcaster.' Working in the shipping and wharfing world myself, I was pleased to hear from her that 'Andrewes' father was a seafaring man who, in his later years, was a Master of Trinity House'. I myself often had to take documents about Thames pilots to the headquarters of Trinity House on Tower Hill – which, alas, was bombed, like so many other ancient City buildings.

King's College, London

I did not learn more about Andrewes until I got to King's College, London, in 1946, to begin training for ordination. I had to begin to learn Hebrew, Latin and New Testament Greek – first of all at evening classes at King's – and I envied Andrewes' facility with languages. According to Thomas Fuller, the seventeenth-century historian and writer, 'Andrewes became so skilled in all, especially oriental, languages, that some conceive he might (if then living) almost have served as an interpreter-general at the confusion of tongues.'

My mentor, the Dean of King's, Eric Abbott – who, of course, became also my close friend – was the next person to teach me to love and admire Andrewes. He was particularly fond of Andrewes' Passiontide sermons. Rather than describe or analyse them, I think it best to offer some further quotations from an Andrewes' sermon, but first let me simply say that Eric Abbott set Andrewes' Passiontide sermons before us who were training for ordination, not primarily as an example of his preaching style but rather of his profound spirituality and as an example of how biblical and devotional addresses could and should nevertheless be skilful, memorable and fascinating: attractive in the deepest sense. They could be teaching sermons without losing their profoundly spiritual aspect.

Each of Andrewes' Passiontide sermons has memorable passages. On Good Friday 1597, for instance, he said:

> He was pierced with love no less than with grief, and it was that wound of love which made him so constantly to endure all the others. Which love we may read in the palms of his hands . . . Christ pierced on the Cross is *liber caritatis*, the very book of love laid open before us.

Good Friday, 1604

The sermon from which I must quote at length was preached before the King's Majesty at Whitehall on 6 April 1604, being Good Friday. Andrewes' text was Lamentations 1:12: 'Have ye no regard, O all ye that pass by the way? Consider, and behold, if ever there were sorrow like My sorrow, which was done unto Me, wherewith the Lord did afflict Me in the day of the fierceness of His wrath.'

Andrewes begins:

> *If ever there were sorrow like my sorrow*
> At the very reading or hearing of which verse, there is none but will presently conceive, it is the voice of a party in great extremity. In great extremity two ways: first, in such distress as never was any, 'If ever there were sorrow like My sorrow'; and then in that distress, having none to regard Him; 'Have ye no regard, all ye?'
>
> To be afflicted, and so afflicted as none ever was, is very much. In that affliction, to find none to respect him or care for him, what can be more? In all our sufferings, it is a comfort to us that we have a *sicut*, that nothing has befallen us, but such as others have felt the like. But here, *si fuerit sicut*, 'If ever the like were' – that is, never the like was.
>
> Again, in our greatest pains it is a kind of ease, even to find some

regard. Naturally we desire it, if we cannot be delivered, if we cannot be relieved, yet to be pitied. It sheweth there be yet some that are touched with the sense of our misery, that wish us well, and would wish us ease if they could. But this Afflicted here findeth not so much, neither the one nor the other; but is even as He were an out-cast both of Heaven and earth. Now verily an heavy case, and worthy to be put in this Book of Lamentations . . .

O consider and behold

Be it then to us, as to them it was, and as most properly it is, the speech of the Son of God, as this day hanging on the Cross, to a sort of careless people, that go up and down without any manner of regard of these His sorrows and sufferings, so worthy of all regard. 'Have ye no regard? O all ye that pass by the way, consider and behold, if ever there were sorrow like to my sorrow, which was done unto me, wherewith the Lord afflicted me in the day of the fierceness of His wrath.'

Here is a complaint, and here is a request. A complaint that we have not, a request that we would have the pains and Passions of our Saviour Christ in some regard. For first He complaineth, and not without cause, 'Have ye no regard?' And then, as willing to forget their former neglect, so they will yet do it, He falleth to entreat, 'O consider and behold!'

And what is it that we should consider? The sorrow which He suffereth, and in two things: the quality, and the cause. First: the quality, *si fuerit sicut*, 'if ever the like were'; and that either in respect of *Dolor*, or *Dolor Meus*, 'the sorrow suffered' or 'the Person suffering'. Second: the cause: that is God that in His wrath, in His fierce wrath, doth all this to Him. Which cause will not leave us, till it have led us to another cause in ourselves, and to another yet in Him; all which serve to ripen us to regard . . .

Who is to regard?

'Have ye no regard all ye that pass by?' To ease this complaint, and to grant this request, we are to regard; and that we may regard, we are to consider the pains of His Passion . . .

Our very eye will tell us

Our very eye will soon tell us no place was left in His body, where
He might be smitten and was not. His skin and flesh rent with
the whips and scourges, His hands and feet wounded with the
nails, His head with the thorns, His very heart with the spear-
point: all His senses, all His parts laden with whatsoever wit or
malice could invent. His blessed body given as an anvil to be
beaten upon with the violent hands of those barbarous miscreants,
till they brought Him into this case of *si fuerit sicut* – 'if ever there
were the like . . .'

The very soul of sorrow

In this one, peradventure, some *sicut* may be found, in the pains of
the body; but 'in the second, the sorrow of the soul, I am sure, none.
And indeed, the pain of the body is but the body of pain; the very
soul of sorrow and pain is the soul's sorrow and pain . . .'

never the like sweat, never the like sorrow

'He began to be troubled in soul,' saith St John; 'to be in an agony,'
saith St Luke; 'to be in anguish of mind and deep distress,' saith St
Mark. To have his soul round about on every side environed with
sorrow, and that sorrow to the death. Here is trouble, anguish, agony,
sorrow, and deadly sorrow; but it must be such, as never the like: so it
was too.

The estimate whereof we may take from His sweat in the garden;
strange and the like whereof was never heard or seen.

No manner violence offered Him in body, no man touching Him
or being near Him; in a cold night, for they were fain to have a fire
within doors, lying abroad in the air and upon the cold earth, to be
all of a sweat, and that sweat to be blood; and not as they call it
diaphoreticus, 'a thin faint sweat', but *grumosus*, 'of great drops'; and
those so many, so plenteous, as they went through his apparel and all;
and through all streamed to the ground, and that in great abundance;
– read, enquire, and consider, *si fuerit sudor sicut sudor iste*: 'if ever
there were sweat like this sweat of His'. Never the like sweat certainly,
and therefore never the like sorrow.

Andrewes moves then from Gethsemane to Calvary: to his disciples forsaking him:

> *the most sorrowful complaint of all others*
> And that was His most sorrowful complaint of all others; not that his friends upon earth, but that His Father from Heaven had forsaken Him; that neither Heaven nor earth yielded Him any regard, but that between the passioned powers of His soul, and whatsoever might any ways refresh Him, there was a traverse drawn, and He left in the state of a weather-beaten tree, all desolate and forlorn. Evident, too evident, by that His most dreadful cry, which at once moved all the powers in Heaven and earth: 'My God, my God, why hast Thou forsaken Me?' Weigh well that cry, consider it well, and tell me, *si fuerit clamor sicut clamor iste*, 'if ever there were cry like that of His?': never the like cry, and therefore never the like sorrow.

Of the twenty pages in print of that great sermon I have quoted you less than four. But there is one sentence that I must not omit. Andrewes says: 'Mangled and massacred in most pitiful strange manner; wounded in Body, wounded in Spirit, left utterly desolate. O consider this well, and confess the case is truly put, *si fuerit Dolor sicut Dolor Meus* – if there be sorrow like unto my sorrow. Never, never the like person; and if as the person is, the passion be, never the like Passion to His.' There are ten pages after that sentence. Let me quote just the last paragraphs of the sermon – which is quiet and calm.

> *stay a little*
> It is kindly to consider *opus diei in die suo* 'the work of the day in the day it was wrought'; and this day it was wrought. This day, therefore, whatsoever business be, to lay them aside a little; whatsoever our haste, yet to stay a little, and to spend a few thoughts in calling to mind and taking to regard what this day the Son of God did and suffered for us; and all for this end, that what He was then we might not be, and what He is now we might be for ever.
> Which Almighty God grant we may do, more or less, even every one of us, according to the several measures of His grace in us.

That sermon I first read fifty years ago, in my last year of training at King's College, London, before ordination. Certainly no sermon has influenced me more. And no preacher has been more a pattern and example to me – in spite of the nearly four hundred years since Andrewes preached.

In our last year at King's, which those of us then reading theology spent at Warminster, we were asked to write a major essay: a kind of thesis. I chose Lancelot Andrewes for my subject – not only for his sermons but also because his preaching seemed to me to arise out of his studies, his friendships, his prayers, and his experience of the world around, and because, though his sermons were not 'designed to be read as literature', they revealed nevertheless what literary gifts could achieve when nature and grace were brought together.

Westminster Abbey and Eric Abbott

After I was ordained, I served a curacy in Westminster, which had King's College Theological Hostel within the parish, and, therefore, the home of Eric Abbott, Dean of King's – who, as I've said, had introduced me to the sermons of Andrewes. After Christmas one year we went to stay in Cambridge for a few days – little did I know my next appointment would be in Cambridge. Eric Abbott wanted to show me the Cambridge he loved. When he took me to Pembroke College he made it clear it was Andrewes' College, and in later years, when I have entered or passed Pembroke, I have often thought of it thus.

Andrewes was first a scholar there in 1571; then a Fellow; then, finally, Master of the College in 1589. The years he spent in residence bore much fruit. When he became a Fellow he learnt a new language each year. He was ordained deacon in 1580 and priest in 1581. He was appointed Catechist to the College in 1578 and gave a course of weekend lectures on the decalogue, to which town and gown came in growing numbers. It was clear that, in spite of his learning, he was in close touch with ordinary people.

The years that Andrewes spent at Cambridge were full of theological turbulence, yet were also years when weariness of that turbulence was evident. Andrewes was a man of peace. He said in a sermon in 1606,

'There is not a greater bar, a more fatal or forcible opposition to His entry than discord or disunited minds.' That was the keynote of Andrewes' life.

Gray's Inn

This is not the place to work systematically through all Andrewes' appointments and career. But I think you will understand how glad I was when I was made Preacher of Gray's Inn, in 1978, to learn that Andrewes had been admitted to the Inn – presumably in an honorary capacity – on 16 March 1590. There's a stained glass window in the Chapel, which commemorates Andrewes' association with the Inn. It may have been that association which introduced Andrewes to Francis Bacon. That they were intimate friends there is no doubt. Bacon often submitted his writings to Andrewes' literary judgement. Their friendship lasted many years, and, when Bishop of Ely, Andrewes would have lived in Ely Place – along Holborn from Gray's Inn – where the Bishops of Ely had their London house from the thirteenth century until 1772.

However, when Bacon was Lord Chancellor, and confessed to corruption, Andrewes must have been greatly embarrassed and, indeed, pained. The complications of that case need not detain us now.

I must record the fact that when Eric Abbott was made Dean of Westminster, in 1959, it was one of his chief delights that he was a successor to Andrewes. It was in July 1601 that Andrewes was appointed Dean. The sermon on Good Friday 1604 – to which we've already given our attention – was preached therefore when Andrewes was Dean of Westminster, and began the tradition, which lasts to the present day, by which the Dean preaches the Good Friday sermon to the Court.

Eric Abbott's delight in his predecessor Andrewes related not least to the fact that he was among those King James had appointed to translate the Bible, and was chairman of one of the six companies into which translators were divided. Andrewes' company had a membership of ten, and was responsible for the books from Genesis to 2 Kings. Not until 1611 was the translation completed.

When Eric Abbott first took me into the Jerusalem Chamber of the Abbey – 'Jerusalem' as he called it – he said, reflectively, 'Here, boy' (it was forty years ago) 'is where Lancelot Andrewes sat with his fellow translators.'

The political sermons and the public role

There is no great surprise in the fact that most of Andrewes' published sermons were for the major festivals of the Church – Christmas, Easter, Whitsun. But there are nineteen sermons known as the 'political' sermons. These have gained a rather negative rating from many modern critics. They were preached to commemorate the Gunpowder Plot and a not dissimilar conspiracy, or alleged conspiracy, in Scotland called 'The Gowries'.

When you are called upon to preach about major national events in which you yourself may have been caught up in some way, preaching may, of course, be particularly demanding. I well remember having to scrap my prepared sermon when Princess Diana was killed, and having to prepare another – during the night – for the Church where, it so happened, Princess Diana had worked at the attached kindergarten: St Saviour's, Pimlico. Then, the next Sunday, I had to preach at the Southwark Diocese official service to commemorate the death of Diana – the day after the funeral service in Westminster Abbey. My thoughts for that Southwark service were shaped and concentrated not least by a silent hour I was privileged to spend that previous week, in my capacity as a Queen's Chaplain, locked in the Chapel Royal at St James's alone with the coffin of the Princess. The crowds queued outside; but, inside the Palace, the coffin seemed, and indeed was, isolated, alone and lonely.

When I had been asked to be a Chaplain to Her Majesty the Queen I did not find the decision easy. I realized it was, of course, an honour, but I also remembered that the saintly Andrewes had been a royal chaplain – and was probably misled by an uncritical, even sycophantic, attitude to the Divine Right of Kings. It is not easy to be or to remain a loyal, admiring, yet critical member of a royal household.

But it must also be said that Andrewes was struggling to set forth a *Christian theology of the state*. In November 1601, for instance, he said, 'God impeacheth not Caesar . . . In the high and heavenly task of the preservation of all our lives, persons, estates and goods, in safety, peace and quietness . . . He hath associated Caesar to Himself.'

The Gunpowder Plot

These thoughts I, of set purpose, share with you before I ask you to remember the context of Andrewes' Guy Fawkes sermons. He was consecrated Bishop – All Saints' Day 1605 – the very day the existence of the Gunpowder Plot was revealed. Had the plot not been revealed, the explosion would have taken place on the day that Andrewes was for the first time qualified to sit in the House of Lords. In his first extant sermon after the plot, preaching on Christmas Day 1605, Andrewes refers to a deliverance from a danger 'so great and so fearful as the like was never imagined before'. The following Easter he compared it with the deliverance of Isaac from sacrifice by his father, Abraham.

Andrewes' selection of texts for his Gowrie and Gunpowder Plot sermons is powerful, to say the least:

- 'That we being delivered from the hands of our enemies might serve him without fear: in holiness and righteousness before him all the days of our life' (Luke 1:74–75)
- 'Touch not mine Anointed' (1 Chronicles 16:22a)
- 'And Chushi answered, The enemies of my Lord the King, and all that rise against thee to do thee hurt, be as that young man is.' (2 Samuel 8:32)
- 'By me Kings reign' (Proverbs 8:15a)
- 'My son, fear thou the Lord and the King; and meddle not with them that are given to change. For their destruction shall rise suddenly; and who knoweth the destruction of them both. These things also belong to the wise.' (Proverbs 24:21–23).

These sermons were all to members of the Court, and you can almost see his hearers hanging on his words. Certainly, if you want to read a first-hand description of what it felt like to be caught up in the first November 5th, you will find no better account than Andrewes' sermon preached on the first anniversary of November 5th.

Canon Paul Welsby – not an uncritical biographer of Andrewes – writes nevertheless:

It is therefore not for us who 'know better' to criticise unduly the attitude of Andrewes, although we may deplore his lack of charity and the vehemence of his expression. He and his contemporaries were only too anxiously aware of a fact which later historians cannot fully appreciate, that whether the Plot was representative of the designs of the English Romanists as a whole or not, if it had been successful, the King, the bishops, the whole body of judges, councillors and elder statesmen would have disappeared and the whole apparatus of government would have collapsed at one stroke. The consequences can be imagined even by us; how much more by those who lived through and were closest to these events.

The fundamental spirituality

It is, I think, somewhat misleading simply to call Andrewes' Gowrie and Gunpowder sermons 'political'. Andrewes' fundamental spirituality is plain in all his sermons. Let me quote just the last paragraph of his Gunpowder Plot sermon of 1615:

> Glory be to Thee, O Lord, glory be to Thee; glory be to Thee, and glory be to thy mercy, the *super omnia*, the most glorious of all thy great and high perfections. Glory be to Thee, and glory be to it – to it in Thee, and to Thee for it; and that by all Thy works, and above them all, by us here; by the hearts and lungs of us all, in this place, this day, for this day, and for the mercy of this day; for the mercy of it above all mercies, and for the work of this day above all the works of it. And not this day only, but all the days of our life, even as long as Thy mercy endureth, and that 'endureth for ever' – for ever in this world, for ever in the world to come; per, 'through' the cistern and conduit of all thy Mercies, Jesus Christ.

Nicholas Lossky, the Russian Orthodox lay theologian, in his book on *Lancelot Andrewes the Preacher*, says of Andrewes: he is 'someone who has made deeply his own the experience of the Church . . . for whom theology is not a system of thought, or an intellectual construction, but a

progression in the experience of the mystery, the way of union with God
in the communion of the Church.'

Preces Privatae

You may be surprised that I have left till last any comment on Andrewes'
book of prayers, compiled by him for his own personal use, known as
Preces Privatae.

There are several brief comments I should like to make on that volume:

- First: it was, as the title says, private – a book of private and personal
  prayer. Although there is one copy, on the cover of which is inscribed
  'My reverend friend Bishop Andrewes gave me this Booke a little before
  his death. W Bath et Welles' – that is to say, William Laud – it was
  never purposed by Andrewes that its contents should be used generally.
- Secondly: any edition that we use today is almost certainly a translation
  of a translation, and may even be a translation of that. The Greek and
  Latin originals will have been translated into English, but not the
  English of Andrewes.
- Thirdly: it is a classic of English piety, but it is undeniably a scholar's
  prayer book. And if, as his contemporary, Bishop Buckeridge, averred,
  Andrewes spent five hours each day in prayer and devotion to God, he
  had clearly a life with obligations different from most of us – though if
  we had five hours free each day it is unlikely that most of us would
  spend them in prayer and devotion to God.
- Fourthly: Andrewes was undoubtedly a man of method, system, discipline and order. Speaking for myself, I am a man of what I can only call
  consecrated chaos. My filing system is of the 'deep litter' variety. I think
  therefore my study and pattern of prayer, such as it is, might well have
  driven Andrewes mad – in minutes – though he might also have learnt
  patience with people like me through his prayer.

Mercifully, Dom John Chapman said: 'Pray as you can and do not try
to pray as you can't.' I think that means he would have said: 'Do not try to
be Lancelot Andrewes. Give thanks for him. But be yourself; and let
Andrewes help you. You will need something of his discipline, order,

method, system, structure and persistence. But if you don't learn that outside your prayer, it's unlikely you will learn it inside it.'

'Let Andrewes help you.' What might that mean? It means, surely, 'Do not let Andrewes dominate you. Let him serve you. Do not be afraid of using only fragments of Andrewes – and using them in your own way.

For instance: *Thursday morning*. Andrewes suggests we say in thanksgiving:

O my Lord, my Lord,
For that I am –
    that I am alive –
    that I am rational . . .

I suggest that such phrases of Andrewes will be quite enough to evoke prayer from many of us. To go on and on slavishly with all that Andrewes provides for Thursday morning, would be to substitute Andrewes' prayer for ours. We need to go over much that Andrewes provides with a kind of diviner's rod, and respond if and when the rod trembles.

Of course, Andrewes' prayer book may encourage us to make our own private prayer book. But let it be our own.

So let Andrewes renew in us our desire to be holy, with the raw material that God has given us, just as Andrewes longed to be holy with the raw material God had given him, which is manifest in his sermons, his prayers and his life.

It is marvellous that the original manuscript of Andrewes' *Preces Privatae* was said to be 'slubbered with his pious hands, and watered with his penitential tears', but before we indulge in an excess of admiration at his obvious sanctity, he, I am sure, would prefer us to ask searching questions about our own prayer, penitence and thankfulness – for and in the world we inhabit.

Finally – which Andrewes, the preacher, would never have allowed himself to say! – There is a lecture on *Lancelot Andrewes as a representative of Anglican principles*, given in 1898 by Walter Howard Frere – Superior and a Founder of the Community of the Resurrection, and, later, Bishop of Truro – in which he speaks of his love for Andrewes' and of Andrewes' influence on him, which is apparent in Frere's own written prayers. Some of those prayers were commended to me fifty years ago by Eric Abbott. So I end, not with Andrewes' own prayers, but with Andrewes' influence on Frere, and thus on Eric Abbot, and thus on me – and, I hope, on you. No prayer has influenced me more than this prayer, which Frere wrote under the acknowledged influence of Andrewes:

My God, I desire to love Thee perfectly:
With all my heart which Thou madest for Thyself,
With all my mind which only Thou canst satisfy,
With all my soul which fain would soar to Thee,
With all my strength, my feeble strength, which shrinks before so
great a task,
and yet can choose nought else but spend itself in loving Thee.
Claim Thou my heart, Fill Thou my mind,
Uplift my soul, and Reinforce my strength,
That where I fail Thou mayest succeed in me, and make me love
Thee perfectly.

Amen.

8 Sydney Smith

I have decided to write not primarily about Sydney himself. I want to discuss a question which I think is highly appropriate for me to raise: should Sydney Smith ever have been ordained? Let me hasten to say, I do not want to discuss the morals of Sydney, or, indeed, his spiritual and/or personal pastoral gifts. I want rather to draw attention to the culture that surrounded Sydney, out of which he, so to speak, emerged – as a priest of and to the people of his age and era.

I think I can best introduce my subject with a fragment of auto-biography. When, nearly fifty years ago, I went up to Trinity College, Cambridge, as a Chaplain, I was utterly ignorant of Cambridge: town and gown. I was myself a product of King's College, London, having matric-ulated through its evening classes, after seven years' work on London's riverside. Soon after the beginning of term, I found myself sitting at dinner, at High Table, next to G.M. Trevelyan, the former Master, by then a lonely widower. 'I'm Trevelyan,' he said. 'You're our new Chaplain. Welcome! I may be anti-clerical but I'm not anti-cleric!'

'What has this to do with *Sydney Smith?*' you may ask. Strictly speaking, very little. But Trevelyan was, of course, the author of the wartime best-seller, *English Social History*, published in 1942 and reprinted again and again – and again. Not only was Trevelyan not 'anti-cleric', he loved talking about clerical life, not least in the eighteenth century. The agnostic Trevelyan was the first person to teach me to see the clergy in the context of English Social History – where, of course, he also placed Sydney, and Parson Woodforde, and, indeed, 'the Parson'.

There was one other Fellow of Trinity who undoubtedly assisted with my education – the Chestertonian George Kitson-Clark, who was at work on his Ford Lectures, to be delivered in Oxford in 1960: 'The Making of

Victorian England'. He, too, furnished me with the background to Sydney Smith. As we walked the Backs at Cambridge of an afternoon, Kitson would boom out what he was preparing to say in Oxford, not really caring what I had to say by way of comment. I was alongside him simply as audience, gratefully gathering the crumbs that fell from the rich man's table.

I left Trinity and Cambridge in 1959, to be Warden of the Trinity College Mission in South London, St George's Camberwell. It was there, in December 1961, that I welcomed one of Kitson's research students, Peter Virgin, who was, of course, to write as brilliant a biography of Sydney Smith as has yet been written – published in 1994. He had preceded it in 1989 with another erudite volume, *The Church in an Age of Negligence*, which is essential reading for anyone who, like me, wants to understand 'the culture that surrounded Sydney, out of which he emerged as a priest'. I have, in fact, learnt more about Sydney Smith from Peter Virgin, who I am privileged to count as a close friend, than from any other scholar. Peter comes out with gnomic sayings from time to time, when I succeed in enticing him from his Rotherhithe lodgings to the cafés of Kennington.

'Never forget, Eric,' he said one evening, 'Oxford and Cambridge colleges in Sydney's time were virtually seminaries.' Put that way, I experienced a sudden sense of shock. But Peter was able, of course, immediately to produce the statistics to support his aphorism. 'In 1820 seventy per cent of Cambridge graduates became clergy.' And so on.

It may help, at this juncture, to share with you another fragment of autobiography. I have recently celebrated the fiftieth anniversary of my ordination to the priesthood. During this half century, I have had much to do with those who have felt themselves called to ordination in the Church of England. One sentence in the examination of candidates for ordination always seems to me almost unbearably powerful: the question directly addressed by the bishop to the candidates for ordination: 'Do you think in your heart that you be truly called according to the will of our Lord Jesus Christ and the order of this Church of England, to the Order and Ministry of Priesthood?'

It is an undeniably crucial question, and the English of the Book of Common Prayer in which it is couched serves only to articulate and emphasize that importance. I can clearly remember when that question was asked of me fifty years ago; and I've never heard it, in all the intervening years, at ordinations, without being moved.

I understand what a scholar like Peter Virgin means when he says that there has been a massive cultural shift in the understanding of what divides the sacred and the secular since Sydney Smith offered himself for ordination. The fact that so many clergy were, for instance, magistrates, and held a significant place in society, means that someone like Sydney would view the work of a parson somewhat differently from how an ordinand of today might view it. But ministry and magistracy were rarely combined without danger and, indeed, loss.

When Sydney contemplated ordination, clergy were getting significantly wealthier – if they secured the right living. And I can imagine Sydney, when his elder brother Bobus got married to Caroline Vernon, who was extremely well connected (to the Russells, the Foxes, the Lansdownes and the Hollands), thinking there might be literally a 'living' available to him from one or other of these 'connections'. But ministry and patronage were also rarely combined without danger and sometimes loss. And I am bound to say it baffles me how such a sensitive person as Sydney – sensitive to language and its significance and to the subtleties of argument and reason, as well as in humour but also logic, in human sympathy and wisdom – should be insensitive to the plain meaning of that question in the Ordinal. And I found myself asking not only what Sydney Smith understood by that question, but what the bishop who ordained him understood by it when he put it to Sydney; that is, to someone who, there can be no doubt, would have infinitely preferred to follow in his elder brother's footsteps, to the Bar, had that course of action received his father's approval and financial support.

My research into the mind and heart of the bishop who ordained Sydney was, however, destined to be somewhat limited, to say the least. There is no doubt that Sydney was ordained by Bishop Edward Smallwell, Bishop of Oxford. But what we can know of Smallwell is, alas, not much. Surprisingly, he is not mentioned in the *Dictionary of National Biography*. We know he was born in 1721; went to Westminster School; took his BA at Christ Church, Oxford in 1743, his MA in 1746/7, and his BD in 1755. We know he was Rector of Batsford in the Diocese of Gloucester from 1755 to 1799; that he was made Doctor of Divinity and a Canon of the Third Prebendary of Christ Church, Oxford in 1775, and was both Censor and Librarian there. We know he was consecrated Bishop of St David's in 1783 and translated to Oxford in 1788. We know that his lordship's death in 1799 was rather sudden, though, I quote: 'he had been a considerable time afflicted with a dropsical complaint'.

But when I asked my friend Richard Harries, the present Bishop of Oxford – at whose Consecration I was privileged to preach – what he knew about his predecessor, he replied, 'Sorry. Never heard of him.' And when I asked the archivist at Christ Church, Judith Curthoys, what information she had concerning Smallwell, she was unable to add more than that he was a curate of Cowley, in Oxford; and that there was a record of some correspondence between Smallwell and the Duke of Portland existing at Nottingham University – almost certainly William Henry Cavendish-Bentinck, third Duke of Portland. That University, alas, knew of no such correspondence. However, my friend at Gray's Inn, Lord Justice Roch, who was Presiding Judge of the Welsh and Chester Circuit, was able to tell me that there is a letter dated 20 July 1764, written by the Duchess of Portland to the third Duke, asking him to consider Smallwell for the living of Bothal, near Morpeth in Northumberland – to which, however, he was not appointed. But what is clear is that Smallwell had to go in search of livings, as, of course, Sydney did.

However, Lord Justice Roch, who lives in the Diocese of St David's, was also able to tell me that on 30 July 1784, Smallwell, as Bishop of St David's, preached the sermon at the Abbey Church, Westminster, to the Lords Spiritual and Temporal, on the 'day of general thanksgiving'; that the sermon was published; and that while Bishop of Oxford he preached on Friday, 18 February 1791 to the Incorporated Society for the Propagation of the Gospel in Foreign Parts at their anniversary meeting at St Mary-le-Bow. Furthermore, the Lord Justice told me, should we wish to read either of the bishop's published sermons, the Librarian at the University Library at Yale will gladly make copies of them available. Otherwise, our knowledge of Bishop Smallwell is, as I say, small indeed.

It's not only odd, it's also greatly dismaying that we know so much about Sydney but know – and can know – so little about the bishop who ordained him; for it is difficult to believe that the bishop had no thoughts about Sydney, who had been at New College from 1789 until the bishop ordained him in 1794 (the bishop, incidentally, died only five years after he had ordained Sydney).

To return though to Sydney, I have deliberately avoided writing of him as though he was primarily a wit – though it might have been more entertaining for you had I done so. But it has occurred to me, as erstwhile Director of the charity Christian Action for over seventeen years – a charity which amongst other things strongly supported the successful campaign for the abolition of capital punishment – that it would be appropriate for me to end what I have to say by quoting a passage from a sermon of Sydney which reveals a somewhat unusual but important aspect of him. It is a passage from a sermon he preached on behalf of 'The Society for the Diffusion of Knowledge upon the Punishment of Death and the Improvement of Prison Discipline' – a society founded in 1808.

Sydney preached the sermon towards the end of his life, when he was a canon of St Paul's. He took as his text Psalm 102: 19–20 – the Authorized Version: 'For he hath looked down from the height of his sanctuary: from heaven did the Lord behold the earth. To hear the groaning of the prisoners; to loose those that are appointed to death.' I shall quote only a small part from the sermon – though it is not a short one! As one hears it, it is important to see Sydney preaching under the great dome of St Paul's, with, of course, none of the benefits of a modern public address system.

After announcing his text, he begins his sermon:

> A question has been raised by some humane men, whether or not it is lawful to take away life as a punishment for crime. The argument has been carried on with great force and great ingenuity: the humane reasoner almost wishes that the objection to capital punishment could be made good, and that reason and reflection could be led to disapprove a practice at which every feeling of humanity trembles; but whatever be the difference of opinion among thoughtful men upon this important topic, there is one observation to which all men have agreed and *must* agree; and that is, that you yourself must not have taught the man you put to death the very crime for which he dies; that the executioner ought not to be the master; that the pupil ought not to be the victim; that the corruption worthy of death

should not have been instilled by him in whose hands the instrument of death is placed.

If there be cruelty upon earth – this it is! If there is a mockery of justice – that is it! What has been the state of our prisons before the late exertions of this valuable society, and what blood guiltiness laid upon us? A young man led out to execution in the flower of his youth, and sent before his God and his Redeemer, with all the solemn and appalling forms of justice! But what cruelty, you will ask, is there in all this? Was he not fairly tried? Yes. Was he not fairly heard? Certainly he was. Is there any doubt of his having committed the offence? None! But where did he learn to commit the offence? What blackened his soul? Where did he acquire that portion of hell which drove him to murder and to rob? You found him when a boy in the commission of some trifling offence, and you placed him in prison, among grown-up thieves and murderers; and no one came to see the poor wretch; and no one warned him. Howard [John Howard] was gone – and that blessed woman [Elizabeth Fry] who visits dungeons had not begun her labours of the Gospel; and day after day the poor youth was encouraged to murder and to steal – and the law smote him – and his soul is in the torments of hell! This is the foundation of our Society! Upon this plea we ask for your association and your assistance, that we may prevent crime, may prevent prisons from becoming the school of crime; that we may classify, assort, and separate in prisons; that we may avoid that awful responsibility and un-Christian feeling, that the victim of the law has become a victim of the law through our negligence, callousness, and coldness of heart; that we have grudged the expense of preparing proper receptacles; that we have grudged the time for inspection, and parental care; that the only activity and alacrity we have shown is in the infliction of those condign punishments which are never just but when everything has been done to render them infrequent and improbable.

What eloquence! What humanity! What courage! And what a fascinating paragraph of thoughts on Prison and Punishment to compare and contrast with our thinking today! I am not, of course, pretending that those two paragraphs adequately represent all that needs to be said on Sydney and Social Justice. Much more could be written on that.

I have not been able to do more than scratch the surface of the important question I set myself: should Sydney Smith ever have been ordained? But I am myself glad there was such a one as Sydney in the ordained ministry of the Church of England in the eighteenth and early nineteenth century, if only to preach such a sermon in such a place as St Paul's as that from which I have quoted.

9 Father Dolling

Fr Robert William Radclyffe Dolling was, without doubt, the right person to minister as a priest in a Portsmouth slum in the 1880s and 1890s. He did something significant and dramatic about what we now call an 'urban priority area', and about 'excluded people', in Victorian Portsmouth. I write neither as an historian nor, indeed, as a biographer, but I write to salute the memory of one who may yet help us, over a century later, to face some of the problems of our contemporary Church and society.

There are pockets of poverty in Britain today not altogether unlike that Victorian slum, and there are people who can help us to identify them. The Department of the Environment can now tell us immediately the fifty most deprived local authority districts in the land, as shown by the Index of Local Deprivation. Those districts that lie at the worst end of the scale are predominantly in the cities of the North and in several of the inner boroughs of London. But, thank God, Church Action on Poverty and the Church Urban Fund are at work in many of those districts, helping the local church and working with the local authorities.

Yet only a brief look at Dolling will alert us to the problems of providing a Dolling for the urban priority areas of today. Dolling was undoubtedly a complex personality. If he was the subject of enthusiastic – and often uncritical – admiration, he was no less the cause of utter exasperation. He himself admitted to being 'a crank and a fanatic'. Without doubt, few men could have been more difficult for any appointments committee to handle.

He was made deacon by Bishop Moberly, in Salisbury Cathedral, on 20 May 1883. He had been at theological college barely a year. He was ordained to a curacy in West Dorset, but the appointment was only nominal. He worked most of his time as a deacon not in Dorset but in Holy

Trinity, Stepney, which Magdalen College, Oxford, had adopted as its Mission.

Bishop Walsham How – suffragan bishop then of East London, and a kind of episcopal Betjeman – wrote a sonnet in praise of Dolling. Frederick Temple, How's diocesan Bishop of London, nevertheless refused to ordain Dolling as a priest to the kind of 'mission ministry' that How desired for Dolling. He had told Temple unashamedly that he had been too busy to read! Temple insisted he should be ordained to an ordinary curacy. This may have been more indicative of the strained relations between Temple and How than a judgement upon Dolling, but it was the cause of the first of Dolling's resignations – within weeks of his ordination to the priesthood. Thus Stepney's loss became Portsmouth's gain – though Davidson, then Bishop of Winchester, would have smiled a wry smile at that phrase, for, eventually, Dolling was to resign from his diocese also, of which Portsmouth was then, of course, a part.

Let us just glance at the earlier years of Dolling that brought him to priesthood and to Portsmouth. He was born in 1851, in Northern Ireland, the sixth child and the eldest son of a family of nine: in the old rectory of the parish of which his grandfather, a migrant to Ireland, had been rector. His father managed the estates of the Mercers' Company in County Derry. On his fourth birthday, it is recorded that the young Dolling was seriously ill. When his birthday cake was brought to his bed, he remarked – overpiously, at that age, one might think – 'Cut a piece for everyone in the house – and for those in the kitchen.' Many have observed that throughout his life Dolling never forgot 'those in the kitchen'.

When he was ten, he was sent to England, to a prep school at Stevenage – from which he endeavoured to escape with another boy. From there, he went to Harrow, where both the future Archbishop of Canterbury, Davidson, and Bishop Gore, were also schoolboys.

In 1868, as a 17-year-old, he went up to Trinity College, Cambridge, but stayed only a year. Eye trouble, it was averred, made study difficult for him. He spent most of the next year in Italy. In January 1870, after his mother's death, he returned to Ireland, to assist his father in his work, but he combined that work as a land agent with caring for the people in the community, especially boys and young men. In 1879, his father died, and Dolling went to London. There he came under the influence of

Fr Stanton, at St Alban's, Holborn. After two years, he decided to get ordained, and, in 1882, entered Salisbury Theological College.

The principal of Salisbury, E.B. Ottley, said that Dolling 'did not settle to serious study'; indeed, that 'it was almost impossible to induce him to read'. His fellow students christened him 'the Land Agent'. He rarely bothered to attend lectures, and 'thinly disguised his contempt for formal study'. He found the choral services in the cathedral a great trial, and – this may be somewhat of a surprise – 'used to read a book in the anthem'. He spent as much time as possible in the mission parish of St Martin, Salisbury, and became a great influence on the young men and boys of the parish, many of whom were wont to visit him in his college rooms.

The best summary of the work of Dolling in Portsmouth is to be found, I think, in the thirteenth chapter of the first volume of Bell's magisterial biography of Archbishop Davidson, which he began to write when he was Dean of Canterbury, having been Davidson's chaplain at Lambeth. (Later, he would be Bishop of Chichester.) He wrote:

> It was a singular misfortune that Bishop Davidson, at the very outset of his Winchester episcopate, found himself in conflict with one of the most remarkable clergy in the Diocese of Winchester, or in any diocese of that day. Robert Radclyffe Dolling was an Irishman of a most unconventional kind . . . At the age of thirty-two, he was ordained and ran a short-lived mission in the East End with what he called 'a sort of Chapel and music-hall combined'. Two years later, he found himself Vicar-designate of St Agatha's, Landport, and Priest-in-charge of the Winchester College Mission. He has written an account of his life at Landport in *Ten Years in a Portsmouth Slum*. His work was magnificent. The heart of it was the Parsonage, and the Mission Chapel was its soul. The Parsonage had a gymnasium attached with cubicles and hammocks for sailors to sleep in at night. It had also a common table, where all sorts and conditions rubbed shoulders with one another – soldiers, sailors, unemployed, Winchester College men, emigrants, down-and-outs. And Father Dolling presided over all, rotund, laughter-loving, affectionate, wearing a cassock and biretta, with a cigar or clay pipe sticking out of his mouth. At the end of six years, he was able to claim that, besides

114

much else, he had reformed 25 thieves just out of gaol, rescued 144 fallen women, started in life 100 young men living in the Parsonage, and closed 50 brothels in the district. No wonder that Mr John Pares, a well-known layman of the diocese, should write to Bishop Davidson at the end of Father Dolling's time: 'I have seen one of the worst "slums" of Portsmouth completely changed in character, and hundreds of souls brought to Christ by Mr Dolling's life and devotion.'

With the College itself, which supported the Missioner, he was no less successful. As the headmaster, Dr Fearon, said: 'His relation to Winchester College was pure, unbroken sunshine.' Wykehamists loved him, and he loved them. He was himself a boy to the end of his life, and he revelled in the fun and jokes of boys. He touched their hearts. He did not talk much about the Mission, but he got the boys to visit it year after year for weekends. He was astonishingly good in his talk to the boys in the Big School, in the Chapel, and the Chantry, and in their studies. He was a great rollicking, serious, irrepressible Christian gentleman – one of the institutions of Winchester during the ten years he was their missioner.

It may help at this juncture if I gather a kind of *catena* of comments that were made on Dolling.

We have noted already a most complimentary comment on him by Fearon, the headmaster of Winchester, but he also said: 'With Dolling one has to accept perpetually the prospect of a crisis.' Concerning Dolling's dramatic resignation from Portsmouth – when he had already resolved to retire a few months later – Bernard Palmer wrote: 'He seemed in fact to crave a martyr's crown.' Lord Northcliffe, the newspaper magnate, said of Dolling: 'He appealed to me primarily by reason of his great power of organisation. He not only knew how things ought to be done, but was able to make the most unlikely people do them. He knew how to make weak people self-reliant.' Osborne, Dolling's curate, and later his biographer, called him 'an ecclesiastical Cecil Rhodes' – and the remark was clearly intended as a compliment, to describe Dolling's capacity to plan ever fresh developments. (For a vicar to be a hero to his curate surely says something significant about his vicar!) The future Superior of the

Community of the Resurrection, Edward Keble Talbot, was so moved by one of Dolling's sermons when he was a boy at Winchester, that he put a pound – a whole half-term's pocket money – in the collection.

After his death, *The Times* said of Dolling that he 'elevated injudiciousness into a fine art'.

There is just one other person whose comments I think we should hear: the Modernist theologian, George Tyrrell, who eventually became a Jesuit. He was a native of Dublin, of Evangelical upbringing. At an early age he came under the influence of Dolling, and described him as 'my best and dearest friend'. He wrote: 'He entrusted me with the library – chiefly theological – which he was then collecting.' (That's a surprise in itself!) 'With many hours devoted to the task, an acquaintance grew into that lasting friendship which I account as one of the greatest graces of my life.' 'Himself an apostle born and not made', Tyrrell continues 'the governing motive of his life, and therefore of his thought, was a deep and affectionate love of the individual soul – the love of a man for men, not the love of a man for a system or religion for which he was to secure proselytes or victims.' Tyrrell says of Dolling, as the Warden of a House in Borough Road, near the Elephant and Castle – to which Fr Stanton had appointed him – before he was ordained: 'It was there that I saw him in his full glory as a Christian Socialist.' That term needs, of course, careful handling, but it is a remark not to be ignored.

Let me remind you that Dolling was in Portsmouth for only ten years. Canon Alan Wilkinson, in his Scott Holland lectures for 1998, states baldly: 'When Dolling left, in 1896, the parish never recovered.' Clearly the problem of continuity is not one we can ignore. We are, I think, getting closer to being able to confront the question: 'What has Dolling to say to us today?' Yet I think I should utter at this point a warning. John Donne said 'comparisons are odious'. (Shakespeare said they were 'odorous'!) Yet we need to make them – carefully. And as soon as we begin to compare the Church in inner-city Portsmouth in the Victorian era with the Church in urban priority areas today, we see some of the reasons for the comparative success of Dolling.

The Winchester College Mission in Portsmouth related to a population of, at most, 7000 poor and crowded people: part of a parish of 27,000. (Professor Kenneth Inglis in his study *Churches and the Working Classes in*

Victorian England gives the population of the area of the Winchester Mission as only 5000.) For that area, in Dolling's decade, there were always two or three assistant clergy to Dolling. There were resident lay-men, often candidates for Holy Orders, perhaps the most notable of which was Conrad Noel, later, of course, the great Socialist Vicar of Thaxted. There were also lady workers and district visitors. This large staff of fellow workers, clerical and lay, enabled Dolling to claim, without exaggeration, that he touched 'every room in the most crowded courts and lanes around St Agatha's'. Such a concentration of ministry required, of course, money. Dolling, the 'Land Agent', knew that well. Not the least of his gifts was that of extracting money from, for instance, the well-heeled Winchester College parents. Continuity, however, implies, not least, con-tinuity of finance. And the collapse of St Agatha's after Dolling's departure raises important questions concerning relating finance primarily to the ministry of particular people with particular gifts.

There is at least one other hugely important factor to be noted in any comparison of the ministry of Dolling with ministry in urban priority areas today. The Welfare State as we know it now had hardly begun to see the light of day in Dolling's day. Dolling saw St Agatha's, and I quote, as 'the chief centre for social righteousness to the whole district', providing for 'man – body, soul and spirit', 'treated as a whole'. It was marvellous that Dolling should have been, in the name of Christ, such a beacon of social righteousness. It gives meaning not least to what Dolling meant by a 'Christian Socialist'. But it would not be long before the state would begin to take up that task to which Dolling and others challenged it. And then the role of the priest in Portsmouth was bound to change. The Church would need to collaborate with the state as well as continue to challenge it. The work of the priest would inevitably be less visible. What was never claimed for Dolling, in his remarkable ten years at Portsmouth, was that, to any significant extent, he challenged the conclusions of Charles Booth, in his great study of *The Life and Labour of the People of London*, published in 1902. Booth summed up his conclusions:

> The great section of the population, which passes by the name of the working classes, lying socially between the lower middle class and the 'poor', remains, as a whole, outside of all the religious bodies,

whether organised as churches or as missions; and as those of them who do join any church become almost indistinguishable from the class with which they then mix, the change that has really come about is not so much *of* as *out of* the class to which they have belonged.

All the evidence is that the social and religious realities of Portsmouth were not greatly dissimilar to those in London. But, for a century, the danger has been that the Church would look back romantically rather than realistically on the days of Dolling, and allow his ten-year success, in one limited area, with exceptional resources, to mask the truth of the overall situation, with wistful cries of 'If only . . .': 'If only we had Dolling's gifts . . . Dolling's resources . . . a Dolling-sized parish'; and so on.

Dolling can, in fact, help us to face the complex realities of today. But I don't think we shall get much further with the questions he raises unless we go first to the heart of the matter, and ask: 'What was the priesthood to which Robert William Radclyffe Dolling said he felt called?' I am aware that to answer that question fully would mean consulting the libraries of books which have been written on the nature of priesthood. But it's not that kind of answer that I think we need here and now.

I cannot myself forget that at Michaelmas 1952, when I went to St Paul's Cathedral to be ordained priest, a letter was waiting for me from my friend and mentor, Eric Abbott, then Dean of King's College, London, where I had trained for ordination. Eric reminded me that I would not become a priest in a moment, in the twinkling of an eye, when the bishop's hands were laid upon me the next day. What would happen then would be that the priesthood which had been gradually becoming manifest in me over the years, would be recognized by the Church. That remark has encouraged me throughout my ministry to be constantly on the lookout for signs of priesthood in others; and I have rejoiced at it sometimes in surprising situations and people. That, surely, has something to say to the Church today: about the need to watch for the spark of priesthood and to fan it into a flame. There is evidence that people recognized in Robert Dolling such signs of priesthood long before he was ordained.

Let me then add that it was Eric Abbott who introduced me to a kind of prayer-cum-poem about priesthood – by the seventeenth-century bishop, Thomas Ken – which I have kept on my bedroom windowsill from my first days of priesthood until now. It has reminded me often not only of my own vocation but also of the vocation of others, as yet unrecognized:

> Give me the Priest these Graces shall possess:
> Of an Ambassador the just Address,
> A Father's Tenderness, a Shepherd's Care,
> A Leader's Courage, which the Cross can bear,
> A Ruler's Arm, a Watchman's wakeful Eye,
> A Pilot's Skill, the Helm in Storms to ply,
> A Fisher's Patience and a Lab'rers Toil,
> A Guide's Dexterity to disembroil,
> A Prophet's Inspiration from Above,
> A Teacher's Knowledge, and a Saviour's Love.
> Give me the Priest, a Light upon a Hill,
> Whose Rays his whole Circumference can fill;
> In God's own Word, and sacred Learning vers'd,
> Deep in the Study of the Heart immers'd,
> Who in such Souls can the Disease descry
> And wisely fit Restoratives apply.

I do not doubt that Dolling would have wanted to make those lines of Bishop Ken his own.

There is a third 'definition' – if that's the right word – which I would like to set before you. In 1962, when I'd been ordained priest ten years, and was Vicar of St George's, Camberwell – an inner-city parish in South London, which was raising for me acute questions about the nature of priesthood at that time – I began to write my first book. Subtitled *The Shape of the Ministry Today*, I called it *Odd Man Out?* While I was writing it, an aristocratic and eccentric old lady, Hilda Grenfell – a Lyttelton by birth – introduced me to the writings of Pierre Teilhard de Chardin, which she herself had translated from the French. I included in my book, as its penultimate paragraph hitherto unpublished in England, which de Chardin had written, in 1918, in a brief monograph he had simply called *Le Prêtre*. He wrote:

To the full extent of my powers, because I am a priest, I wish from now on to be the first to become conscious of all that the world loves, pursues, suffers. I would be the first to seek, to sympathise, to suffer; the first to open myself out and sacrifice myself – to become more widely human and more nobly of the earth than any of the world's servants.

After that paragraph, I simply wrote, to end my book: 'There speaks a priest of this century the truth of priesthood which this century waits to hear; for in the truth of priesthood there is the truth of man himself.' I am still satisfied with those three 'definitions' of priesthood.

We do not know precisely when Dolling's vocation to the priesthood first manifested itself. We do know that Fr Stanton, at St Alban's, Holborn, did much to encourage it. In 1877, Stanton had initiated a most remarkable piece of pastoral work at St Alban's, Holborn. He had formed the St Martin's League for postmen. It was open to all employed by the Post Office, without religious distinction. Stanton was president. He wrote to members of the League:

'Right away, I urge, see to our object to try and love one another. You smile as you read this, as you always do when I tell you this is our bounden duty. We are not only to put up with one another, but to love one another with all that that word 'love' implies – choice, sacrifice, and union . . . 'How can a fellow love a fellow?' I answer 'How can he *not* and live with him – what is League or Life without Love? . . .'

Almost all the League were young unmarried postmen. Robert Dolling – 'Brother Bob' as he was soon called – came to London and to St Alban's in 1879, and was soon made Warden of the League's house for the South East Postmen's District, in Borough Road, near the Elephant and Castle, for about a year.

In February 1882, Archbishop Tait preached to 500 members of the League of St Martin-in-the-Fields. The League's total membership was 700. It has never been recognized as such, but the League was, surely, one of the first and most important precursors of Industrial Mission. Dolling gave much time to it and received much from it. There was always tea at St Alban's on Sundays for the postmen – and for the 'hooligans', as they were called, from the slums surrounding St Alban's.

To involve the 28-year-old Dolling in the pastoral work of the St Martin's League, as well as in the worship at St Alban's, was an imaginative pastoral act in itself. It should surely provoke us to think today what the Church is doing – and might yet do – in youth and community work and in social action, and how the laity of the Church can be involved in that and other pastoral work.

I have not changed my mind since I wrote in a preparatory essay I was asked to write for the Lambeth Conference of 1968:

> In addition to the present method of recruitment for ordained ministry, which relies primarily on the call subjectively experienced, recruitment for the ministry should be woven into the whole structure of the local church. For this to be more than a pious hope, the local congregation will need some regular inescapable confrontation. Each year, for instance, at a special meeting of the congregation (at, say, Whitsuntide), the whole congregation should be called together to consider who – if any – should be nominated from the parish or electoral roll, as candidates for further training for ministry . . .

I went on to underline that such a method of recruitment needed to be related to training for ministry for all, in which what was involved in 'varieties of ministry' – particular kinds of ministry – was specified.

To be a member of a congregation should mean being inescapably confronted by the question: 'What ministry am I called to?' And: 'What further training do I need?' Dolling's work as a Land Agent and his community work in Ireland was ministry, and it led to other forms of ministry. Fr Stanton soon spotted Dolling's gifts, possibilities and potential. St Alban's was not simply 'smells and bells'. It was the significance of worship, and the interrelatedness of worship and pastoral ministry, that Dolling discovered at St Alban's, and he learnt there also what he might later do in Portsmouth.

So far, we have reflected little on the important work of encouraging vocations like Dolling's. It is clear, from the number of ordinands Dolling had to live with him at Portsmouth – after the failure of the training at Salisbury to engage his enthusiasm – that he had his own ideas as to what training for ministry in areas like St Agatha's should involve. It needed to be more what we would now call 'contextual' – closely related to the context of places like the slums of Portsmouth. We have also already noted, in passing, that money for ministry is an important subject.

That great Bishop of Sheffield, Leslie Hunter – whose biography, by several hands, was aptly entitled *Strategist for the Spirit* – when he was Archdeacon of Northumberland, published in 1937, an important pamphlet called *Men, Money and the Ministry*. He followed that, in 1941, with *Putting Our House in Order*. It was the beginning of a movement for radical reform in the Church of England of the payment, care and deployment of the clergy. It was not until twenty years later that, on 14 July 1960, the subject was taken up by the Church Assembly, who decided to ask Dr Leslie Paul, a sociologist, to make a report, which was published in 1964. *The Paul Report* was followed by the Morley Commission of which I was a member. Its Report, *Partners in Ministry*, was published in 1967.

I resigned as Vicar of St George's, Camberwell in 1964, in order to 'stump the country' as Director of the organization *Parish and People*, to put before the Church what, basically, Leslie Hunter had appealed for in the thirties: an organizational structure which would enable there to be Dollings financed, cared for and deployed where they were most needed. I myself became a member of the Morley Commission. The recommendations of the Report of the Morley Commission were, alas, castrated by the Church Assembly – shortly to be succeeded in 1970 by the General Synod. It needs to be understood and underlined that the Morley Report was not simply about the Payment and Deployment of the Clergy. Because it covered that, it was therefore about such thorny subjects as the care and support, the dependence, independence and interdependence of the clergy and the laity: hence its title *Partners in Ministry*.

Let me relate what I've said on the subject to the life and ministry of Fr Dolling, and vice versa: It was a private patron, Winchester College, that appointed Dolling to Portsmouth, and it is very doubtful indeed whether he would have gone to Portsmouth without such a patron. It was private patronage at its best, and it warns us about the dangers of ecclesiastical power when it is given only to a bishop, or to a committee that, in reality, is in the power of a bishop. Power – the power of patronage and appointment – dare not be despised or neglected by those who have the needs of the inner-city at heart. Nor dare we evade the question: 'Would a Dolling be ordained – and appointed – today?' Has the desire for bishops to speak with one voice – with a kind of corporate curial loyalty and unanimity – so triumphed as to quench the Spirit, and so suffocate that gift of prophecy that is part of priesthood? (And prophecy is not simply in words: Dolling was a prophet primarily as a pastor.) Can a Dolling-like 'Odd Man Out' now survive the system?

Dolling raised most of the funds he needed from those who appointed him, but it was a hit-and-miss affair. As soon as Dolling had gone, the funds dried up. Such a system has little to commend it.

Now, after Morley, there is a disbursement of funds to all dioceses and to all parishes that is – at least in theory – much less dependent on the initiative of the local priest or patron. But I believe the time has come to look again at *Men, Money and the Ministry*, to ensure that the Urban Priority Areas of today get the ministry of men and women that they need and deserve. There are, without doubt, several new factors – not least, but not only, financial – which affect payment, care, support and deployment.

There is, of course, now the fact of the ordination of women, and there is also the employment of clergy wives. In practice, it is often now the job of the wife of the priest (and sometimes of the husband?) that is one of the main factors in deployment. There are certain factors which specially affect the deployment of clergy in UPAs, particularly clergy with families.

Not long ago, I was asked to go away with about twenty clergy, men and women, who come from the Deanery of Tower Hamlets, in the East End of London. Their parishes all lie between the Isle of Dogs and the Tower of London. They had given their annual residential conference the significant title 'An exploration of Anger within God's world and within ourselves', and had invited me to give what help I could, by way of some addresses. I felt very privileged to do so, because I know well their places of ministry, and that they are a sorely tried and tested group of people. In the first session, I asked each member of the conference to say, in three minutes, what personal and social anger meant for them, in their particular circumstances. The first person told us that in the previous week every window of his home had been suddenly smashed by a gang of teenagers, and when he rushed out, they set on him, and he was left in the gutter with damage to his ribcage from which he would take several weeks to recover. It was good of him to come to our conference at all. He was still in considerable pain. He was a mild sort of man, but he was, very understandably, quite angry. The second person talked of the double murder which had taken place a few doors away from the vicarage during the previous week. As it happened, he knew the family well, and was feeling a bit guilty at coming away from the parish to a conference at such a time of need. But, as he said, every week in that parish brings its fresh crop of violence.

The first stories were not entirely untypical, I'm sad to say, of what most of the members of the conference had to report. They were clearly living in, and describing, a very violent society, and they themselves were, of course, not without violence in their reaction, however much they tried to control it and bottle it up. What was clear was that they were living in a society in which the perception of the role of the clergy had changed almost out of all recognition from the days of Fr Dolling.

When I lived in inner Southwark, in the sixties, my canonry – an erstwhile vicarage – was next door to a block of flats which still had a foundation stone visible describing it as 'police barracks', and people would often talk of what had once been a 'no-go area' even for police, except in pairs; but everyone said the clergy of Southwark and Bermondsey were then 'father figures' – as, clearly, Father Dolling was. Many factors, however, not least drugs, have radically changed that perception – as, for example, anyone travelling late at night in a dog-collar on the underground near, say, the Elephant and Castle, may well now discover.

It is worth noting that when Dolling served his brief spell in the East End of London, it was even then a complex multi-racial society. There was, as there still is, an Italian community – with its church – near St Alban's, Holborn. Since 1870 Jewish migrants had greatly diminished the number of those who belonged to the Church of England in the parish of Whitechapel. There was a large population of Irish Roman Catholics in London, many of them poverty-stricken. And in Portsmouth Dolling was soon made aware that the sailors who lodged there belonged to many nations.

Yet it is clear that since 1945, inner-city areas in Britain have often become multi-cultural, multi-racial and multi-faith to a degree that was not even imagined in the 1880s. This provides new challenges and opportunities, and – there is no need to deny it – new difficulties for parochial ministry. Hindus in Britain now number 400,000; Muslims one million; Sikhs 400,000. Britain's oldest minority, the Jews, number 300,000. These communities are overwhelmingly concentrated in inner urban areas. The theological questions posed by other religions cannot be avoided, and these questions challenge the Church's understanding of itself.

There is one other subject which I might prefer to, but cannot, ignore, because, for me, it rises directly out of any reflection upon the subject of the ministry of Fr Dolling and ministry in urban priority areas. It is stated clearly, time and gain, in biographical writings about Dolling, that he was 'good with men and boys': not least with the schoolboys of Winchester College and with the training-ship boys and sailors of Portsmouth. The Revd the Hon. James Adderley, in an essay on Dolling in *Great Christians* refers quite naturally to 'one of his boys', who ran away but returned to Dolling. We must, of course, remember that Dolling's Victorian era was still, paradoxically, a masculine world. Dolling was unmarried, and it is a sober conclusion that he was in all probability homosexual. There is, indeed, every likelihood that he was one of the many gay priests – as we now call them – who have done marvellous work in the slums of great cities, and in that world and ministry have found themselves totally fulfilled. Inner-city ministry would have been decimated without them.

The recent declarations of the Lambeth Bishops on homosexuality and priesthood have, however, made many priests in inner-cities, and many ordinands who might have served in them, think again. Some priests I know – priests of great quality – have resigned their full-time posts and sought secular employment. Some ordinands I know have decided not to be ordained, though there was every prospect that they would have made marvellous priests in the inner-city. I believe the bishops should be asked to think again: to think what their declarations have done, particularly to ordained ministry in the inner-city, and what they have done to prevent individuals finding that fulfilment in priesthood that Dolling so clearly found.

Of course, in Dolling's time the whole subject of sex was 'under wraps', but in our post-Freudian age it is impossible to keep sexuality quiet, so to speak. Let me quote from a letter published this summer in *CR*, the quarterly review of the Community of the Resurrection. The writer, a theological graduate, but alas, now an erstwhile ordinand, wrote: 'No wonder that I am so unhappy, because it was through the emphasis on the doctrine of the "incarnation" and the Anglican church's claim to be truly Catholic that I first realised this was the place where I belonged.' He ended his letter no less movingly. He referred to the 'crucible of pain, hurt, doubt, paradox and fear that is symbolised in the Cross' and said: 'I guess it is to this Cross that I now have to look in deciding whether the ultimate sign of my calling to the priesthood will be a sacrificing of it and all that it means to me as I choose not to seek ordination in God's church or whether I should continue.'

It is, of course, places like Mirfield which have the heavy responsibility of both interpreting the Bishops' Lambeth declarations and of training future Dollings – once they have been *selected* for training. 'Ay, there's the rub.'

And what of the gospel Dolling preached and the gospel preached today? I have been able to find few published sermons of Dolling. He was an orator of undoubted eloquence rather than one who wrote his sermons. There is, however, in *Sermons and Society* (an Anglican anthology edited by Canon Paul Welsby in 1970) an extract from a sermon by Dolling entitled 'Soldiers and Sailors' preached at St Edmund's, Lombard Street, in Lent 1898 – one of a course of sermons organized for City businessmen by the London branch of the Christian Social Union. That sermon is almost entirely concerned with conditions in the armed services from the perspective of someone who daily had to deal with them in Portsmouth. It underlines what Stephen Mayor said of Dolling in *The Churches and the Labour Movement* in 1967: 'He was essentially a parish priest, unafraid of public controversy, but chiefly concerned to minister to the needs of the poor around his church.'

Dolling, I believe, would be one with those who today insist that urban theology involves a call from God to reflect with people, in the midst of decay and despair, upon the realities of their situation, and upon what the gospel says to us; and would insist also, I suspect, that it was because Jesus lived with the poor that he could say with integrity, 'Blessed are the poor'. Dolling did not believe the Church was constituted simply by those who believed the gospel with their minds. He believed passionately that they needed also to act out the good news. The parish regularly fed two hundred children and twenty old people twice a week. There was a communal meal for eighteen on weekdays and for forty on Sundays.

I quoted earlier the comments of Lord Northcliffe on the ministry of Dolling, and noted that he gave Dolling considerable financial support. Northcliffe was born in 1865. He was 20 when Dolling went to Portsmouth. He was one of the five Harmsworth brothers who became famous as British newspaper magnates and politicians. It was said that in later years if Dolling was preaching anywhere near, Northcliffe would be in the pew, and would always be ready with princely benefactions. Dolling's influence on Northcliffe, it has to be said, is anything but immediately obvious in his later life: as proprietor of the *Evening News* from 1894; the *Daily Mail* from 1896; the *Daily Mirror* from 1903; and *The Times* from 1908. Northcliffe died in 1922. Few people had had more opportunity to influence the policies and politics, and, indeed, the life of our nation.

Since *Faith in the City* – the Report of the Archbishop's Commission on Urban Priority Areas, published in 1985 – I have had the great privilege of seeing its effects on the life of the Church of England in all the principal cities of our land. I can only be grateful for what it has achieved both in Church and state. I have already paid tribute to the work of the Church Urban Fund and Church Action on Poverty. But it would be idle for me to pretend that *Faith in the City* changed the face of England or of the Church of England. We are still two nations – and, indeed, two churches. Go to a meeting in, say, Hastings – a place today of much unemployment – and you will not find much concern with the homeless and the unemployed there from those who live more than a few miles from Hastings. Go to, say, Sunderland, and you will find a different world from the South of England. Unemployment and poverty in the North are a world apart from the employment and housing in the South.

Dolling did great work helping the boys of Winchester College to have some understanding of the slums of Portsmouth. He did it, not least, by keeping an open house where men and women of all kinds congregated. 'It was an amazing Family which gathered round Dolling, not one but loved him, not one who ever felt he was despaired of or forgotten or despised.' So wrote James Adderley. 'He had a wonderful power to enthral', so wrote Canon Scott Holland. 'He shocked us out of our nervous proprieties.'

The tragedy is that within five years of his leaving Portsmouth, Dolling was dead. For eighteen months he had been out of work. He wrote his bestseller *Ten Years in a Portsmouth Slum*. He preached not only all round England but also in the United States. In 1898 he went to St Saviour's, Poplar, but lasted only three years there. Portsmouth had worn him out. He was 51 when he died in 1902.

When I was a curate, in the early fifties, at St Stephen's, Rochester Row, there was a devout old lady of fourscore years, who 'departed not from the temple', and, indeed, set all the curates – and the vicar – an example of prayer. When she had them to tea, she would diffidently press upon them a copy of her biography of her brother, *Mark Napier Trollope*, who became Bishop of Korea in 1911. He had returned as a missionary from Korea in 1902, on account of his father's failing health, and in the first years of that interlude in England he was appointed Fr Dolling's successor at St Saviour's, Poplar.

Constance Trollope's chapter on Poplar provides one of the most interesting accounts of the Church there at the beginning of the century. Miss Trollope first of all quotes an assistant priest at St Saviour's in Mark Napier Trollope's time: 'The appointment of a successor to Father Dolling', he says, 'was a difficult task, even though his regime at St Saviour's had been short. Lives of Dolling minimise his achievement in Poplar, but though Poplar was different to Landport, the parish was transformed. Somehow the spirit of the man was a felt pressure and influence.' That is surely a very important tribute.

For the life and ministry of Robert Dolling we give thanks. But the point of this chapter cannot be primarily to look back to the past. It is surely to make some contribution, however small, in this rapidly changing world, particularly in inner-city areas, to ensure that people with Dolling-like gifts of ministry shall be enabled to use them where they are most needed and best used. And I remind you that it was Lord Northcliffe who said that one of Dolling's great gifts was to enable others to realize and use their gifts. This rather contradicts James Adderley, who said of Dolling that he was 'an original sort of spiritual Dictator', and that 'the secret of Dolling' lay in large part in 'his natural capacity for generalship'.

There are still, alas, Anglican priests who run '*their* parish' – the possessive is important! – like a dictator. And if, and when, they go, it all collapses – as it did when Dolling departed – unless and until another dictator is appointed. Dolling, it might be said, would have been even more successful if one of his main aims had been to work himself out of a job. Maybe, after all, it is not just more Dollings that we need in our UPAs but also a ministry the main ambition of which is to liberate the gifts of ministry of those who live in the Landports of today.

Having resisted the temptation to begin this chapter with 'Hello Dolling', I must now stiffen that resistance and refuse to end it with 'Goodbye Dolling, I must leave you'. I should end, I believe, simply by giving thanks that, for ten years, over a century ago, Dolling set an example which is still valid: an example of ministry in a fragmented society that, in the name and in the power of Christ, did something to heal that society and bring it together. Winnington-Ingram, Bishop of London, said of Dolling at his funeral 'When everybody else had given a man up, it was always said "Dolling will take him".' To conclude I must proclaim my belief and share my conviction, after roughly half a century of ministry, that the Church and, not least, its ordained ministry, still has a unique opportunity, living where it ministers, to continue that work of healing, particularly in our inner-cities and urban priority areas today.

10 Charles Gore: the preacher

It was in December 1876 that Charles Gore heard the words, unforgettable to him who hears them spoken to himself, 'Take thou authority to read the Gospel and to preach the same, if thou be licensed thereto by the bishop himself.' Gore was then a young fellow of Trinity College, Oxford.

Gore delivered his last sermon on 22 August 1931, at the Grosvenor Chapel. Significantly, it was on 'Social Righteousness and the Christian'. That very week Ramsay Macdonald resigned as head of the Labour Government and formed a National Government to balance the budget.

It is impossible to recover and record, now, all the influences that went towards the making of Gore's ministry. There was undoubtedly the influence of his aristocratic home. He wrote once, in a birthday letter to his mother: 'I do indeed feel, whenever I think, that I owe you almost everything that is worth having in me.' From his sister we know that Gore preached his first sermon in a nightgown, to the nursery, from the pulpit of a towel-horse.

Amongst the near-neighbours to their forty-acre home at Wimbledon was Henry Scott Holland, six years older than Gore, who was to become one of Gore's closest and most intimate friends, and as great a preacher, if not greater.

The influence of Gore's schooldays is clearly crucial. Gore was at Harrow when Montagu Butler was headmaster. But even more significant is the fact that Brooke Foss Westcott was one of the young assistant masters. Gore himself later confessed that a sermon on 'The Disciplined Life' which Westcott preached in 1868 had an indelible effect upon the 15-year-old future founder of the Community of the Resurrection. 'Seldom has there been such a preacher, seldom such a listener', wrote Albert Mansbridge.

By the time he was 17, Gore was escaping the ordinary English ways of his family. His letters to George Russell describe expeditions to St Alban's, Holborn, and to St Michael's, Shoreditch. In 1871, he writes: 'Such a splendid service at St Alban's, with the Hallelujah chorus at the end of Mass, accompanied by a full band. Such a magnificent sermon from Father Stanton.' Fr Stanton taught him to make his confession, to love the Mass, and to fast on Fridays. But Holborn and Shoreditch in those days were places where the poor lived. Westcott it was who taught the young Charles Gore – for life – to love the poor: no trivial contribution to the ministry of a preacher.

Having carried off a packet of prizes at Harrow – for Greek Epigrams, Latin Elegiacs and Latin Essay, and English Literature – all of which would leave some mark on his preaching, Gore went up to Balliol. Oxford, then, was dominated by T.H. Green, but there were Jowett's sermons, too, in Balliol Chapel, and Liddon at Christ Church, and R.M. Benson at Cowley.

But Oxford for Gore was the place of the *meeting* of friends, and his Oxford friends – the circle that gradually grew into the Lux Mundi group – were no inconsiderable influence upon his ministry as a preacher: Henry Scott Holland, Edward Stuart Talbot, J.R. Illingworth, Francis Paget, R.C. Moberly, Arthur Lyttleton, R.L. Ottley, Aubrey Moore, Walter Lock, W.J.H. Campion.

Yet Bishop Michael Ramsey, in a lecture more than forty years ago, reminded his hearers of perhaps the supreme influence on Gore, the preacher: the Bible itself: 'The Bible was the pasture ground of his mind: and with it the themes of judgement and catastrophe, of a God who punishes, chastens and raises from death. His mind and conscience wrestled with the reconciling of the data of human experience with that faith in the God of the Bible by which he lived.'

Gore was elected a Fellow of Trinity College, Oxford, in 1875, was made deacon by Bishop Mackarness in 1876, and was ordained priest in 1878. It rarely gains sufficient attention that Gore, while his Fellowship at Trinity continued to run, undertook assistant curacies at Christ Church, Bottle, where he preached twenty-one sermons in three months, and then at St Margaret's, Princes Road, Liverpool. That confrontation with the urban realities of Liverpool, at weekends and in vacations, would have contributed much to the message of Gore.

In 1879, at 26 years of age, he became Vice Principal of Cuddesdon, and Prestige records that 'his sermons, both in the College chapel and in the parish church, brought home to the students a new realization of the meaning of self-dedication and of membership in the Christian society'. He adds:

> His reading of the Lessons was then as ever an inspiration in itself, as with arresting voice he unfolded the argument of the passage. Gore knew his Bible well, and with the sense of the passage in his mind went far to identify himself, as he read, with the sacred writer. He would retire further and further from the lectern, with the hand of either arm thrust into the cassock sleeve of the other; then suddenly release his hands and hurry forward to turn over the page.

Pusey died, at the age of 82, in 1882 and in the course of a year £25,000 had been collected to build the 'Dr Pusey Memorial Library', commonly known as Pusey House. In November 1883 Gore was appointed Principal Librarian. It was not least Gore, the preacher, the selectors had in mind. Although there would be a good-sized oratory in the House, there was also a scheme – 'Keep this utterly dark,' wrote Scott Holland – to obtain the full use of St Mary's on Sunday evenings: 'King and you – together there: would not that be an opening?!!'

In the very month that Gore was appointed Principal Librarian, he preached before the University of Oxford the first of many of his sermons that would be the cause of controversy. It is one of his first published sermons, on 'The Permanence of Christianity'. Its subject is evolution. He observed that:

> the horror – with which, not wisely perhaps, but certainly not unnaturally, new conceptions of evolution in nature were at first regarded by theologians and Christian teachers – is passing away; and they at least are declaring on all sides, and in all good faith, that they do not find their frankest acceptance at all inconsistent with a Christian belief.

It was a foreshadowing of the approach of Lux Mundi, in 1889. A letter published in the press said that if that passage were deliberately penned 'surely the sooner the subscribers to the Pusey Memorial looked elsewhere for their champion the better'.

But Gore was soon to be cut off from such controversy. The Cambridge Mission to Delhi had been founded in 1877; and whilst Gore was in Liverpool, Edward King, then Professor of Pastoral Theology, had called a meeting at which the Oxford Mission to Calcutta had been initiated. Two Liverpool curates, both Oxford graduates, one a Scholar of Trinity when Gore was elected to his Fellowship, went out with Marsham Argles, a close school-friend of Gore's, and Edward Willis, Vice-Principal of Cuddesdon, as founder members of the Brotherhood of the Epiphany. But, in 1883, Argles' health had broken down, and he died a fortnight after his return to England; Willis also collapsed. Gore was therefore determined to give what he could to Calcutta during the interval before the opening of Pusey House. He sailed for India a month after he preached his sermon before the University. His letters home during the voyage record that 'on Sundays and on Christmas day a service was held in the saloon at which I officiated and praught for ten minutes in various degrees of swell; and on Sunday nights I go and talk to the sailors at the other end of the ship, and that I like better.' The following Lent he was preaching in the great Cathedral at Calcutta. He records how he was irritated by the operation of the punkahs 'they swing low enough to just touch one's hair when one is standing up'. Prestige comments: 'Those who have had the privilege of observing Gore's normal restlessness in the pulpit can well imagine the hardly suppressed fury with which he must have experienced this novel punctuation of his discourse.' In Madras he preached by an interpreter to one of the Tamil congregations. 'I hate preaching by an interpreter', he says. 'I am always filled with suspicions that he is talking what he pleases.' Without doubt his visit to India made an indelible impression on him. Preaching on behalf of the Oxford Mission to Calcutta, in 1888, he said:

> Christianity does not depreciate the good in other religions. It does not depreciate the good in Judaism, but supersedes it; and in like manner it supersedes other religions. Granted that Mohammedanism preaches a living God, granted that Buddhism preaches a holy God; but Christianity preaches a God who is both holy and living, and

declares that without holiness no man shall see the Lord. It supersedes other religions by including in a vaster and more complete whole the broken elements of truth which they possess.

In 1890, Gore in fact returned to India and Calcutta for a brief visit when the Superior since 1886 joined the Roman Church. Gore was able to preach on the Feast of the Epiphany to the priest associates of the Brotherhood – I read his sermon while I was myself staying with the Brotherhood in May 1972. He paid his third and last visit to India between November 1930 and April 1931. He preached in Bombay and Calcutta and Delhi, and pleased the Parsee community when he hailed Zoroaster as a prophetic witness to ethical monotheism. But that last sacrificial trip to India of the 78-year-old Gore – which was too much for his heart – showed how much India had meant to him through that first visit to the Oxford Mission.

Gore was at Pusey House, the 'Puseyum' as he called it, for ten years – from 1883 to 1893. J.H. Adderley wrote in 1888: 'Pusey House was to the Oxford of that day what St Mary's was to the Oxford of the days of Newman. Gore's influence was the greatest in Oxford since John Henry Newman.'

At the time of Gore's death in 1932 that remarkable poet-missionary to Rhodesia, Arthur Shearly Cripps, wrote a poem, *Charles Gore at Oxford*, which gives some feeling of how, forty years later, Cripps remembered the grip of this spiritual guide upon the hearts and minds of his generation. The poem describes Gore preaching at St Barnabas, Oxford, a favourite place for those of Gore's persuasion:

> Whom went we forth – we boys of old – to hear?
> One with wan face, rough brows, and hermit's beard,
> A brooding preacher. How o'ercast and blear'd
> Were his encavern'd eyes, how slow to clear!
>
> How blindly groped his hands, as tho' they'd tear
> Pillars like fumbling Samson's! Ere it near'd
> Its cataracts – how cok'd his speech appear'd –
> A dull brook trickling thro' the marshlands drear!

Then that light blaz'd at last, that Whirlwind blew:
He bow'd himself before the o'erruling might
Of driving gusts with furious lightnings bright;
To a prophet's stature, while we gaz'd, he grew –
Beside himself, possess'd by God anew –
An oblate – ear to ground – on Horeb's height!

In the last years of that decade of Gore's at Pusey there were three events of great significance in his life as a whole which were also central thereafter to the content of his preaching.

The first was the publication of *Lux Mundi* in 1889, foreshadowed, as we have said, by the University Sermon on Evolution. But *Lux Mundi* was equally about Biblical criticism. It can be safely said that no one did more than Charles Gore to show to a generation bewildered by the conflicts of faith and criticism how devotion, churchmanship and a faith centred upon the Bible could yet be combined with contemporary critical thought; and he did that not least through his preaching.

It was from the Bible, and thus through an incarnational theology, that the second central event of that decade at Pusey sprang. In the very same year that *Lux Mundi* was published, Gore, Holland and Westcott founded the Oxford Branch of the Christian Social Union at a meeting in Pusey itself. The work of the Union was carried on with great activity up and down the country by means of meetings and addresses and sermons in which Gore took his full share. Again, no one did more than Gore to arouse the social conscience of the Church and to deepen its social thinking and, later, to raise up a younger generation, like William Temple, to continue the work. His very last sermon, as we have already noted, was on 'Social Righteousness and the Christian'. Gore would speak of 'the apostleship of justice and the responsibility of wealth'. It was basically biblical theology rather than political philosophy that he preached. 'There are moments when a Christian may legitimately, like his Lord in the garden of Gethsemane, be engrossed in bearing his own burden, but in the main a Christian ought, like his Lord or like St Paul, to have his own burden so well in hand, that he is able to leave the large spaces of his heart for other people to lay their sorrows upon.' As Prestige says, Gore was demanding not conduct merely but character. Christ spoke in the Sermon on the Mount, he believed, to a sacramental society, not to a state or a world or to individuals who had no larger frame of reference than themselves. Gore based his social doctrine on the specifically Christian concept of the Fatherhood of God and on common sonship in the divine family. But as time went on, the more he concerned himself not simply with the principles but with the details of social and economic action. And it was by his sermons, later, at Westminster, that Albert Mansbridge was inspired to found the Workers Educational Association.

Sacramental society; divine family: those words lead naturally to the third event of that deeply significant decade in Gore's life. On St James' Day, 25 July 1892, Gore and five of his friends made their profession as founder members of the Community of the Resurrection. Gore is remembered now as the founder and pioneer of the Community rather than as a member of it. As he said sorrowfully to Fr Paul Bull on one occasion after leaving the Community: 'All I have to do to make any institution prosper is to leave it.' But Gore never allowed the Church to forget the significance of the Religious life. One of his finest sermons, delivered at Cowley, in 1915, has the explicit title: 'The Revival of the Religious Life', and on the Feast of the Transfiguration 1924 he preached at St George's Bloomsbury, the parish where R.M. Benson was born, a memorable sermon to mark the centenary of his birth.

'Sacrifice and Self-Surrender', 'The Life of Sacrifice': this is a constant theme of his preaching. Nor does the theme betoken an isolated piety. He spent a Sunday every year of his years at Oxford preaching in the woollen district of the West Riding. In the very year he founded the Community of the Resurrection he also conducted a Mission in Walsall. It was Gore's desire that eventually the Community should be established in the industrial North.

Before that took place the Brothers migrated five miles from Oxford, to Radley, where Gore the preacher took the Three Hours, and prepared his sermons carefully, and taught himself to address simple folk intelligently. But it is not without significance that on the wheel of an ordinary village parish the health and heart of Gore was broken. Inducted Vicar of Radley on 21 September 1893, by the end of 1894 he had accepted a canonry at Westminster. And if that year at Radley was Gore's unhappiest, the years at Westminster were with little doubt the happiest years of his life.

Let us pause at this watershed in the life of Gore the preacher. Gore is 41. Let us hear from John Gore what it was like at Westminster in those memorable days; forgiving the somewhat roseate if not purple pen of a nephew writing of him who described himself as 'Nuncle'.

> There are vivid recollections of those Sunday and Monday afternoon sermons which filled the Abbey to overflowing and raised traffic problems for the solution of which the question of building him a tabernacle was seriously propounded . . .
>
> The popularity of his sermons and the furore which his preaching caused brought him an enormous amount of correspondence . . . And while he was evidently gratified by the sight of the crowds thronging the cloisters and aisles long before the services began, his popularity brought in its train a variety of unpleasant consequences. He detested publicity and loathed the attentions of egotists and busybodies who satisfied their own craving for self-expression by letters of flattery and adulation, often carried to the point of absurdity . . . He was no stained-glass saint. On the contrary, he was intensely human. When overwrought, he could be irritable, hasty, and short. The pains he took with those famous sermons few people at the time probably appreciated. He would spend an hour at a busy time running to ground the exact reference of some text or the precise wording of some half-remembered quotation. He was uncertain as to how his voice carried to distant parts of the Abbey, and on more than one occasion he asked his secretary, Mr Lawrence, to test it by sitting at agreed points during the service. For a time, in the middle of a series of addresses, his sight gave trouble, and he was compelled to rely in the pulpit on a half sheet of notes done out in large print and representing in outline his argument, which was arranged in his mind only. His memory in things material was extraordinarily good, but in things unmaterial – it was a family failing – he was often extremely absent-minded. He would mislay something at a critical moment and be unable to find the name for the object to be sought, and when time pressed, he was sometimes reduced to a state of real exasperation. For, above all, he dreaded to be

late for a service or an appointment. In a word, he was grossly overworked at Westminster, and his nerves, temper, and health suffered.

But the impression of his teaching at Westminster remained – strong and ineffaceable. In those few years he had altered the very nature of the Abbey's great appeal to Englishmen. He, more than any in our time, helped to make that memorial to the illustrious dead a place once more of hope and comfort for the living. The mists of the dead past yielded to the sunlight of present comfort and hope for the future. Men and women of every class and type, busy men, sick men, men who rarely went to church, were drawn to those Lenten services, attracted to a man who practised what he preached and preached nothing beyond the compass of ordinary men to understand and to do. They would spend precious half hours in the waiting queue rather than risk the disappointment of being turned away. And when the doors opened, every available space from which the preacher's voice could be heard was quickly and silently filled. It was a strangely moving sight. The soft light of a hundred candles dimly lit the choir and its carved oak stalls, and threw a still fainter light on time-worn arches and the chancel's vaulted roof, and on the pale and delicate tracery of lancet windows. A single candle burned on either side of the altar, but through the south-west windows the last rays of the sun streamed in, flooding in pools of purple and crimson, floor and columns and carved wood. Beyond this dim yet gorgeous setting in the choir, deep shadows lay on silent and empty spaces beneath the mighty vault. There in the jewelled light was life and hope, and beyond was emptiness and death. And again and again in the waiting congregation men looked up, fascinated by the perspective and the indescribable beauty and contrasts of the scene. Then at last the great bell struck the hour and the procession came in sight. The choirboys in their pageantry of white and red, the clergy following, and last, the preacher whose conviction and magnetism had brought the great congregation together. And when evensong was finished and he went up into the pulpit, there was in his eyes a hint of perplexity, of wistfulness, almost of doubt, as he looked down on that sea of upturned faces;

till, with a characteristic twist of his shoulders, he shook off a
momentary mood of contemplation, and his clearly enunciating
and penetrating voice broke the silence. He said nothing that the
youngest could not understand nor the wisest fail to appreciate as
essential truth and the refined ore of intense labour and research
and behind every simple statement of faith he put the force of his
own triumphant conviction. Before that argument, that plain tale
told so plainly (and yet with such consummate art) difficulties of
faith seemed to vanish away and even workaday anxieties to fade.
When the strangely mixed congregation streamed out at last, it
would have been hard to assess the value of that virtue gone out of
him, the hope and inspiration and comfort carried out into the busy
streets and into the lives of all sorts and conditions of men. Certain
it is that none went away empty, with the echo of that magic voice
in his ears: 'The peace of God which passes all understanding keep
your hearts and minds.'

After such an account, the question that will not go away is: what went
they out to see – and hear – at Westminster in those seven years of Gore's
canonry? – seven years of plenty, by any standards: of sermons and
addresses preached; of people eager to hear the preacher's word; of food for
thought provided.

Arthur Shearly Cripps' poem provides part of the answer, for Gore at
Oxford was not essentially different from Gore at Westminster. But
Westminster is a world away from Oxford. Those queues of ordinary,
ordinary people: what went they out to see?

We need to remind ourselves of the very nature of preaching. Preaching
partakes of the particularity of the gospel itself. A preacher is a particular
person, with a particular voice, particular looks, particular gestures, par-
ticular gifts. He is a particular parson, with a particular experience, par-
ticular convictions. He addresses us at a particular time, in a particular
place. There are many books on preaching which tell us precisely what a
sermon is and what it's not. But a great preacher – like Gore – can expand
the very idea of a sermon. Oddly, you will not find Gore in any notable
book on preaching, in spite of the crowds he drew. Why? Perhaps because
most of his sermons are so unlike what people have come to expect of a

preacher. There are no purple passages; few illustrations; fewer personal anecdotes. Out of George Reindorp's *Ten Points for Preachers* he might perhaps score two. His sermons were most often lectures and addresses, sometimes explicitly so. His lectures and addresses were often sermons. Yet men went out to hear them.

It was H.H. Farmer, in that quintessential book on preaching, *The Servant of the Word*, who wrote:

> It was said of a certain theological professor in my hearing, by one of his students, that to hear any of his lectures, profound and technically learned as they were, was like listening to a powerful sermon, or even at times being present at a communion service. That was high praise. I am not suggesting that a sermon could ever with profit become a theological lecture, but that even a theological lecture in the right hands can become a sermon does at least illustrate my point. Similarly, I have heard Charles Gore or George Lansbury speak on social questions in a way that made the whole utterance a preaching of the Word. Everything depends on carrying with you a sense of the living, saving, present activity of God in Christ.

Where Gore is concerned, I believe Farmer might even have gone further. Gore proved the theological lecture could become a sermon in the right hands and the sermon a theological lecture – in his particular hands.

Those green-gold books of Gore published by John Murray – the *Sermon on the Mount*, published in 1896; *St Paul's Epistle to the Ephesians*, published in 1898; *St Paul's Epistle to the Romans, Volume I*, 1899, *Volume II*, 1900 – Gore may say in his introduction that they have little connection with the lectures delivered in the Abbey, but what he delivered in the Abbey were lectures – on the Sermon on the Mount, and on Romans and Ephesians. And there was a series on St John's First Epistle delivered in Lent 1900, and another on the Apocalypse delivered in 1901 which were only printed in the *Church Times* and were far less worked over for publication than those published by John Murray. And if you go to Gore's sermons proper there are few that are not more lecture than sermon as sermon is usually understood.

In the offices of the *Church Times* (to whose proprietors I am very greatly indebted for generous hospitality), in great blue bound volumes of past numbers, there are over a hundred sermons and addresses by Charles Gore. Let us look briefly at one, preached in the dying hours of the nineteenth century: Evensong, 31 December 1899. On what would Gore choose to preach to ring out the old and ring in the new? The news from South Africa was sombre indeed. Ladysmith was invested. Defeat had followed defeat – though the news of Churchill's dramatic escape had reached London only a few days before. Gore had already that year denounced and rebuked the demands for revenge against the Boers.

He chose that New Year's Eve – that New Century's Eve – to preach on 'Divine Correspondence'. His text, was from the Epistle to the Hebrews, 'Let us go on to perfection'. It is a characteristic sermon, characteristically profound, on 'Progress'. Progress does not consist in the lapse of time, he says. Progress, if you seek to get to the heart of it, lies in the consciousness and willing correspondence of man with God. The scientific mode of progress is through unconscious adaptation. With us it is different, as individuals and as nations. A nation that progresses is a nation that owns the sovereignty of God and regards his will.

On such an evening a preacher was bound to ask his hearers to look back over the century that was coming to an end. It is a fascinating panorama that he unfolds. He claims that 'not only in the material but in the moral and spiritual parts of life there had been great progress – the Christian conscience awakened, missionary expansion', and so on. Then he talks of 'the ambiguity of gifts' – like the diffusion of popular education, and the ability to read – and speaks of the visions of peace which had retired out of view and the grinding of commercial competition which heralded no better prospect for mankind. Imperialism was dominant – the worship of our unregenerate British selves without morality or fear of God. Then follows a very simple 'recipe', so to speak, for correspondence with God in such a situation: prayer, reading the Bible, and the Communion of the Body and Blood of Christ. And, finally, he points his hearers to the perfection of the City of God:

> So that perfected City of the saints: that City in which God dwells,
> shall be a city the materials of which have been found and fashioned
> in the materials of our common life, in the human character, in the

men and women amongst whom we are, in that material of human passion, and human capacity, and human fellowship, in the midst of which we are labouring and enjoying ourselves, and bustling and hurrying today. It is the common life in which we are being tempted, and falling, and rising, and living, and in various ways affecting and influencing one another: it is the common life out of which only can be built up the City of God.

And the question for you and me is whether we really know that humanity is destined for a real progress towards a real perfecting; whether we really realise that progress for man is a precious thing, that it depends on correspondence with God.

So look to your duty, look to your privileges, and look to your responsibilities, and as you form your plans for the coming year and wonder about the coming century, remember this always, that the part that you and I will play in the life of society, in the life of the Church, and in our own lives, depends on this one thing, that we maintain our correspondence with God.

We may say: 'There's nothing very remarkable there.' True. But we have not heard Gore's voice, or seen his hands or the flashing of his eyes. We have received the sacrament of the word: but only in one kind – his written words:

> *We are the music-makers,*
> *   And we are the dreamers of dreams,*
> *Wandering by lone sea-breakers*
> *   And sitting by desolate streams;*
> *World-losers and world-forsakers*
> *   On whom the pale moon gleams:*
> *Yet we are the movers and shakers*
> *   Of the world for ever, it seems.*
> (From 'The Music-Makers' by Arthur O'Shaughnessy)

Gore, the preacher, was in his own particular way, a music-maker and a dreamer of dreams, and enabled others to dream dreams. That New Year's Eve we cannot doubt Gore, who is now

> *. . . in the ages lying*
> *In the buried past of the earth*

gave to people as they went out into the cold night air of Westminster, as few others of his generation could have given them, a sense that

> *. . . each age is a dream that is dying,*
> *Or one that is coming to birth.*

And so he did, week after week, for those seven plenteous years. He did it not by burdening his hearers with instruction, but by bearing in front of them his own burden of making sense of his own experience, and thus helping them to bear theirs. He personified with the authority of his intellect and experience a way of coping with life; yet that personification and authority did not banish all mystery and ambiguity. Gore steadied people, enabled them to face their problems, and gradually, as a kind of vision, to master them. If you did not feel he had all the answers, you yet felt he had a way of so tackling one question as to enable you to go on to the next.

Hensley Henson, on his own admission temperamentally opposed to Gore, expressing nevertheless his affection for him and his admiration for his ability and courage, wrote:

> Gore brought a new kind of preaching into the Abbey pulpit . . . The
> great Abbey congregation which filled the Abbey Church to hear him
> preach had little understanding, or sympathy with, its distinctive
> traditions. They would have followed him as readily anywhere else,
> but, since it was in the Abbey that he preached, he strengthened
> notably the reputation of the pulpit, while he revolutionised the type
> of its preaching, and threatened the survival of the type of
> Anglicanism which it had expressed. Under his influence
> Westminster Abbey, long regarded with disfavour by the orthodox as
> a citadel of obsolescent latitudinarianism, began to acquire a new
> attractiveness as the sounding board of the more fashionable version
> of Anglican religion, blending the distinctive doctrines of the Oxford
> Movement with the newer enthusiasms of the Christian Social
> Union.

It was whilst Gore was at Westminster that he began to preach on a subject which is a natural, some would say inescapable, development from his former convictions, but which to some of his friends had a different and a disconcerting ring about it: the subject of Church Reform. The Church Reform League had been founded in 1895. Gore spoke at its first conference. But he was even more radical than the League. In 1898, his speech at the annual meeting of the League was published in 'Advent Sermons on Church Reform', and that same year the volume of 'Essays in Aid of Church Reform' he had edited was published.

What Gore was preaching for was liberty for the Church to manage her own affairs, in parishes and dioceses and provinces. He realized very well that this would not be given without the joining of laity and clergy in church government. He asked for 'hierarchy – if hierarchy it can be called – tempered by spiritual democracy'. He pleaded for votes for women in church government, and a place for the laity in the election of those who are consecrated to the sacred ministry. He wanted an end to nominal church membership, and to all that smacked of feudalism and imperialism in the Church. He called for the limitation of the rights of patrons and the right to remove clergy who were no longer pastors but stumbling blocks, and the end of the arbitrary incumbent. He was calling for counsel and consent. It was twenty years – and it needed the Life and Liberty Movement – before Gore got some of what he wanted in the Enabling Act. It was seventy years before he got other things he wanted in the Synodical Government Measure – many years too late to affect him personally. But other reforms in Crown appointments and patronage and freehold still wait the assent of the Church let alone the Royal assent, though it must be said in fairness that many a bishop who has been a poacher before consecration becomes a gamekeeper by the laying on of hands, and within a few years of his consecration Gore proved himself to be no exception.

It was on 23 February 1902 that Gore, after many protests, was consecrated Bishop of Worcester. R.C. Moberly was the preacher. It would not have been inappropriate for him to have said what, as we noted earlier, that great preacher F.A. Simpson was to say at the consecration of Mervyn Stockwood, in 1959 (F.A. Simpson, greatly and lately lamented, at the turn of the century lived with Armitage Robinson in the deanery, alongside Charles Gore.) 'To you', Simpson said, 'has been given a measure of

eloquence; a rare gift, a noble gift, although unharnessed it can be a
dangerous gift. But harnessed, not shackled, it will be all the more valuable
in your new office, since not many holders of that office possess it.'

For seventeen years Gore was to preach and teach as a bishop of a
diocese, with all the preaching and teaching, day in day out, that requires.
Some of the comments of Prestige on Gore's episcopal preaching are
worth recollecting:

> His charge to the candidates on the eve of the ordination was always
> most impressive. 'Tomorrow I shall say to you, wilt thou, wilt thou,
> wilt thou? But there will come a day to you when another will say to
> you, hast thou, hast thou, hast thou?'
>
> His charge transcended in its richness of affection any formal
> relationship of bishop and ordinands. He addressed them as the sons
> whom on the morrow he was to beget in Jesus Christ. 'You are the
> children whom God has given to me.'
>
> Gore's addresses to his clergy were always very interesting and full
> of matter. He sent them away with a clear knowledge of what they
> had to do and more than ever determined on trying to do it. But he
> sometimes gave them the impression that religion was a stern, hard
> business. It seemed to contain more duty than love. 'He felt it was a
> battle' one of them has written, and he exulted in the struggle, and he
> knew that he had in the Christian creed the weapons which would
> carry him through. But a battle is not very much fun.
>
> At his Confirmations Gore would often walk up and down the
> aisle, delivering to the candidates addresses which were as simple as
> they were full of teaching, insisting on the goodness and patience of
> God, urging his hearers never to despair, crying in a voice that
> thrilled with emotion, 'God will never, never give you up.'
>
> Each year in Birmingham, he delivered a course of Lent lectures to
> large congregations, mainly of men, at the Cathedral.
>
> Gore preached assiduously, visiting as many parishes as he could.
> He tried when possible to pay not two but three parochial visits in
> one Sunday, in order to see a great number of parishes. It was
> characteristic of his preaching that he never minded repeating
> himself. Having taken pains to discover the best method of

presenting a subject, he adhered to the same plan, and even to the same phrases, insomuch that priests preparing candidates for Confirmation sometimes ventured to inform them beforehand of some of the points which the Bishop would emphasise in his own address at the service. The *Church Times* reported at an interval of a few years two sermons which he preached on prayer.

On comparison of the printed discourses it was found that, apart from a topical introduction, the two sermons were almost identical. But he did not cease to be impressive. Nearly always the phrases which he reiterated and the illustrations which he repeated were so precisely apt that to change them would involve real loss. He was never known to talk rubbish, and so powerful and illuminating was his treatment that often his addresses could be remembered easily after a single hearing, in substance and in form. Sermons so good did not jar when they were heard a second time.

We might usefully repeat here the words of F.A. Simpson, of Trinity, Cambridge; 'It is always better to hear a good sermon twice than a bad sermon once.'

Gore's pulpit mannerisms – the spectacles worn over the top of his brow; the poise on tiptoe; the clutch of his folded arms; the occasional reverse-motion which directed his discourse at a pillar or blank wall instead of his hearers; the unusual and emphatic pronunciation of certain favourite words, like 'eggs-tray-ordinary'; the use of characteristic phrases, such as 'I am pro-fownd-ly convinced' or 'it is luminously clear' – all this produced a sense of vividness and variety which, taken with his intense seriousness and passion of conviction, maintained the interest and preserved the sermon from any trace of staleness.

Gore was enthroned as Bishop of Birmingham in 1905 and succeeded Francis Paget as Bishop of Oxford in 1911. In the latter part of 1915 the idea of holding a National Mission of Repentance and Hope was mooted. To Gore the idea was in principle a good one. But he did not believe the time was opportune, either for Church or for nation. The clergy were discouraged and the people unresponsive. Of the words 'national mission' he wrote, 'I am very much afraid that at present such large words will sound hollow.' What Gore did was to summon all the clergy of the diocese into retreat, in the premises of four of the large public schools of his diocese – Wellington, Radley, Bradfield and Wycombe Abbey. Gore himself took one of the retreats. In all, over 600 priests attended.

But Gore's diocesan preaching did not diminish the demands upon him by the Church beyond his dioceses.

Before the Church Congress of 1906 he preached a famous sermon. Its burden was that the Church was still the Church of the well-to-do. It had condescended to the poor instead of becoming identified with them. 'This sermon', said Gore in a characteristic phrase, 'is only the cry of a permanently troubled conscience.'

In 1914, there was the Mission to the University of Oxford – born of Neville Talbot and backed by Scott Holland, who eventually persuaded Gore to undertake it. Bishop Walter Carey, who was a member of the planning committee, describes how Arthur Burroughs, later Bishop of Ripon, proposed that undergraduates should be stationed outside St Mary's to stop passers-by and induce them to come in. 'No, no, we must have no accorsting [*sic*] – no, no, please no accorsting [*sic*],' said Gore. The proposal fell dead under the repeated strokes of the word 'accorsting'. Neville Talbot says that, on the first night, Gore opened uncertainly, but after the third night there was no looking back. Walter Carey describes the final service:

> There were probably 600 undergraduates at the final Communion at St Mary Magdalen's. When Gore looked in and saw them there, all kneeling, it was too much for him. Whether it was a prophetic instinct that told him that most of them would be dead in a few months, or whether it was the mere sight of so much youth kneeling in real humility and love towards God, I just don't know. All I saw was that he knelt in the vestry and sobbed his heart out. At last I had to act, so I laid my hand on his shoulder and said that I was so very sorry to butt in, but that he simply must get up and go in and take the service. This he very humbly did at once, but it left an ineffaceable mark on us who saw it.

Gore had paid his first visit to America when he was still a Canon of Westminster. In 1918, he paid a second visit involving much preaching and speaking.

In 1919, Gore retired. He was 66 years old. He refused a canonry at Westminster, and resisted the blandishments of Dick Sheppard, who was anxious to persuade Gore to preach regularly at St Martin-in-the-Fields. He did not want a great public apostolate. He accepted a curate's licence at the Grosvenor Chapel, preached there once a month and delivered courses of sermons. Like most of his addresses, they seldom lasted for less than three-quarters of an hour. He did not by then write out his sermons beforehand. He took into the pulpit a half-sheet of notepaper on which he had set down his chief points. His sermons were packed with thought, with humanity, and had an undercurrent of wit. His eloquence, his learning and his character attracted a crowd of intelligent men and women to hear him. There were a number of memorable occasions in those last years that were made even more memorable by a sermon from Charles Gore: for instance the Solemn Requiem for Frank Weston at St Matthew's Westminster, 15 November 1924.

In 1922, Mowbray's published four sermons on the Deity of Christ which had been preached the previous Advent by Charles Gore in the Grosvenor Chapel. In his preface Gore states that they were not designed for publication, but they were taken down by a skilful reporter. Nevertheless, they give an impression of Gore in these later years which the sermons that had been more prepared for publication do not. They reveal him preaching with authority, persuading, convincing – and, in fact, it must be said, overconvincing. But the dynamism of it all reveals something of the secret of his success as a preacher and teacher. Let us hear just two paragraphs from Gore at the Grosvenor Chapel:

> What then is this supernaturally-conceived being, so human yet so divine – this Jesus of the Gospels – so tender and so tremendous, so loving and so stern, so miraculous and so natural? I say to myself as I read that story, told in the simplest language without any pretension, 'I am touching reality! This passes the wit of man to invent or to imagine!'
>
> And then make a little enquiry, and you will find that these documents have been subjected to the most searching criticism to which any documents on earth have ever been subjected. Every possible doubt has exercised itself upon them; but I am not

exaggerating when I say that they have been given back to us with the best guarantees. There is no reasonable doubt that the second Gospel was written by John Mark; and we know who this John Mark was. He was brought up in his mother's house at Jerusalem. We find him there about fourteen years after the Crucifixion. His mother's house was a large house, so that the company of Christians could assemble there – a large number of people – for prayer when Peter was in prison. It must also have been a large house because it had an outer gateway into a courtyard, and a porteress whose name we know, Rhoda; and it was plainly the place of common gathering of the followers of Jesus. There Mark had been brought up. I do not think it is possible to doubt, myself, that in his Gospel, when he suddenly introduces the incident of the young man in the linen garment – which has no connection with anything that goes before and after – he means by this to say, 'I was that young man, I saw Jesus taken.' It is just as in an Italian picture of the fifteenth century, when you see one quite incongruous figure introduced into the sacred subject, you say: Either this was the donor or it was the painter? So when you see these few phrases, quite unconnected with what goes before and after about the young man in the linen garment who was there when they took Jesus, you say: That was young Mark; there is no other reason why he should have put it in . . .

That was the kind of sermon Gore was still preaching ten years later when, as an old man of 78, he preached his last sermon, as licensed curate of the Grosvenor Chapel.

In this chapter on Gore the preacher I have had to ask several intractable questions. I have had to ask, 'What is a sermon?' – that the crowds at Westminster, and at Oxford and elsewhere could be so drawn to hear Gore preaching. I have had to ask, 'What was it about Gore's preaching that made his preaching draw the crowds in a way which few other preachers of his generation, if any, had been able to do?' And because as a painting arises largely through what a painter does when he is not painting, so also a sermon arises largely through what a preacher does when he is not preaching, I have not been able entirely to avoid the major question: 'Who was Charles Gore?'

It might be thought that with Prestige's magisterial biography, and all that has been written on Gore in the last forty years, the answer to that question would be clear. But Prestige's Gore was written within three years of his death, and when there was still the tradition of reticence in episcopal biography. We await yet an analysis of the very complex material of Gore's character which could make him, all in a moment, gruff and terrifying and embarrassingly affectionate, rude and irritable and full of fun and wit and humour. We know little at any depth from Prestige – though more from Mansbridge – of Gore's human relationships. The reasons for his isolation, dejection and pessimism are not all necessarily theological. It is important to know something more of the underlying causes of his streak of authoritarianism which made him at times almost a persecutor. Perhaps it was the intensity of his early conflicts which left a permanent mark on his sensitive and highly strung nature, and made him so habitually gladiatorial, but perhaps the cause lay earlier and deeper. Again, to be a rebel and in opposition all your life may say something more about a man than simply that he is one of God's prophets. It was the sympathetic Mansbridge who wrote that Gore was completely known to very few people, if any, and that he was a man of many parts and kept the parts separate. I have found myself greatly desiring a study of the psycho-pathology of Gore because it is only honest to recognize that in the force of Gore's preaching there is some evidence of the energies of a temperament that has not only found its security but is still engaged in passionate pursuit of it. Hensley Henson, in the *Retrospect*, obviously trying to be just and appreciative, wrote that in Gore there was a strange blending of opposites, 'an alert even sceptical intellect kept unrestful company in him with a deeply devotional temperament, a strong domineering will, with an affectionate sympathy'.

There is one final question that I must briefly ask and as briefly answer: 'What has the phenomenon of the preaching of Charles Gore to say concerning Christian apologetic today?'

We have said that preaching relates to a particular person, a particular place, and a particular time. Well, there is no one around today quite like Charles Gore, that's for sure; and, undeniably, times have considerably changed. Westminster Abbey, it is true, remains, but not *entirely* as it was in Gore's day!

But preachers are primarily interpreters of God and man; part of that company – amongst whom Charles Gore should certainly be numbered – whom Isaiah addressed when he said: 'Behold all ye that kindle a fire, that compass yourself about with sparks; walk in the light of your fire, and in the sparks that ye have kindled.' That company includes not only preachers but playwrights, poets, novelists, journalists, artists, musicians, people whose gifts are manifest in broadcasting and television, and so on.

When, for instance, I read Housman's lines:

> They say my verse is sad: no wonder;
> Its narrow measure spans
> Tears of eternity, and sorrow,
> Not mine, but man's.

I think immediately not only of poets like Housman but of preachers like Gore – Gore who was an artist, with the observing eye of an artist, and who was thus 'sorrowful, yet always rejoicing'.

I believe that what Dame Helen Gardner writes of the art of T.S. Eliot, has much to say both of Charles Gore's preaching and of Christian apologetic today: 'It is not the poet's business to make us believe what he believes,' she writes, 'but to make us believe that he believes. He must convince us that what he believes genuinely interprets, makes sense of, experience which we recognise as our own. Although we may not accept his interpretation, we must feel it is a real interpretation.' 'But,' she continues,

> in an age like ours, with no accepted system of belief, in which the traditional system is not so much actively disbelieved as ignored, such an interpretation can only convince if the poet forgoes what earlier Christian writers loved to employ: the language of the Bible and of the common prayers of the Church. The problem of communication for a religious poet in an age where his religious beliefs are not widely held is a special aspect of the general problem of communication for the poet in the modern world.

To the ecclesiastic, the preacher today may not seem to be under the full burden of the poet's handicap, as Dame Helen Gardner describes it. If that is so, I am profoundly convinced, his eyes are holden. Certainly, the phenomenon of Charles Gore, the preacher – with the soul of a prophet – should not cause us simply to think furiously how to bring back the golden age of Victorian and Edwardian preaching in Westminster Abbey. It should cause us rather to think prophetically how we can follow Gore's example of accepting the whole of experience yet continuing to act creatively, to interpret that experience creatively, well aware of the cost in the bearing of pain.

Paradoxically, though this may lead us to examine our preaching today, it will certainly cause us to think of other media than preaching, and other places than churches. It will cause us to think of how, and where, and in what way we can best be interpreters of man and God if people are to apprehend what we have to share with them: the mystery of our Lord's revelation of God. For it was because Charles Gore spoke of his mystery where people were then prepared to hear him, in a way that they could then best hear what he had to say to them, at the time of their need, that over a century ago they went out to see and hear what he had to say.

11 Trevor Huddleston: from a biographer's chair

It was in 1986, at the seventieth birthday of Dame Diana Collins, the widow of Canon John Collins, erstwhile Dean of Oriel, Canon of St Paul's and founder of Christian Action, that Trevor Huddleston, who had been reading my biography of Bishop John Robinson, surprised me with the remark that he would like me to write his biography; but, he added, 'I'm not having one written while I'm alive.' I said I rather approved of that, but that I didn't see why we shouldn't meet regularly so that I could at least begin the task and perhaps preserve memories which might otherwise be lost. So, for nearly ten years, Bishop Trevor and I met, roughly every six weeks, for a meal and a talk together. I also did quite a lot of research: into his childhood and schooldays; his time at Oxford and theological college; his years as a curate and as a novice at Mirfield; and I followed in his footsteps in South Africa, Tanzania, and in the Indian Ocean.

Then I had a stroke, confining me to hospital, followed by one or two of what they call 'TIAs'; and it became clear that I should not and could not do all the work that remained to be done. I'd written over 60,000 words, but, alas, I'd not begun to research Trevor's time at Stepney; and there were complications to his life which didn't make it a simple matter to finish the book. Someone once said: 'No one putting their hand to the plough should throw up the sponge'; but that is what, reluctantly and regretfully, I had to do.

Yet I suppose I'd got to know Trevor Huddleston – of whom Nelson Mandela had said simply: 'No white person has done more for South Africa' – as well as anyone ever did. So instead of a biography I have produced this essay on Trevor, which I have called *Trevor Huddleston: from a biographer's chair* – echoing Anthony Clare's *In the Psychiatrist's Chair*.

First of all, I want to say something about Trevor's childhood. Trevor

153

was born in 1913, the son of Captain Sir Ernest Whiteside Huddleston, who eventually commanded the Royal Indian Navy. 1913 was of course the year before the First World War, and Captain Huddleston was absent in India when Trevor was born. He did not see his father till he was 7. His mother, too, was often absent in India. Trevor could only remember two or three times when his parents were at home together in England, before his father's permanent return when Trevor was 12. He was brought up in Hampstead, by a wealthy widowed aunt, nicknamed 'Potsa', and by a nanny, Ada Pateman.

I shall never forget how, early on in our meetings together, when I asked Trevor, 'What kind of childhood did you have?', he answered immediately that his childhood was 'idyllic', but quickly followed that remark by telling me that whenever he was lonely he talked to his imaginary companion, whom he called by the rather odd name 'Gilkert'. He said he played with him and talked with him a lot – rather, I gathered, as Carl Jung used to talk with his fantasy figure 'Philemon'. Trevor had a very vivid mental picture of 'Gilkert'. He described him as a 'wraith-like, wispy figure, with fair, almost white hair'. I was reminded of Robert Louis Stevenson's poem *The Unseen Playmate*:

> When children are playing alone on the green,
> In comes the playmate that never was seen.
> When children are happy and lonely and good,
> The Friend of the Children comes out of the wood.

It's not unusual for children to devise ways of bearing what Graham Greene called 'the burden of childhood'; the terrible departure of parents, for instance, and their no less painful absences; but it is unusual for such children to maintain that their childhood was 'idyllic'. Certainly, in later life, Trevor seldom seemed like a son who had had an 'idyllic' childhood.

Fr Aelred Stubbs CR, in his obituary of Trevor in the Community of the Resurrection's *CR*, wrote: 'It is hard not to believe that the deprivation of a mother's love and an adored father's presence did not leave a deep wound.' And he asks if Trevor's uninhibited affection for children – 'an affection instantly and multitudinously reciprocated' – was 'a compensation for what he had lacked in his own childhood?'

Trevor was in many ways a typical 'son of the Raj'.

I am clear that any profound understanding of Trevor has to begin with his childhood. Prayer itself is, after all, a kind of conversation with the 'Unseen Playmate'. And, to ask another question that Fr Aelred Stubbs asks: 'Was his [Trevor's] anger with God at the end of his life "in whom 98 per cent of me", he said, "does not believe" – at least in part an anger of the child with the father who was never there?'

Well, I could say several thousand more words to you on Trevor's childhood: on Trevor as 'boat boy' at St Michael's, Golders Green; on Trevor playing 'churches', using a laundry basket for a pulpit, and a bed-spread for a chasuble. He remembered how, when he was 6, he was taken to hear 'Woodbine Willie' – Studdert Kennedy – at a Golders Green cinema. Trevor could never remember a time when he did not want to be a priest. And, several years before his own confirmation, when his sister was confirmed at St Paul's, Bedford, Trevor clearly remembered looking in wonder at Michael Furse, Bishop of St Albans, clad in cope, and saying to himself: 'I am going to be a bishop'.

But no more on Trevor's childhood, except to say: 'Birdie' Bowers, who died with Scott of the Antarctic, before Trevor was born, had been a close friend of his father's. So from childhood Scott of the Antarctic was almost part of Trevor's 'religion'; and Kipling's poem *If* was, so to speak, one of the hymns of that religion.

After his childhood, came Trevor's schooldays at Lancing College. They were hugely important to him. Trevor got me to read Evelyn Waugh's description of Lancing in his short story *Charles Rider's Schooldays*, early on in our exchanges together.

Such was Trevor's love for Lancing that, in spite of his reputation in later years – and his claim – to be a Christian Socialist, he was never known to utter a word of criticism or, indeed, of questioning of the public school system.

Trevor told me how, when he was on parade with the OTC at Lancing, he was brought the desolating news of his aunt Potsa's death, in her early fifties. No one realized how bereaved he was. He had to go on with the parade, and keep his bereavement to himself.

He played the trumpet in the school orchestra at Lancing, little realizing how in later years that would stand him in good stead in South Africa, when he got black boys, like Hugh Masekela (who played the trumpet at his Memorial Service in Westminster Abbey) to form a school band.

He was Lancing's secretary for Toc H, and the memories of his visit to the Movement's birthplace, Talbot House, with its upper-room chapel – a converted hay loft – at Poperinge, and to the First World War battlefields of the Ypres salient, were indelible.

In 1909, Lancing College founded its Mission in Camberwell, South London. Trevor would say that the Lancing College Mission was his first introduction to social deprivation, and to the social divide within his country.

Trevor was the editor of the school's magazine; and he wrote, significantly, in his last editorial, as he took leave of Lancing: 'It is the loss of ourselves that causes us real sorrow – the dreadful thought that before we can be noticed again we must compete not with a school of 400, but with the world.'

That year, 1931, Trevor also lost his mother, who died of cancer. That year, too, Trevor went up to Oxford, to Christ Church: to read Modern History, not Theology. Two men above all made Christ Church memorable for Trevor, and a place to which he was bound by bonds of gratitude and affection: Keith Feiling and J.C. Masterman. Feiling helped Churchill with his biography of Marlborough. Masterman, as Trevor's tutor, helped him to begin to awaken to the realities of the European and international political scene. Not least when he was himself a major figure of the South African scene, Trevor would remember with gratitude those who had helped him to grapple with the complexities of Modern History. It was in his first year at Oxford that Tawney's *Equality* had been published.

At Pusey House, Miles Sargent was an outstanding pastor, through whom Trevor got to know Fr Basil Jellicoe, a priest who had become a public figure through his fight for better housing of the poor of St Pancras. Trevor had first heard him, when he was 12, preaching in All Saints' Margaret Street, and saying 'Slums are the devil's sacrament: the outward and visible sign of an inward and spiritual disgrace.'

Miles Sargent arranged for food and bedding for the hunger marchers who marched through Oxford. He also drew Trevor into a group he called the Fellowship of the Transfiguration. And it was with Miles Sergeant and members of that Fellowship that Trevor joined a Mission to Hop Pickers at East Peckham, in Kent, in two of his summer vacations.

Trevor suggested I should look at Miles Sargent's book *St Francis of the Hopfields*. I did. And it was very revealing – but not exactly as Trevor had imagined. I found it embarrassingly condescending: much of it written in transliterated pseudo-Cockney.

> See that crahd up by my 'ut this afternoon, Father? It was my son bashin' 'is missus. Saucy piece she is, and 'as been arstin' for it for a long time. Now she's got it – I thort I'd just let yer know it wasn't nothin' to worry abaht, Father . . .

'With hardly any exceptions,' Miles Sargent continues, 'the pickers are really good to their children, as far as their intelligence goes; but unfortunately that isn't very far . . .'

It was from this extraordinarily condescending Christianity that Trevor, the public schoolboy and Oxford undergraduate, nevertheless learnt and received much. It would be another forty years before Trevor would be concerned with raising up a local ministry from within the East End of London, and it would be several years before he began to question the condescending paternalism within church and society. But he began that journey at Oxford, attending in 1932 the Anglo-Catholic School of Sociology on *Marxism and Christianity*. The School was the child of Maurice Reckett and the 'Christendom Group'. It introduced Trevor to people like Canon V.A. Demant and the notorious Conrad Noel, Vicar of the 'Red' Church of Thaxted. T.S. Eliot and Nicholas Berdyaev addressed the conference.

It was all a bit beyond Trevor, but gave him the conviction that the Church – and especially the Catholic wing of its Anglican branch – had a real and powerful contribution to make in the modern world.

There was one other incident in Trevor's years at Oxford that had a life-long effect on him. Miles Sargent enticed him to go on a mission to Bournemouth. The mission was largely the initiative of Max Warren, later head of the Church Missionary Society. Mervyn Stockwood, as yet unordained, was also lured to help him with the mission. The chief missioners were Canon Bryan Green and Fr Harold Ellis CR. One of the assistant missioners was the Mirfield novice, Andrew Blair, who had been a curate at St Mark's, Swindon, where – it was no coincidence – Trevor would serve his title. Trevor was billeted with Andrew Blair on a Mrs Smythe, a wealthy widow woman, who sustained them both with an ever memorable abundance of whisky and soda – so beginning a habit of 'sundowners' which Trevor continued to his last days. There is no doubt that it was from the days of the Mission to Bournemouth that Trevor warmly entertained the thought of Mirfield and the Community of the Resurrection. Harold Ellis became his spiritual director from that time, and would write to Trevor each week, having given him a strict rule of prayer, daily offices and daily Mass. Soon after the Mission, Trevor made his first visit to Mirfield.

The meeting Trevor most remembered from that visit was with the Superior, Fr Keble Talbot. Fr Talbot was no narrow ecclesiastic. The son of Edward Stuart Talbot, Bishop of Rochester and Southwark, and, later, Winchester, he cherished all that was best in the religion and culture of his day: books, painting, music and not least, splendid talk. At their first meeting, Trevor and Fr Talbot were talking together when Fr Talbot stopped in his tracks and said, suddenly, 'You know, what will be most demanding for you will be having no children.' Trevor was, at the time, surprised by the remark, but in later years came to realize just how perceptive it was.

Trevor celebrated his 21st birthday in the June that he went down from Oxford – 1934. His father had married again, and was not happy with his son's choice of a future career. He saw it as the desire of an inexperienced young man to be a priest rather than a sailor – like him – and, more recently, a monk. He encouraged Trevor to set sail and see the world. So, immediately after his birthday, Trevor embarked on a freighter for Ceylon. There he joined the Vicar of St Michael's, Colombo, John Hardy, travelling in Ceylon for four months, and travelling thence to Burma. After their journey together, Trevor went on to visit many of the cities of India he'd heard so much about from his parents. Finally, he sailed to the Holy Land, to spend Holy Week and Easter there. It was the year that H.V. Morton's *In the Steps of the Master* was published, and Trevor found it an invaluable companion. But he was also travelling there in the steps of Charles de Foucauld; René Bazin's book on de Foucauld was another that was a great influence on him. The memory of the two words JESUS-CARITAS painted on the door of de Foucauld's hermitage at Beni-Abbas would remain imprinted on Trevor's memory for the rest of his life, as would de Foucauld's injunction to himself and his followers: 'Be kind and compassionate. Let no distress leave you unmoved.'

It was in the summer of 1935 that Trevor, having completed his 'Grand Tour', began his training for ordination at Wells Theological College. It has to be said that the 'Grand Tour' had certainly not achieved the change of heart his father had hoped for.

The Palace, the deanery, and the college at Wells were still in those days rather Trollopian. The ordinands were more concerned with shootin', huntin' and fishin' than with theology and the soul. The bishop, St John Willson, had been a public school headmaster most of his life. The dean went about in a top hat and frock coat and was verged each afternoon from the deanery to the Cathedral – which led one irreverent observer to exclaim; 'Doesn't the old bugger know his way yet?'

There was one man on the staff of the college who would never be part of the Trollopian Church: John Ramsbotham, Bishop of Wakefield from 1958–67, Vice-Principal of the college when Trevor arrived. Bishop Ramsbotham remembered very clearly – in his 83rd year – that there was a certain 'hiddenness' about Trevor's participation in the life of the College. Trevor himself said unashamedly, 'I tried to make my soul a bit at Wells.' Having read no theology at Oxford he also needed to study hard.

There was one priest who had a particularly powerful influence on Trevor at Wells: Father Briscoe of Bagborough. He had known Trevor's parents in Bedford, and in 1904 had become 'squarson' of West Bagborough, in Somerset, at the foot of the Quantock hills. Briscoe was a somewhat contradictory character. In 1929 he had re-edited the *Priest's Book of Private Devotions* that was used by virtually every Anglo-Catholic priest of that era. He lived a life of astringent abstinence and asceticism. He was an authority on ascetical and mystical theology and was a leader among Anglo-Catholics of the opposition to birth-control. He was a diligent parish priest, but his damnation of what he understood to be sin had a fierceness and severity – albeit delivered in a gentle voice – which was a legend in the locality.

He taught that a priest who had surrendered himself to God could not share that life with a wife. When a priest married, Briscoe entered the remarkable record in his diary, 'One gone'; and would at once cease either to meet with or write to him.

Trevor would cycle the thirty or so miles from Wells to Bagborough on, for instance, Feast Days, to lunch with Fr Briscoe, who was to him a second Curé D'Ars. It is, however, difficult for me to believe that in Fr Briscoe Trevor had found the wise pastor he needed at that time, who could help him to understand and love the complex psycho-sexual nature with which he had been endowed – with which he must already have become familiar – and who would help him, in St Julian of Norwich's phrase, to turn his 'wounds into worships'.

Trevor was ordained deacon in Bristol Cathedral at Michaelmas 1936 by Bishop C.S. Woodward, to serve in the parish of St Mark's, Swindon. (Mervyn Stockwood was ordained at the same time in the same place.)

Swindon, in 1936, was a very different town from today. It was of one greatly preponderant industry: the Great Western Railway, which employed 12,000 workers out of a population of 66,000. The sound of the hooter when they got up and when they knocked off work governed their life. 1936 was still the height of the Depression. Several thousand Swindon railway workers were unemployed, and Trevor was soon to meet dire poverty and distress. It was a marvellous working-class parish in which to begin his work as a priest.

Many of the congregation of St Mark's were employees of the railway, in its offices and works. The church had been built in 1845, when the directors of the GWR saw the need for it and employed Sir Gilbert Scott to build it.

Canon Ross, Trevor's vicar, was a wealthy Etonian who paid Trevor's stipend out of his own pocket. There was daily Mass on weekdays, and sacramental confession, and, on Sundays, Sung Mass at 10.30 a.m. Trevor was one of a staff comprising the vicar, five curates, and the sisters – sometimes eight of them – of the Community of St Mary the Virgin, Wantage. The sisters lived in their own Mission house. There were five daughter churches, built as the town expanded.

The 70-year-old Canon Ross had spent the whole of his ministerial life, since his ordination in 1891, in the parish. He lived alone, was very shy, and had a speech impediment. He did not enjoy visiting or pastoral work, was eccentric and past his prime, but was generous and humble. Every Sunday after Evensong, the curates were summoned to dinner, and everyone had to give a précis of the sermon he had preached that day. It had to be short, and Ross would write it down in a big book. He would give a comment on the précis, which was usually acerbic.

Trevor was the fortieth and last deacon to serve under Canon Ross, who was succeeded in 1937 by Fr Ronald Royle – whom I knew when I was a deacon, as Vicar of St Matthew's Westminster. Royle was a martinet who worked the curates hard. He made them move into the vicarage with him. Trevor was not greatly enamoured of him, but Royle nevertheless remembered Trevor as 'a very handsome young man who got on exceedingly well with the railway workers'.

There is little evidence that Swindon caused Trevor radically to reflect on 'Church and People in an Industrial City', as, for instance, Sheffield was to cause Ted Wickham, later Bishop of Middleton, to reflect less than a decade later. Trevor the pastor was nurtured at Swindon. Trevor the prophet had yet to be born. He was impatient now to get to Mirfield.

Alan Wilkinson's marvellous centenary history of the Community of the Resurrection and Nicholas Mosley's biography of Raymond Raynes provide us with all the background we need to know to the Community into which Trevor was entering. But let me underline that at the turn of the century the CR had been wanting to get away from London and Oxford to the North, and Walsham How, first Bishop of Wakefield, had suggested a house he had refused as his Bishop's Palace, Hall Croft, at Mirfield, an ugly stone building that had belonged to a rich mill-owner. The advantage of Mirfield was that it was in the middle of the industrial area of Leeds and Huddersfield. The Community moved there in 1898. The new Superior, after Gore, was Walter Howard Frere, who was Superior from 1903–22. The college was founded in 1902, and, later, set up a hostel in Leeds. The second step was in South Africa, to which the Community sent three brothers, also in 1902. In 1923 Frere became Bishop of Truro, and Talbot was appointed Superior.

The testing of Trevor's vocation meant first that he must go to Mirfield and stay there – go there, able-bodied, in June 1939, 26 years of age, and stay there – when every other able-bodied young man was being called up: first, through the months of the gathering storm before the Second World

War; then through the months of the 'phoney war'; then through the fateful years of Dunkirk and the fall of France, the threat of invasion (Britain's 'darkest hour'), the Battle of Britain, and the 'blitz'. All this time Trevor had to believe, and go on believing, that his post, in the Providence of God, was at Mirfield. When Nehemiah was building the walls of Jerusalem, his enemies sought to draw him away from the work, but he replied: 'I am doing a great work, so that I cannot come down.' The testing of Trevor's vocation was, first, to believe that, cut off from the war at Mirfield, he was, nevertheless, in the right place, and must not 'come down'.

'When Trevor arrived', Fr Hugh Bishop, one of his fellow novices wrote, 'he was dangerously near to being the perfect novice. He never did anything wrong. He would always do anything he could to help people.' Trevor seemed to Hugh to be 'censoring the things he said before the words came out of his mouth'. When Hugh, who later went to war as a chaplain, was taken prisoner in North Africa, Trevor was given the duty of writing to him once a week in his prison camp.

Harold Ellis, the new Novice Guardian, was a simple sort of man, the son of an Evangelical clergyman who had become an extreme Anglo-Catholic; he was himself a papalist Anglo-Catholic. He was the kind of preacher given to gestures, and, in his daily life, remained a preacher who was something of an actor. He was also given to dramatic aphorisms. 'To preach, all you need is the Bible and Spurgeon's sermons', he would say. And, 'Every true Religious has a shaven head' – so Trevor's head was shaven. 'The good novice', he said, 'leaps as if on fire at the sound of the rising bell.' Fr Ellis would speak of 'my novices'. He encouraged Trevor to devote much time and care to a study of the life and writings of William, the twelfth-century abbot of St Thierry. A characteristic saying of William's, which left its mark on Trevor, was, 'The love of truth drives us from the world to God; and the truth of love drives us from God to the world.'

Fr Ellis was clearly fond of Trevor. Fr Mark Tweedy, who was a novice with Trevor, remembered a retreatant at Mirfield asking him concerning the monk, with a white scapular, who had served them at lunch: 'Who is that young man with the face of an angel who would gladly go to the fires of Smithfield?'

On St Mark's Day, April 1941, Trevor was professed as a full member of the Community. His father could not be there because of the war, but, in any case, he was deeply troubled about the life his son had chosen. Trevor had no doubts.

It was in January 1943 that Raymond Raynes – then Prior of the Community's South Africa House and parish priest of Sophiatown, Johannesburg – was elected Superior of the Community. The day he arrived back at Mirfield, after acting as a chaplain on board a troop-ship, and spending Holy Week and Easter at sea, he arrived without warning. Trevor was on kitchen duty that day – *servitor* – so also answered the doorbell. Trevor said, 'There was Fr Raynes, looking like death. I knew who it was from his photographs. He did not, of course, know me. He announced himself. "Well, I'm Trevor," I said.'

Soon after, Raymond took to his bed, with flu, and Trevor was given the task of looking after him. The sick man was still relatively young – 39 – and full of ideas. They talked for hours about South Africa, with Trevor doing most of the listening. 'I was immediately captivated by him,' wrote Trevor. 'He was a very attractive person. From then on I loved him dearly and got to know him well. I kindled to all he said.'

After only a fortnight, Raymond told Trevor that he wanted him to go and take over in Sophiatown. Trevor said that Raymond must talk to his spiritual director – the Novice Guardian – who would tell him that he was too inexperienced and quiet a character for such a job, though Trevor had long known that the high probability was that he would some time, sooner or later, be sent to South Africa, as were all the younger brethren, to gain experience. Raymond, almost immediately, announced Trevor's appointment. The Novice Guardian turned out to be in full support.

Raymond had been perceptive with almost a sixth sense concerning Trevor's potential. There were, of course, those who thought the appointment rash, but since it was the new Superior's first appointment they were unlikely to voice any objection.

It may seem curious to us now – fifty years on – that no special mission-ary training was then required for priests. Trevor was unaccustomed to public speaking and had no experience of the media and modern publicity.

It was, not at all inconsistent with the role of the 'British Raj' in those days that a 30-year-old white priest, the product of public school, Oxford, a three-year curacy in working-class Swindon, and four cloistered years in community, as a monk at Mirfield, should be sent out, untried and untrained, to take charge of a huge parish of 60,000 Africans at Sophiatown and another 40,000 miles away at Orlando, and head up the team of workers, because, supremely, he was the Superior's choice. On the one hand the risk was huge and the gamble great; on the other, it was virtually impossible to describe the actuality of Sophiatown and Orlando, let alone train for it. Trevor was being thrown in at the deep end. He would sink or swim.

To put the situation thus is, of course, to put it 'humanly speaking'; but, in the end, that is the only way we can put it. Trevor himself did not believe the decision was simply his, or even his and his Superior's. He himself had been praying day after day, and for four years: 'O thou that hast prepared a place for my soul, prepare my soul for that place . . .'

Trevor's ship, the *Themistocles* had to sail in convoy from Liverpool. As soon as he had got on board, he tossed his gas mask over the side, in a gesture that signified his resolve to put the past behind him. But the past was not so easily dismissed. There was still a war on. Off Portugal, the convoy was bombed. Trevor had the alarming experience of seeing another ship in the convoy sunk, and his narrowly missed. Then the engine of the *Themistocles* broke down, and it had to drop out of convoy and limp into Freetown, Sierra Leone. Out of convoy, the journey was even more hazardous. Trevor was seven weeks at sea. This son of a commander of the Royal Indian Navy had never really enjoyed travelling by sea, and it was a man much relieved and thankful who eventually arrived at Capetown, 'the haven where he would be'.

What became of Trevor in South Africa he has, of course, written himself in *Naught for Your Comfort*, published in 1956. If you are interested in him you will, no doubt, have read or will read it. It would be impertinent of me to think I could improve upon it.

But there is one paragraph that Archbishop Tutu has written recently which I think speaks volumes:

> If Trevor wore a white cassock, it did not remain clean for long, as he
> trundled the dusty streets of Sophiatown, with little urchins and
> grubby fingers always waiting to touch him, and calling out 'Fader',

with obvious affection in their little voices. He loved us –
tremendous! He was fond of letting you sit on his lap, and in 1978,
when I told people at the Lambeth Conference that I used to sit on
Trevor's lap, they looked at me, looking so decrepit, and him still
very sprightly, and I don't think they believed me.

When I was engaged in writing the South Africa chapter of Trevor's life,
a BBC correspondent approached me with the question: 'Is there one
incident in that period which sums up the South African years of Trevor?'
I thought hard, and made my selection and asked Trevor whether he
approved. I was gratified that Trevor warmly approved. Here is my record
of my that crucial incident:

The 28 June 1953 was a Sophiatown Sunday like so many other
Sophiatown Sundays. The weather was bright and clear, for
Johannesburg is six thousand feet above sea level. But it was also a
very special and significant Sunday, and the people of Sophiatown
knew it. The 'authorities' had announced their Western Areas
Removal Scheme. Sophiatown was to be the first area removed. In
some ways the scheme could be said to be 'slum clearance'.
Sophiatown was undoubtedly, by many definitions, a slum: a shanty-
town slum; but it was also one of the few areas where it was open to
the people to occupy their own *freehold* property. Those rights were
to be not only ignored but trampled upon. 60,000 people were to be
removed. That removal was not because of some carefully prepared
scheme of slum clearance, but because white Johannesburg had
encroached upon black Johannesburg; so, with neither discussion
nor consultation, black Johannesburg must move on. That removal
was the direct result of the South African government policy of
apartheid.

Fr Huddleston had by then been in South Africa ten years. He had
lived alongside the people of Sophiatown as Prior of the Community
of the Resurrection. He was aware of both the plight and the
possibilities of the people as few other white men or women had ever
been. He had walked the streets of Sophiatown and visited the homes
of the people day after day. He had become their recognized leader.

When, for instance, the Odin Cinema had been built, just round the corner from the Church, it was Fr Huddleston who had been asked by the manager to stand surety to the authorities that all the legalities would be observed. Now it was to Fr Huddleston that the people turned when they needed someone to chair their Western Areas Protest Committee, and its inaugural meeting that Sunday morning – in the Odin Cinema.

Fr Huddleston hurried to the cinema when Mass was over. When he arrived, there were already over a thousand people filling the cinema, and more outside. When he reached the vestibule he was confronted by a group of Europeans who said they were the CID. They were arguing with Indians and Africans, and asserting that they, the CID, had every right to be there. With great presence of mind, Fr Huddleston quietly slipped into a neighbouring shop and phoned a friend in the law, Harry Bloom QC, who confirmed that the CID had no such right. Fr Huddleston returned to the cinema and requested them to leave, which, very reluctantly, they did; and the meeting began.

It was just after Fr Huddleston had finished speaking that the entrance doors burst open, and a body of police marched up the centre aisle of the cinema and on to the stage, and arrested Yusuf Cachalia, a prominent leader of the Indian Congress. Outraged, the people rose to their feet and exploded with anger. Fr Huddleston was well aware of the acute danger of the situation and the possibility of violence. He knew he must deal with the police. But at the door of the cinema he was confronted by a policeman with a tommy-gun at the ready. Several more police were in the foyer, and outside were a hundred or more armed African police. The people inside the cinema could have rushed the door – on to the tommy-gun; and the result would probably have been a massacre. Fr Huddleston protested to the officer-in-charge and tried to make him see reason, but was himself threatened with arrest. 'If you will call off the police, I will see that the meeting ends peacefully', he promised. Fr Huddleston could secure a disciplined response from the people, but the police had not yet finished their work.

In 1952, Walter Sisulu and Nelson Mandela and seventeen others had been tried under the Suppression of Communism Act, and had been sentenced in December 1952 to nine months imprisonment – reduced to six months' banning. The ban had only expired that week. When the police spotted Mandela and Sisulu outside the cinema they attempted to arrest them. Fr Huddleston again threw himself in front of the police and told them 'You cannot do that! They have only just been released.' His action was decisive.

The people could see that his courage and determination had saved Mandela and Sisulu – at least, for the moment. And, later, Yusuf Cachalia, too, was released, when Trevor went to the police station; for there was no charge to answer.

Mandela was 35 at the time, and Deputy President of the ANC. Sisulu was 41, and Secretary General of the ANC.

The arrest of Yusuf Cachalia was of crucial significance to Fr Huddleston. From that day he felt the need to use every means open to him to make known abroad as well as within South Africa the fearful lengths to which South Africa had gone in the suppression of civil and personal liberties. It was no longer for him 'simply a matter of patience'.

The meeting in the Odin Cinema, too, was crucial. Fr Huddleston knew now he must identify himself with the African people with more than words and speeches. He resolved to join the African National Congress.

It has been suggested that this act was a fatal error: inevitably leading him into too deep a political identification. It is true that Fr Huddleston at that time – not for the first or the last time – felt that the Church was distant from the problems of the people of Sophiatown. It is true that even some members of his own Community did not understand, and felt he was 'going too far' in politics. To Trevor Huddleston his action was as much spiritual as political. 'For the Christian,' he wrote, 'it is this mystery of identification which finds its expression in the Stable of Bethlehem – God Almighty and Eternal, identifying himself with man at his most helpless, with man in his utter littleness and poverty. Surely, if the Incarnation means anything at all, it must mean the breaking down of barriers not by words but by deeds, by acts, by *identification*.'

There's just one other event of his South African years I want to discuss, which concerned both Trevor and his Superior, Raymond Raynes: the removal of Trevor from South Africa, which Trevor never accepted as right, though he obeyed his Superior's orders.

In the years he had been in South Africa, Trevor had changed from the 30-year-old innocent abroad to the experienced man of the world. He was now a South African citizen, and Johannesburg, where he lived, was home. Each day in his recitation of the Daily Office he said Psalm 119 verse 96: 'I see that all things come to an end: but thy commandment is exceeding broad.' But he never envisaged his time in South Africa coming to an end.

There were two people who had the power to effect such a termination. The first was the Superior of his Community, Raymond Raynes; the second, the Archbishop of Cape Town, Geoffrey Clayton (who had been Trevor's bishop in Johannesburg), who held the position of Visitor to the Community of the Resurrection. There was, in fact, a good deal of cooperation between the Visitor and the Superior.

Nicholas Mosley, in his *Life of Raymond Raynes*, writes:

> [Raynes] . . . backed up Father Huddleston in everything he had done and he knew he would have done the same himself. It was sometimes difficult for him to remember that as Fr Huddleston's Superior he had a responsibility towards him beyond that of being wholeheartedly on his side. It so happened that in 1955 the Community found themselves in need of a new Novice Guardian. There was no one at Mirfield suitable. This was an unusual situation. It was also a vital one, for there were a large number of novices, and upon their training the future of the Community depended . . . At the General Chapter of July 1955 . . . [it was agreed] to bring Fr Huddleston home and appoint him Novice Guardian.

Bishop Trevor never believed he was brought home simply to make him Novice Guardian. He thought Clayton had advised Raynes to recall him. This was, however, strenuously denied by Raynes in a sermon which he preached in St Mary's Cathedral, Johannesburg on 4 December 1955. He said:

Twelve years ago it was my duty as Superior of the Community to send one of its members to take charge of the mission at Sophiatown, and I sent Father Huddleston. I have no need to say much of what Father Huddleston has done since – save this – that I personally and the whole Community thank God for giving us such a Brother, and we thank God that he has so continuously and so courageously, yet with persistent patience and charity, witnessed, by his life, his words and actions, to those fundamental principles which are held and shared by all his Brethren.

In a remarkable manner, he has expounded by word and action the Christian approach to the racial, social and political problems of the world, and that in a country where they are most acute.

It has been said that his recall to England is due to the fact that I disagree with him or am embarrassed by his attitude. Nothing could be further from the truth. I remember nothing with which I disagree . . .

It has been continually and persistently suggested that pressure has been brought to bear that he should be removed; the source of the pressure being either Church authorities, big business or the Governments of South Africa or the United Kingdom. There has been no pressure from any of these sources. People must either believe me or not. On that I can say no more, save that, had there been such pressure, I should not have been much influenced by it.

There has, however, been very strong pressure upon me to reconsider Fr Huddleston's recall. I have been deeply moved by the representations made to me by people and groups of all races and of all creeds. I have considered them all most carefully, but I am still convinced that he should return to the home of the Community, for the work to which he has been appointed.

It is the duty of the Superior to safeguard the life of the Community in all its aspects and, further, so seek its increase, growth and development, and this, not for its own comfort and security, but that it may serve God and the Church more strongly . . . The position of Novice Master in any Religious Order is one of the utmost importance; a thing which it is perhaps not easy to understand for those outside. For long I have thought that

Fr Huddleston was the right person – an opinion supported by responsible people whom I have consulted. There are some who urge that, though this is true, this is not the time. They may be right: but equally the Community may be right.

In all this, strategy and long-term policy must not be overlooked, and to move a leader from one part of the field to another, which may appear to be less important, is often required. The decision to do so is no easy one, and no one is infallible. I must accept the fact that I may be mistaken. I can only say that I am seeking to do what I believe to be right, and to God I must answer for it. He is a merciful judge, who knows the secrets of our hearts. I know, and it is heavy on my heart, what personal loss to very many Fr Huddleston's departure must mean. Yet on earth and in the Church Militant such partings and separations are inevitable and necessary in this our pilgrimage.

Trevor felt that Clayton's threat to resign as Visitor to the Community 'must have influenced Fr Raynes and that the decision to recall him possibly related to that incident'.

Alan Wilkinson, the historian of the Community of the Resurrection, has given particular and careful attention to the recall of Trevor from South Africa. Here is what he has to say:

In June 1954 Raynes made a special visit to Johannesburg to see Trevor Huddleston, believing that Trevor would not be allowed back if he came to Mirfield for his regular consultation as Provincial. In December Clayton decided to resign as South African Visitor because (he wrote to Raynes) Huddleston, the Provincial, showed by private letters and public articles that he had no confidence in his leadership. Huddleston immediately went to see Clayton who reacted with unprecedented affection and, amazingly, withdrew his resignation on the spot. (Clayton's moods would change suddenly.) Huddleston reporting this to Raynes added: 'I think it was my fault in writing too strongly: I have been pretty "wore-out" by this endless crisis and said too much.'

Clayton had also complained to the Archbishop of Canterbury

(Fisher). In 1955, Fisher came to inaugurate the Anglican Province of Central Africa at Salisbury Cathedral. He had heard that there were two experiences he must not miss: the Copper Belt and Huddleston. When they met at Penhalonga, in May, Fisher told him that his methods were 'entirely wrong'. After the argument, Fisher proclaimed sunnily 'the score is about deuce' and insisted on being photographed arm in arm with his adversary.

Wilkinson continues:

In February 1955, Raynes despatched Jonathan Graham on a tour of African Houses. He reached Rosettenville on 23 March. Raynes seems to have already decided in principle to recall Huddleston. One of Graham's tasks was to test possible reactions. So he spoke with two brethren (Sidebotham and Rakale), with Oliver Tambo (who wept at the idea) and finally, in June, with Clayton, who reacted: 'He has too much to give; and what is best for him must be best for the Church.' Graham arrived back for July Chapter and spoke about Huddleston with deep admiration (such a display of unqualified emotion was very unusual for him). Though Graham was reserved and conformist, he understood perfectly how Huddleston's prayer and pastoral love had led him to make a stand and to seek world-wide publicity. 'TH incomparable' he noted in his diary, but recommended his recall. Huddleston was under enormous strain. Police followed him everywhere. They ransacked the Priory and took away papers. There was the constant threat of imprisonment or deportation. The authorities were waging a personal war against him. It was said that the destruction of Sophiatown was speeded up to spite him. Meanwhile there were seventeen novices at Mirfield; the Novice Guardian was 'a dear', but ineffective. So after a night of prayer Raynes took the most difficult decision of his life.

When the news broke in October 1955, supporters in England and Africa were dumbfounded. Some were outraged. They put great pressure on Raynes (who had also once returned from Africa against his will) to change his mind. Trelawney-Ross wrote to Mirfield that the South African brethren felt devastated, as if Montgomery had been withdrawn just after El Alamein. What answer could they give to the bewildered multitudes who were asking 'why?' and 'why just at this time?' Though some brethren thought Trevor too impulsive and that all the publicity was giving the government an excuse to take drastic action against CR, they all loved him. The official statement said that the recall was 'a perfectly natural and normal occurrence', that a new Novice Guardian was needed (which was true) and Trevor was the best man for the job (which turned out not to be the case). Raynes flew to Johannesburg in November. He told brethren that he would have been even more extreme than Trevor, 'the more brethren and bishops arrested, the better!'

No one who knew Raynes thought he was acting at the behest of the Archbishop of Canterbury or the South African government . . . Clayton's letter certainly did not cause Trevor's recall.

Trevor said, nevertheless, to the young Michael Worsnip, the South African theologian, in 1984:

> I was recalled, as I believe now, because the Superior of my Community felt, first of all, that I was in danger (because I would certainly have been among the Treason Trialists if I had stayed there). But I don't think he was so influenced by that as by the fact that he felt that my relationship with Clayton, who was Visitor to the Community, had made it very difficult for the Community to operate with me as Provincial . . . And although he didn't spell that out, I believe that had a very big influence on him. The two things weighed on him very much.

There is, however, one piece of evidence which I myself have come across which I think throws a spotlight on the Superior's decision. In December 1955, Fr Raynes went to visit Deane and Dorothy Yates in Johannesburg (where Fr Raynes had taught at one time). Deane and Dorothy were very close to Trevor as well as to Raymond. I myself got to know Deane Yates in the late 1950s and visited him and Dorothy in 1992 in Johannesburg. Dorothy kept a diary which she used as an archive for her autobiography, as yet unpublished, in which she wrote:

Raymond loves Trevor, and, having himself been in Sophiatown he knows the value of the work Trevor is doing. But he knows about the threats Trevor has received, and some of the numerous people he has talked to believe that Trevor could be imprisoned. He is a diabetic, and a spell in prison without the proper insulin could bring serious illness, or even death. 'I am his Father in God', Raymond says, 'and I feel the responsibility is awesome.'

Deane also vividly remembers the meeting with Raymond. Deane recalls he was in bed with an incipient duodenal ulcer. When Raymond arrived, Deane said, he saw how tense he was.

He did the talking and we just listened. It seemed he was using us as a sounding board. He paced up and down the bedroom, chain-smoking, and talking all the time about the tough decision he had had to take. This is so vivid in my mind, I could only liken it to Raymond's Garden of Gethsemane. I am still quite certain that Raymond was gravely concerned about Trevor's diabetes. Of course, there were other reasons which must have influenced him in taking the decision he did, but I still think that when Raymond talked to us it was the problem of the diabetes that was uppermost in his mind.

Deane added:

It is important to remember the background. Since 1948 the politicians had been making apartheid laws: now, for the first time, they were taking action (forced removals) in accordance with what those laws prescribed. We now know that they were by no means confident that the operation of forced removals would be successful. Indeed, the Minister himself was in direct radio contact with the police CO on the ground, in Sophiatown. Their *eminence grise* was Trevor, and they hated him with a passionate loathing. If they could justifiably get their hands on him, they would do so, and they would make this hated Englishman pay for what he had done. This was the fear of Raymond, and it was the fear of us all.

Deane concluded:

> I believe they felt strong enough to let him rot in gaol, and they were
> certainly thick-skinned enough to take the consequences in the
> resultant world opinion, for in 1955 the world, of course, did not
> know what was going on in South Africa, and had not taken steps to
> rebuke it. That was to come later, not least, through the efforts of
> Trevor himself (outside South Africa).
>
> It needs to be emphasised that Trevor's case was different from
> that of Ambrose Reeves, Bishop of Johannesburg, who subsequently
> was deported. Trevor was a South African citizen. Deportation was
> therefore not really an option. Or, if it was, it was a less desirable
> option for the South African authorities to take. A few years later, an
> Imam, imprisoned under the Ninety Days Rule in Cape Town, died
> mysteriously. His captors said he had slipped on a bar of soap in the
> showers. The death of the diabetic Trevor could have been similarly
> 'arranged', and, like the Imam, the world in time would have
> forgotten about him. That was Raymond's fear, but not only
> Raymond's. And the death of Trevor in prison was a risk he was not
> prepared to take.

Dorothy Yates remembers that Fr Raynes did not sleep at all the night he
was with them, because of his agony of decision over Trevor.

Sending Trevor Huddleston to South Africa is a decision which only a
few Christians in England have ever questioned. Withdrawing him was
questioned by multitudes of black citizens in South Africa. Yet I believe
when Raymond Raynes' reasons for withdrawing him are soberly
considered most people can only approve.

It speaks volumes of Trevor Huddleston that there was such approval
of his being sent to South Africa and such dismay at his withdrawal –
and that dismay expressed, in the main, by the black people of South
Africa.

There is no doubt that Trevor himself was willing to remain in South
Africa, *even if it led to his death*. There may even have been something akin
to a kind of 'death wish' in Trevor – even a streak of spiritual vanity. I say
that because Trevor knew by heart a passage in T.S. Eliot's *Murder in the*

Cathedral which I, several times, heard him recite aloud – as though he was giving himself a severe talking to:

> A Christian martyrdom is never an accident, for Saints are not made by accident. Still less is a Christian martyrdom the effect of a man's will to become a Saint, as a man by willing and contriving may become a ruler of men. A martyrdom is always the design of God, for his love of men, to warn them and to lead them, to bring them back to his ways. It is never the design of man; for the true martyr is he who has become the instrument of God, who has lost his will in the will of God, and who no longer desires anything for himself, not even the glory of being a martyr.

I think of Trevor as someone who knew that *in the end* he needed to lose his will in the will of God, 'no longer desiring anything for himself, not even the glory of being a martyr'.

It was such a person who left South Africa to become Novice Master at Mirfield but in fact became the scourge of apartheid around the world. It was such a person who, in time, became a memorable Bishop of Masasi, in Tanzania; and then, as many can testify, a no less memorable Bishop of multi-racial Stepney; and, finally, a much-loved Archbishop of the Indian Ocean – Mauritius, Madagascar and the Seychelles. It was such a person who, after 1983, spent fifteen years in unquiet retirement.

It was the unquiet Trevor whom I most frequently encountered, in our meetings at six-week intervals in the Vicarage of St James's Piccadilly, or at the Reform Club or the East India Club, where he loved to talk over a meal. I had little doubt that his unquietness was related to his childhood wounds, and the failure of his spiritual advisers, when he was an ordinand and a young priest and a novice, to enable him to understand, and love, and cherish the raw material at the heart of him.

So, when Trevor died, I never more fervently uttered the prayer – which I make again today: 'May he rest in peace'.

12 Spirituality, Shakespeare and royalty

There are at least a dozen reasons why I have decided to take as the subject for this chapter 'Spirituality, Shakespeare and royalty' and I feel it right to spend some time at the beginning spelling out those reasons.

The first is the association during his lifetime of my friend Eric Abbott with the monarchy. He was Chaplain to His Majesty King George VI from 1948 to 1952 and to Her Majesty The Queen from 1952 to 1959; and he prepared three royal princesses for their weddings here. He offici-ated at many other royal occasions, and was a much-loved pastor to the Royal Family. In 1966, Eric was therefore made a Knight Commander of the Royal Victorian Order.

Secondly, on some memorable occasions, my own relationship with Eric involved, let us say, an oblique relationship to the Royal Family.

I well remember telling Eric, in 1952, when, as Dean of King's, he was living in Vincent Square, and I, as a curate at St Stephen's, Rochester Row, was living not far away from him, how I had been invited to go, late at night with the vicar, George Reindorp, and the other curates – all in cassocks – to join the thousands who had waited, in the sleet of that February, to enter Westminster Hall, and file past the catafalque of King George VI, lying in state. The scene was unforgettable; the guards stand-ing motionless in solemn silence; the tall unbleached candles at each cor-ner of the coffin, guttering in the darkness. It would be a poor psychologist who failed to notice the deeply serious core of feeling that accompanied the seemingly endless file of people at that time – a poor psychologist, and, I think, a poor theologian.

But I must also record that the next year, the first year of my priesthood, it was as the guest of Eric, Chaplain to Her Majesty The Queen, that I sat next to him, in a stand immediately opposite Buckingham Palace, at the Coronation of Her Majesty, on 2 June 1953.

I have myself been a Chaplain to Her Majesty The Queen from 1984 to 1995, and have been an Extra Chaplain since 1995. That office requires one primarily to preach in the Chapel Royal, St James's Palace; but preaching without a pastoral concern for the Royal Family, and for its future, is, to my mind, unthinkable.

I myself remarked, when giving a lecture on the first anniversary of Eric's death, that 'not all Eric's friends who visited him were equally positive in their reaction to the galaxy of signed royal photographs with which he was pleased to surround himself'; but I was careful to add 'this was, not least, because not all recognized the profound theology of royalty Eric brought to this aspect of his ministry'. We shall examine some aspects of that theology later in this chapter.

I suspect some people still find it impossible to enter Westminster Abbey without recalling the tragic events of September 1997. On the day of Princess Diana's death, I happened to be preaching at St Saviour's, Pimlico; the church where, in the church hall, Princess Diana had looked after the children of the Young England Kindergarten. After the morning service that day, a young man of about 20 entered the Church, carrying a bunch of flowers, and with them a handwritten message. He asked me where he should place the flowers. I talked to him for a while. He told me how, as a toddler, Princess Diana had looked after him. He said 'there'll always be a place for her in my heart'. Little did I know that that bunch of flowers was but the beginning of an avalanche.

All that week, the Mall was a slowly moving procession of those who mourned the death of Princess Diana. And on the Saturday, there was, of course, the unforgettable funeral. On the Sunday morning I tried to interpret the events of that week to a village congregation in Bedfordshire. In the afternoon, at the invitation of the Bishop of Southwark, I preached to a crowded Southwark Cathedral, at the Diocesan Memorial Service to the Princess.

In the Spring Number of *Prison Report*, the magazine of the Prison Reform Trust, there appeared this letter:

> I am a life sentence prisoner . . . I am on a wing occupied by 100

lifers. The death of Diana profoundly affected the atmosphere on the wing, in a way which is extremely difficult to describe. The general demeanour of both staff and prisoners was certainly one of sadness and regret. Of course, there were exceptions. But those who were not touched by Diana's tragic death were an insignificant minority – even they could not avoid being affected by the sombre mood.

I spoke to many of my fellow prisoners about how I and they felt about the death. It was extraordinary that so many men, from so many different backgrounds, should be as united in grief as we were.

On the morning of the funeral, many of the men gathered in a television room and sat silently throughout the entire proceedings. I saw men surreptitiously wipe tears from their faces as we watched Diana's cortège proceed past the crowds of mourners. Such is the pressure to be tough in prison, this is a sight rarely beheld. I knew that I was not alone in inwardly weeping for the Princess. Just as Diana's coffin was commencing the final leg of its journey to her resting-place, officers started locking us all up for the lunchtime 'bang-up'. An officer came into the television room, took one look at the faces of the men watching the Princess being carried to her grave, and departed without a word.

Several minutes later, as the motorway leg of the funeral journey commenced, we all left the room to go to our cells. I could hardly wait to get behind my door to cry in private. I later discovered that many of my friends did likewise.

Steven Jones, HMP Nottingham

Since that sad week, there has been the service at Westminster Abbey to mark the Golden Wedding of the Queen and the Duke of Edinburgh. Subsequently, the mood of the nation, and of the monarchy, has perceptibly moved. I was privileged, however, to give the first Eric Symes Abbott Memorial Lecture after those tragic days, and what I said then provides the basis for this chapter.

On Eric's gravestone in Westminster Abbey, one of the carefully chosen phrases is 'he loved the Church of England'. I believe he would never have loved it more than when it served the Royal Family, the Church of England, and the whole nation so conspicuously, in shaping, in a few days, a service for the funeral of Princess Diana which voiced the inarticulate prayers of millions of people, not only of this land but of the world. Those prayers provide part of my subject.

So far, however, I have only outlined the easiest part of my subject. There are other reasons why I have chosen spirituality, Shakespeare and royalty as my subjects, and some of them are inescapably controversial.

Canon Alan Wilkinson, the noted Anglican historian and Diocesan Theologian of Portsmouth, wrote an article for the *Independent*, a week after the funeral of Princess Diana, which concluded:

> For Jesus, being anointed meant washing feet, as our monarchs did up to James II, on Maundy Thursday. Can we envisage a reformed monarchy anointed not for wealth and privilege but for servanthood? Though this is a Judaeo-Christian concept, it would appeal to people of other faiths and none as well. We already have hints of that concept in Prince Charles' concern for the inner-city and the unemployed. When things go wrong with hopes and relationships, we often react by wanting to be rid of the source of the pain. This is how many people are reacting to the failures of the monarchy. Ought we to abandon an institution which is woven into every period of our history, out of disappointment or a fit of pique? There is still time to salvage the monarchy, but there is not as much time as some in authority once seemed to assume.

The death of Diana, Princess of Wales, has been the occasion, but not wholly the cause, of many of the questions that people have been asking about the monarchy. But mortality is something close to us all, however much we avert our gaze.

Her Majesty The Queen, I am myself keenly aware, is less than a year younger than I am. The Duke of Edinburgh is but four years older. If the Duke of Edinburgh were to die, would the Queen, without the huge help of a consort alongside her, retire from the scene – like Queen Victoria? Or would she abdicate? Or would she continue to serve as monarch as devotedly as she has done for over forty years? And what would happen were the Queen herself to die?

The Prince of Wales waits in the wings, so to speak, though his waiting is both active and creative. And, in time, he will no doubt have his own thoughts about his role as monarch.

Prince William is now twenty-one.

There is another very relevant question. The government has raised the question of hereditary peers. There is, surely, a certain illogicality – even naïveté – in thinking you can raise, as a matter of principle, the question of hereditary *peers* of the realm, but think you can leave entirely undisturbed the question of the *hereditary monarchy*.

As we contemplate entering a united Europe, we clearly foresee a degree of union with countries which have other models of monarchy, with which we can compare and contrast our own. Membership of the Commonwealth also has something to say to our British model of monarchy. The idea – and, more than the idea, the recent living process of Australia becoming independent of Britain and free of the monarchy, rediscovering its identity – is not without its implications for what we used to call the 'Mother Country'. 'The isle' – this isle – we may yet discover, if we have ears to hear, 'is full of noises'; of voices seeking to rediscover *our* identity. Some of those noises may be made by people who are British and, say, Muslim rather than British and C of E.

Finally, there is the role of monarchy in relation to the Church of England, which Eric Abbott loved.

The title given to the Queen – 'Defender of the Faith' – is one conferred at his own request on Henry VIII, in 1521, by Pope Leo X. Parliament recognized the style as an official title of the English monarch, and it has been borne since that day by all British sovereigns. It would be foolish to think that the future of the monarchy could or should be discussed without the Church of England playing a significant part in the discussion. As the Archbishop of York has said recently, the future of the House of Lords begs the question of the future representation of the Church of England in that House – and, indeed, of other Christian bodies, and other religions – and the relation of the Church of England to those other bodies.

It would also be foolish of *me* to think that within the compass of a single chapter we can discuss at any depth most of these questions. I can only indicate their importance. And I think it is right to call for them to be the subject of public debate. But to call for such a debate without providing the public with some sort of study guide that clearly spells out the main issues of that debate, would surely be unwise.

I respectfully suggest that the archbishops should set up a broad-based Commission on *Church and Nation*, with special reference to the future of the monarchy. So far, the churches have been strangely silent on the modernizing of the monarchy, though, surely, they have much to contribute through what the Bible says on monarchy – not least through the prophets, but most through the self-revelation of God in Jesus, and the model he provides of leadership in his kingdom, in contrast with our all too human requirements of distance, rank, status, possessions, hierarchy (which, of course, meant originally 'rule by the priests') and what Shakespeare called 'degree': 'Take but degree away. Untune that string. And, hark! what discord follows.' Such a Commission would surely have valuable insights for our secular, multi-racial and multi-faith society. Gospel, kingdom, Church, nation, Establishment, monarchy would all be on its agenda.

I cannot myself lay claim to be a professional theologian, but I think what I should do in the rest of this chapter is raise some theological questions about the future of the monarchy.

When I first began my training for ordination, at King's College, London, we had a curious survival custom at the end of term, called 'Collections', when we shook hands with all our mentors, and they said words of wisdom and encouragement – or discouragement – to us. Eric Abbott, then Dean of King's, at one of the first 'Collections' of my academic career, shook hands with me and gave me the gnomic instruction, 'Think theologically, boy.' I didn't know what he meant, and wrote him a letter to say so. He asked me to come and see him and then patiently explained that he thought I had a better mind than I imagined, and that I must now bring to every bit of experience, past, present and future, what I was learning in theology. At the time, there seemed a great gulf fixed between the world I had left – of dockers and riverside wharves, where I had worked for seven wartime years – and the theology which I was being taught. But I have no doubt at all that Eric would want me to 'think theologically' about the monarchy and its future.

At the beginning of my training for ordination, I knew, of course, very little theology, but I knew much more than most people about William

Shakespeare, for reasons already elucidated. When I got to know Eric Abbott, I soon discovered we had William Shakespeare in common. I remember Eric saying one day, with amazement in his voice, 'Shakespeare knew it all, boy!' And that was, of course, particularly true concerning 'this royal throne of kings'. So when, in 1949, I first came across John Danby's penetrating study of *King Lear*, entitled *Shakespeare's Doctrine of Nature*, I soon shared my enthusiasm for it with Eric.

In fact, that study concerns much more than *Lear*. Through *Lear*, *Richard II* and *III*, *King John*, and *Henry IV*, Parts 1 and 2, Danby defines Shakespeare's idea and ideal of monarchy, and reveals his remarkable understanding of a true theology of the royalty of humanity.

Danby's study appealed to Eric Abbott, not least because he penetrated the mind and heart of Shakespeare through what he calls Shakespeare's 'inner biography'. He pictures Shakespeare, the son of a small farmer/leather-merchant/butcher/glove-maker, who'd lost both money and status in his country town, coming up to London to 'snatch at opportunity'. In London, he encounters an age not unlike our own, a society not yet outgrown, its standards come down from another age, assuming a cooperative, reasonable decency in people; God to be worshipped; parents to be honoured; and others to be used by us as we ourselves would be by them. That Old Society existed, cheek-by-jowl, with another, the brash beginnings of another age. In this New Society, even kings 'break faith upon commoditie' – what nowadays we'd probably call 'the Market'. Edmund, in *Lear*, like any outsider today, abjures tradition, crying, 'Wherefore should I stand in the plague of Custom?'

The king himself, the crown of humanity, the figure of God's majesty, his captain, steward, deputy-elect, could be deposed or killed, or lose his wits, or have his eyes put out. Kings could prove to be 'sneaping' kings; the crown, a wretched, cankered, blistered, hollow thing; the majesty of kings all counterfeit, their royalty banished or confounded.

The crown, Shakespeare knew well, had constantly to be defended, but not by mere assertion or assumption. No one's authority in Shakespeare's time could rest secure upon his status or his ancestry. A king, so quickly made, could be unmade as quickly. A king could be a king but have no kingdom. Yes, but if that is so, the questions have to be faced! What is it that makes a king? And what makes human nature royal? Shakespeare underlined the common humanity of royalty. I mentioned earlier how, in 1968, I went with Eric to see Ian McKellen as Richard II, and how after the play, as we walked together down St Martin's Lane, Eric kept repeating Richard's almost unbearably poignant words:

> I live with bread like you, feel want,
> Taste grief, need friends, subjected thus
> How can you say to me I am a king?

The question is, of course, rhetorical. It is, indeed, such humanity that makes a king. And Shakespeare employs a subtle play on words – '*subjected* thus' – to underline that it is the very closeness to his subjects which makes a king, ' 'Tis not vestures which shall make men royal.'

It is significant that in *Lear*, when the blinded Gloucester asks Lear 'Is't not the king?' Lear replies 'Ay, every inch a king.' But it is after he has recognized the sufferings of others, and gone through much suffering himself, that that is *now* his reply.

In *Lear*, almost everything turns on seeing. It is a play about blindness and vision, those two great New Testament words. It is about *royal* vision and blindness, and indeed, about blindness and vision in our royal humanity. Gloucester, blinded, thinks only of suicide, and seeks a guide to the cliff over which he has made up his mind to leap to death. He enters, led by an old man, who has befriended him. It is one of his own tenants, who, by plain intention on the part of Shakespeare, is almost exactly Lear's age. The blinded Gloucester begs his guide to leave him, lest the guide prejudice himself with those in authority, for helping him. 'You cannot see your way', the old man protests. 'I have no way, and therefore want no eyes,' Gloucester replies. 'I stumbled when I saw.'

When Lear meets the blinded Gloucester, he says, 'O, ho! are you there with me? No eyes in your head, nor no money in your purse? Your eyes are in a heavy case, your purse in a light, yet you see how the world goes.' 'I see it *feelingly*', replies Gloucester.

The authority of vision; of what you see; of what you can only see by feeling; of what you see by experiencing and suffering; that there is no more royal feature of human nature than vision. That, certainly, is what *Lear* is about. One of the most moving moments in *Lear* is when, out of his experience of suffering, the king exchanges the arrogant authority that comes from the absence of equal interchange and the flattery of court sycophants for an emerging humility. Seeing through feeling the sufferings of others, he utters a prayer which would have been inconceivable earlier in his reign:

> Poor naked wretches, wheresoe'er you are,
> That bide the pelting of this pitiless storm,
> How shall your houseless heads, and unfed sides,
> Your loop'd and window'd raggedness defend you
> From seasons such as these? O I have ta'en
> Too little care of this. Take physic, pomp,
> Expose thyself to feel what wretches feel,
> That thou may'st shake the superflux to them,
> And show the heavens more just.

Shakespeare was speaking then, surely, as if he had been addressing the royal family of every age and clime, including our own. The life of a royal family can never be truly royal if it 'takes too little care' of, say, homeless families and those on benefit. 'Take physic, pomp' is a wonderfully terse yet realistic instruction; but 'physic' meant to Shakespeare a purgative, and 'pomp' had also a more negative meaning than now – as in the Prayer Book's phrase 'The pomps and vanities of this wicked world'. 'Take physic, pomp', was Shakespeare's dismissal of all courtly pomposity that ignored, or was out of touch with, the social realities.

Lear discovers his royalty not in his riches, but in his poverty, his humbling and his emptying; not in his sanity and wisdom, but in his madness.

But Shakespeare's prayer is not only a prayer for kings. It is a prayer for us all. Shakespeare moved beyond the Divine Right of Kings to the Divine Right of Everyman – whose royalty is all of a piece with kings. As he puts it in *Hamlet*, 'There is a divinity that shapes our ends.' Or, as Edgar says to Gloucester in *Lear*, 'Thy life's a miracle.' It is the priestly role of the king to help the people to discover their royalty, the royalty of their nature; so that the king in Everyman responds to the king on the throne.

The words 'nature', 'natural' and 'unnatural' occur over forty times in *Lear* alone. Shakespeare had no naïve understanding of nature. He had struggled to penetrate the mystery of evil, as well as of good, in nature. 'Let them *anatomize* Regan', Lear cries. 'See what breeds about her heart.' And, bewildered by two of his daughters, he sustains his cry, 'Is there any cause in *nature* that makes these hard hearts?' Mercifully, he has another daughter, who 'redeems nature from the general curse which twain have brought her to'. That daughter is, of course, Cordelia. She reveals the royalty within her nature.

> It seemed she was a Queen
> Over her passion, who, most rebel-like,
> Sought to be king o'er her.

Often, in Shakespeare, you scarcely know whether he's talking of a person, or of a principle, or of a community – like a nation-state. One thing is certain, Shakespeare was familiar with the thoughts of those two great minds of his time, Bacon and Hooker, who had grappled with the problem of nature and society. Shakespeare warns us through such plays as *King Lear* that the future of the monarchy is not a subject that can be left today to the media, or to populist politicians on the make – or, indeed, to preachers! But neither can things be left just as they are. Shakespeare saw the Elizabethan playhouse as the successor to the medieval pulpit. His plays help us to think as profoundly as we can – and must – about nature, and the kind of structure of society and its leadership nature calls for; indeed, demands.

Shakespeare may be full of quotations, but they are not the sound-bites of today that will die on our lips tomorrow. He was calling us to contemplate the mystery of monarchy, on the throne and in each individual. He returned to the subject in almost every play he wrote. We shall not get the subject of monarchy right in a day, nor dare we use that word 'mystery' as an escape. Shakespeare asks sharp questions. He knew – as we do – that part of the problem of royalty is the court, the cult and class that hedge the monarch – for which, of course, the monarch is, in part, to blame. Security is the breeding ground of toadying sycophants. And few of us have the courage to rise above that excessive deference to royalty which defeats its object.

The question needs to be posed again, in our own time, whether the mere accident of birth can ever now be expected to produce a man or woman fit for the role that royalty requires with, from birth, the fierce glare of publicity on the heir's upbringing, education and development, and the investigative frenzy of the media that will accompany his or her making of friends, wooing, and so on. The relation between the private person and the public role, it must be faced, now makes all but impossible demands.

In England, until 1213, the monarch was elected. Maybe the time is returning for election to the task and role. As an Extra Chaplain to Her Majesty, I would want to pay tribute to the devotion with which, I believe, the Queen has served the country as monarch. Nor do I believe that now is the time for an immediate change in our mode of government, but it is surely time for a profound reflection upon and reconsideration of the role of monarch. The problem of hereditary monarchy is obvious and simple. The monarch *now* may be above reproach, but you can never tell what you are *going* to get. And there's not a lot to be said for such a lottery!

Shakespeare, in *Troilus*, said:

> Take but degree away. Untune that string.
> And, hark! what discord follows.

He speaks of:

> The primogeniture and due of birth,
> Prerogative of age, crowns, sceptres, laurels.

Bagehot, the great expert on the English constitution, said that 'in 1802 every hereditary monarch was insane'; but Hilaire Belloc – in, of course, a somewhat different context! – memorably advised

> Always keep a-hold of Nurse
> For fear of finding something worse.

Exactly sixty years ago, Kingsley Martin, then editor of the *New Statesman*, wrote: 'If we want democracy to work we must be sensible. If we cannot be sensible about Monarchy we had better have a Republic and try to be sensible about a President. At present we still believe that Monarchy best suits our traditions and preserves our liberties.' It was clear that Martin thought this would be safer than going for Republicanism. 'The advantages of Constitutional Monarchy', he wrote – in 1937 – 'are more obvious in the post-war than in the pre-war era. If we drop the trappings of Monarchy in the gutter, Germany has taught us that some guttersnipe (or house-painter with a mission) may pick them up.'

None of Martin's asseverations have been more quoted than this. Yet it is a somewhat pessimistic posing of alternatives to the Constitution – as it was in 1937 – or a guttersnipe or house-painter. A mature democracy like ours today surely can, and must, do better.

Tom Nairn, in his not unsympathetic study of Britain and its monarchy entitled *The Enchanted Glass,* published two decades ago, called his readers to look at 'the sociology of grovelling', as he surveyed the nation's attitude to the Royal Family. He looked at 'the royal soap opera', with the help of a fairly typical week of women's magazines. He examined both the illusion of ordinariness and the snobbery that surrounded royalty. 'The present ruler and royal family', he said 'have carried equestrian worship to novel heights of intensity, and show-jumping, polo and horse-carriage driving have all benefited immeasurably from Royal practice and patronage.' No one, reading Tom Nairn's study, is likely to think it a very radical idea that there should be profound reflection upon the role – the *representative* role – of the monarch, and also on how that role should now be initiated and invested.

The Chaplain of an Oxford College – a trustee, as it happens, of the Eric Symes Abbott Memorial Trust – told me recently how, when he played the recording of the 1953 Coronation Service to a group of serious-minded undergraduates, they were reduced to helpless laughter by parts of the service. Clearly much of what the nation wanted to say fifty years ago, and said through the Coronation Service, much of the nation can no longer say.

Edward Carpenter, the revered historian, and erstwhile Dean of Westminster, in his magisterial life of Archbishop Fisher – Archbishop of Canterbury, of course, at the time of the last Coronation – sets out with clarity and authority what I will call the 'Coronation Story: its history, ancient and modern'. He makes clear that the task of drawing up the

Order of Service rests with the Archbishop of Canterbury, but that, in 1952, Archbishop Fisher fully recognized his need of help, and appointed an advisory committee. Carpenter writes of the situation in 1952:

> The Rite was self-evidently medieval and as such its feudal ethos was felt by some no longer to correspond with the special and political realities of post-war Britain. Not surprisingly, therefore, many responsible people thought drastic changes were necessary if the Coronation Rite was to communicate any meaning to a largely industrialised and secular society. Also there were problems created by its exclusively Anglican character which inevitably led many to ask whether other Christian denominations ought not to participate, and beyond this, what about other Faiths within a newly emerging Commonwealth? Such concern and questioning found public expression in a leading article which appeared in *The Times* on 5 May 1952 . . . *The Times* leader writer was not the only one to call for a serious reappraisal.

That was over fifty years ago.

How much more urgent it is now that the archbishop should appoint his advisory body – again, broadly based – to begin work, while there is yet time, on the shape of the next Coronation Service, ere the reign of Queen Elizabeth II be brought to its close; work which should, of course, be carried out in the closest cooperation with the heir to the throne.

It was not Shakespeare, but the Catholic poet and playwright James Shirley, who wrote – half a century later than Shakespeare:

> The glories of our blood and state
> Are shadows, not substantial things;
> There is no armour against Fate;
> Death lays his icy hand on kings:
> Sceptre and Crown
> Must tumble down,
> And in the dust be equal made
> With the poor crooked scythe and spade.

There are two other facets of my subject which I think we must consider. Those who knew my friend Eric Abbott well will remember that he was above all concerned with priesthood. In the number alone of clergy for whose training he was directly responsible he was without equal. Yet Eric would have said he was primarily concerned with the priesthood of humanity. It was thus with the royalty of priesthood that he was concerned, and this led him to be concerned with the priesthood of royalty. Eric would have been the first to recognize that society has need of focal people, and often priests and monarchs fall into this category. Both are representative human beings.

At the time of Princess Diana's death, she was often said to be an 'ikon'. It was a good and important word. We were told that Diana was an 'ikon' of compassion, and this was clearly true. But, for the whole truth's sake, it will not quite do to leave the matter there. There were other 'ikons' of Diana. There was the ikon of her crucifixion in a Mercedes, after a journey at, literally, breakneck speed, along the Via Dolorosa of a motorway and concrete underpass from the Paris Ritz Hotel. There was the ikon of a Princess who, after the tragedy of her broken marriage, was understandably involved in a compulsive search for another companion and partner in a string of affairs. Ikons should neither be romanticized nor oversimplified. And, again, where Princess Diana was concerned, there was the complex contemporary question of the relation between the public and the private self, and its almost impossible demands. Richard Harries, Bishop of Oxford and erstwhile Dean of King's, in a notable article in *The Tablet*, called the Princess 'a mythic figure'. She was without doubt a focal person.

One of the favourite phrases of Eric Abbott, when talking to priests, was to remind them that 'the diaconate is never discarded'. He would quote the words from St John's Gospel, 'I am amongst you as one that serveth' – literally, in the Greek: 'as a deacon' – 'ws diakonwn'. Jesus took upon himself the form of a servant, not least when he washed his disciples' feet. Eric would say, 'Do not discard your diaconate. It is the human basis of your priesthood.'

New translations of the Bible have meant much to us in our age. There is much evidence that the Geneva Bible, published in 1560, four years before the birth of Shakespeare, meant much to him. And if you had pressed him on the subject of the royalty of humanity, I would not myself have been surprised had he turned to his Geneva Bible, and to the thirteenth chapter of St John's Gospel:

> Before the feast of Easter, when Jesus knew that his houre was come
> that he should departe out of this worlde unto the Father,
> forasmuche as he loved his which were in the worlde,
> unto the ende he loved them.
> And when supper was ended
> (after that the devil had put into the hart of Iudas
> Iscariot, Simon's sonne, to betray him),
> Jesus, knowing that the Father had given all thynges into
> his handes, and that he was come from God, and went to God,
> He riseth from supper, and layeth aside his upper garments,
> and took a towel, and girde himself.
> After that, he poured water into a basyn,
> And began to wash his disciples' feet,
> And to wype them with the towel wherewith he was gird . . .
> So, after he had washed their feet and received his garments,
> and was set down again, he said unto them,
> Wot ye what I have done to you?
> Ye call me Master and Lord,
> and ye say well for so am I.
> If I then, your Lord and Master, have washed your fete,
> Ye ought to washe one another's fete.
> For I have given you an ensample, that ye should do as I have done to
> you.

I suggest there has to be something parallel to the diaconate for every monarch to be truly royal. The foot-washing is the means and point of contact with humanity. The monarch has to distribute the Maundy Money, but the symbol has to be steeped in the roughness of human reality. However, whereas the priest can refuse his or her vocation – the choice is there – the monarch has his (or her) vocation thrust upon him/her – simply by the fact of birth; though, before the monarch is crowned, he or she must choose their future, or abdicate it. Abdication ought, surely, to be seen to be an honourable alternative before a coronation, and, indeed, during a reign.

The last aspect of this important but intimidating subject which I have invited you to consider, I would like to relate to the Installation of Eric Abbott as Dean of Westminster on 30 November 1959. Eric was himself the preacher, and it was clear that on this climactic occasion in his ministry, he was saying in his sermon things that were of supreme importance to him. There was one quite demanding passage in that sermon which I believe may have something profound to add to our considerations. Eric said:

> Our prayer to God is partly articulate and partly inarticulate. For most of us it is more inarticulate than articulate. I would appeal to the sense of the inarticulate prayer which I believe every human heart is making and which the Holy Spirit of God is seeking to make articulate in us, as more and more a conscious and deliberate faith is formed.

After the funeral of Princess Diana, and the millions that wanted to share it, I don't think many of us will be entirely surprised by Eric's distinction between 'partly articulate and partly inarticulate' prayer, but I think it is worth posing the question: what kind of prayer lies behind our thought concerning the future of the monarchy?

It may help to return again to Shakespeare. In *Antony and Cleopatra*, Shakespeare gives to Cleopatra, before she ends her own life, a remarkable petition,

> Give me my robe, put on my crown, I have
> Immortal longings in me.

There is, of course, ambiguity about that sentence – as there often is in Shakespeare. Why does Cleopatra need her robe and crown if her longings are truly immortal? Harold C. Goddard, in his great book *The Meaning of Shakespeare*, writes: 'After she renounces the intoxicants of earth, a celestial intoxication comes over her. She feels herself being transmuted from earth into fire and air. Whoever, as he listens to her, does not feel, in however

191

diminished degree, a like effect within himself, misses, I believe, one of the supreme things in Shakespeare.'

'I have immortal longings in me.' It is surely not unreasonable to suggest such immortal longings are inarticulate prayer. And it could be that the death of a young and beautiful princess, a focal person, a 'mythic figure', reminded many people who had never faced the question of their own death, of the immortal longings within them. That is what 'focal people' do.

I think it is helpful to ask what inarticulate prayer there was in Princess Diana. Our wounds can be our prayers. Perhaps the wounds of Princess Diana were her best prayers. I think it is no less helpful to ask what inarticulate prayers were evoked by the Princess. She was, Elton John made clear to millions, 'A Candle in the Wind'. And a candle is of all things something profoundly symbolic. In a materialistic world, it is light and life, yet so easily the victim of the wind. Of all lights, it is the most vulnerable; of all life, the most easily extinguishable. 'Out, out, brief candle', Macbeth soliloquizes. And it is significant, surely, that Solzhenitsyn, in 1960, called his play *Candle in the Wind*. In that play, Alex, the scientist become philosopher, says to Philip, the philosopher become scientist, concerning Alda, his cousin, 'She's a little candle, Philip! She's a little flickering candle in our terrible wind. Don't blow her out! Don't harm her!' Yes, the fact and symbol of royalty, of the vulnerable princess, can, like a fairy tale – a tragic fairy tale – provoke prayers within us all.

To call Shakespeare to our aid for the last time: in *Richard II*, Bolingbroke, afterwards Henry IV, has usurped the throne. Richard is brought before him, and utters words of great pathos:

> Alack! Why am I sent for to a king
> Before I have shook off the regal thoughts
> Wherewith I reign'd? I hardly yet have learn'd
> To insinuate, flatter, bow, and bend my limbs:
> Give sorrow leave awhile to tutor me
> To this submission. Yet I well remember
> The favours of these men; were they not mine?
> Did they not sometimes cry 'All hail' to me?
> So Judas did to Christ; but he, in twelve,

Found truth in all but one; I, in twelve thousand, none.
God save the king! Will no man say, amen?
Am I both priest and clerk? Well then, amen.
God save the king! Although I be not he;
And yet, amen, if heaven do think him me.
To do what service am I sent for hither?

When we pray 'God save the Queen', or sing it, what is the inarticulate prayer behind those oft-repeated words? What lies at the heart of them? I suggest that sometimes that prayer is specific for some member of the Royal Family, but sometimes it is an inarticulate prayer for, say, the future of the nation and its government. 'God save the Queen' may, indeed, be a heartfelt prayer, articulate or inarticulate, for the future of the monarchy – not least when that prayer is shouted in the Coronation Service. And Shakespeare's final question, put into the mouth of Richard II, is relevant: 'To do what service am I sent for hither?' It is an appropriate prayer, in the form of a question, for every member of the Royal Family, and for every member of the royal priesthood of our humanity. To quote Richard Harries, it may express 'the idealism that continues to lurk beneath our cynicism, our ideal of a truly compassionate human life'.

There is one more 'Eric' anecdote, with which I think I may appropriately bring this chapter to an end. One day in 1963, I came past Westminster Abbey when Eric was dean. Clearly there was something of importance going on. Official cars were arriving and departing; flags were flying. There were a lot of people outside the West Door, mostly black, many in national costume. I soon discovered it was a service to celebrate the Independence of Nigeria. 'Who's preaching?' I asked a friendly verger. 'The dean,' he answered. 'May I slip in?' I asked. 'Of course,' he said, and showed me to a seat in the nave. I wondered what Eric, Dean of Westminster, would make of such an occasion. I need not have wondered. The sermon was vintage E.S.A., and everyone, as they left the Abbey, was saying what a marvellous sermon it was. I smiled to myself – not superiorly, but affectionately. I had first heard Eric give that sermon as a devotional address to theological students in the chapel of King's College Theological Hostel, when I was a student. It wasn't that Eric had taken an old sermon out of the 'bin', dusted it, and used it again. He saw his theme to be profoundly true for the Prime Minister, Cabinet Ministers and people of Nigeria – and for the royalty of Great Britain, gathered there, and for the representatives of our government; as profoundly true for them as it had been for theological students. He centred all he had to say on just three words: 'Independence; Dependence; Interdependence', which, characteristically, he frequently reiterated.

It was a sermon which was profoundly Christian yet would speak as profoundly to a Nigerian Muslim. Indeed, that day Eric epitomized in his sermon what he had said in his Installation Sermon, when he had talked of appealing to the 'sense of inarticulate prayer' which he believed 'every human heart is making'.

On Eric's gravestone it refers to his striving to make 'this House of Kings a place of pilgrimage and prayer *for all peoples*'. It is that sense and that striving which I believe should govern the hearts and minds of those who, ere long, should begin to frame and fashion the service for another Coronation. It does not, or should not necessarily, raise controversial questions of 'multi-faith'. It simply raises the question of 'the inarticulate prayer which *every human heart* is making'. It is that inarticulate prayer which I believe makes it appropriate for me to end this chapter with those four familiar words of both articulate and inarticulate prayer: 'God save the Queen'.

13 The spiritual care of the elderly

I must begin by declaring a personal interest in this subject. I am 78 – rising 79. But I must also declare a concern. The title hints, even suggests, that there's a group of people who will neatly fit the description 'the Elderly'. But my experience is that there isn't – thank God! So I must ask, first of all, 'Who are the elderly?' They surely can't be all the retired, for retirement nowadays starts so young. Striplings of 50 are taking retirement now. And I really think it would be safer and wiser for me to talk on 'The spiritual care of those who are growing old'. Maybe they are aware of that, and maybe – for one reason and another – they are not. But what these days is 'old'?

Winston Churchill was 80 when he retired from the office of Prime Minister, and I'm glad I never had the 'spiritual care' of Winston! No doubt he was exceptional. But he reminds us all how differently the ageing process affects each one of us. His last years were a sad contrast to the years when he was in his prime – the prime of the Prime Minister. And those who looked after him in those last years must have been in special need of care themselves.

I suspect that all of us are well aware, perhaps all too aware, of the ageing process. And that fact has suggested to me the first quotation that I want to set before you for your consideration. It was read at the funeral of Bishop John Robinson, Bishop of Woolwich, and author of the sixties' bestseller *Honest to God*. John had asked for it to be read then; and it was read by Alan Hodgkin, the Master of Trinity College, Cambridge, who received the Order of Merit for his work as a physiologist, and so knew a great deal about 'the ageing process'. John Robinson died from cancer at 64 – a relatively young age. In his last six months he learnt a lot – not so much about ageing as about death and dying. But he had been learning about that all his adult life. The passage he asked to be read at his funeral is from a book by the Jesuit Teilhard de Chardin, called *Le Milieu Divin*. As a priest and paleontologist, de Chardin also knew a great deal about the ageing process. He died on Easter Day 1955, aged 74. He was someone who, as a scientist and a priest, was concerned with the evolution and development of the world, and of individuals and of species. He was also concerned with the existence of God, with the nature of God, with the love of God, and with the Cross at the heart of the life of Christ and of God himself. Here is the passage:

> It was a joy to me, O God, in the midst of the struggle, to feel that in developing myself I was increasing the hold that You have upon me; it was a joy to me, too, under the inward thrust of life or amid the favourable play of events, to abandon myself to Your Providence. Now that I have found the joy of utilising all forms of growth to make You, or to let You, grow in me, grant that I may willingly consent to this last phase of communion in the course of which I shall possess You by diminishing in You.
>
> After having perceived You as He who is a 'greater myself', grant, when my hour comes, that I may recognise You under the species of each alien or hostile force that seems bent upon destroying or uprooting me. When the signs of age begin to mark my body (and still more when they touch my mind); when the ill that is to diminish me or carry me off strikes from without or is born within me; when the painful moment comes in which I suddenly awaken to the fact that I am ill or growing old; and above all at that last moment when I feel I am losing hold of myself and am absolutely passive within the hands of the great unknown forces that have formed me; in all those dark moments, O God, grant that I may understand that it is You (provided only my faith is strong enough) who are painfully parting the fibres of my being in order to penetrate to the very marrow of my substance and bear me away within Yourself.
>
> The more deeply and incurably the evil is encrusted in my flesh, the more it will be You that I am harbouring – You as a loving, active principle of purification and detachment. Vouchsafe, therefore,

something more precious still than the grace for which all the faithful pray. It is not enough that I shall die while communicating. Teach me to treat my death as an act of communion.

It is not an easy passage. But it has some profound phrases in it.

There's the agenda, so to speak. And it's some agenda! How do we address ourselves to that agenda? Not by concentrating entirely on ourselves. We, most of us, still have a lot to do: a lot of work with and for others: a lot to contribute, and a lot of development of ourselves. But ageing means a new opportunity to confront the mystery of existence and the mystery of ourselves; and the mystery is personal: above us, around us and within us.

Shakespeare died at an age which, to us, is young; but it is clear that to him he was old. He could write about old age as few others have ever done. *King Lear* is, of course, his great portrait of an old man; and four lines before the end of *Lear* he says, 'Come, let's away . . . and take upon's the mystery of things as if we were God's spies.' I don't think that anyone will ever describe the spirituality of the aged better than that. It describes the final responsibility of each person's life . . . the great responsibility and the great opportunity. Old age is not a time for knowing a lot, in the sense of being able to give explanations and information, necessary as they are . . . in old age our knowledge can easily get out of date. But 'the mystery of things' means that the most trivial and mundane of events is touched by wonder. Wisdom is more related to 'the mystery of things' than knowledge.

There is a meaning to, and new opportunity for us, in the years (or months) that remain to us. There's an invitation to us to go forward towards the mystery – not by ourselves, but in the company of God himself, our Creator and Redeemer: God who loved us into existence, and loves us and will never cease to love us. But how, I ask again, do we address ourselves to that agenda of Teilhard de Chardin?

I agree with Helen Luke who entitled her book *Old Age: Journey into Simplicity*. I want to suggest that we commend to the elderly – not least ourselves! – that they say each day the Prayer Book Collect for the Sixth Sunday after Trinity: 'O God, who hast prepared for them that love thee such good things as pass man's understanding, pour into our hearts such love towards thee, that we, loving thee above all things may obtain thy promises, which exceed all that we can desire.'

That prayer is important because it reminds us of what St Paul says: that 'now we know in part': and that God has prepared for us, in his love, the other part of what in his love he has created us for – which waits for us beyond this life. And that it is the increase of God's gift of his love that we most need and most need to desire as we approach our end. That prayer takes us forward in a most marvellous way – forward into the Unknown – and puts the Unknown in a way which is neither threatening nor intimidating.

St John tells us that 'Perfect love casts out fear' and that 'There is no fear in love'. Fear and anxiety about the future is natural, because it is fear of the Unknown, but this particular prayer replaces fear of the Unknown with the vision of God's love. How else can we go forward to the mystery of God's love? Let me be practical and precise.

I began by using a quotation. And I want to suggest that every one of us needs to gather together a book, or file, or maybe a special shelf, or shelves, of various things that have proved helpful to us on our spiritual journey, and to which we can have recourse from time to time. It is up to everyone to decide what they want to keep in their file, folder, shelves: sayings, quotations, photographs, paintings, music, prayers, and so on. But remember: *Old Age: Journey into Simplicity.*

Alan Ecclestone, a notable Sheffield vicar – who wrote several much valued books, and who died in 1992, aged 88 – called his last book *Gather the Fragments.* That title reflects, of course, the Feeding of the Five Thousand: 'Gather up the fragments that remain, that nothing be lost.' Let me just give you one or two examples of the fragments that I keep by me. I'm not suggesting they should be your fragments, but I'm hoping that they will provoke you to gather yours.

The poet John Donne, who was Dean of St Paul's after being Preacher to Lincoln's Inn – and who died when he was about 59 – wrote 'A Hymn to God in my Sickness', which begins with this verse:

> Since I am coming to that Holy Room,
>   Where, with thy Quire of Saints for evermore,
> I shall be made thy Music: As I come

I tune the instrument here at the door,
And what I do then, think here before.

That verse, I find, immediately concentrates my mind – at all sorts of times – on spirituality, not simply for this elderly person but also for the spiritual care of other elderly folk: helping them to 'tune the instrument at the door'.

Gathering together our own collection of fragments means resorting to one of our gifts which I think becomes more and more important as we age: the gift of memory. Elderly people usually remark on their increased inability to remember names, which is, of course, true – infuriatingly true. Last week I was made a member of a club: the CRAFT Club – CRAFT stands for 'Can't remember a flipping thing'. Its tie is a series of elephants with knots in their trunks and their tails, on a blue background. But most people, nevertheless, as they get older, relish and treasure their memories. 'I remember . . .' is an important part of our spiritual care of ourselves and others. I enjoy saying to old people, 'Tell me about your childhood. Tell me about your grandchildren. Tell me what job you've most enjoyed doing. Tell me what you've loved doing with your spare time.' And seldom do they not seem to enjoy telling me. We need to turn what we remember into thankfulness, wonder, intercession and penitence – but not in any formal way. And all that we remember needs to be remembered within God's love. We must never let recollection of sin, for instance, be outside remembrance of God's love.

So our collection of 'fragments' needs above all to be a collection that renews in us our knowledge of God's love. People, friends, occasions, places – like gardens – remind us of God's love. And then we need to remind ourselves that we haven't yet seen half of God's love! (And again, the Prayer for the Sixth Sunday after Trinity can be a great help here.)

One of my very dearest friends was George Otto Simms. I went to his consecration as Bishop of Cork in 1952. That was where I first met him, and we became friends from that hour. After his consecration in St Finn Barre's Cathedral, Cork, the bishop and his wife and their five children – and I and Eric Abbott, later Dean of Westminster, who had preached the sermon – all played hide-and-seek together in the medieval crypt of the Bishop's Palace.

As I say, we became close friends, and when he was Archbishop of Dublin he asked me in 1962 to conduct a Quiet Day for the clergy of his diocese in Christ Church Cathedral, Dublin. At the end of the day he took me to a bookshop and bought me a copy of the *Irish Church Hymnal*, and showed me various hymns which he loved – most of them Irish hymns – ancient and modern. One hymn he selected that day simply *has* now to go amongst my fragments – 'amongst my souvenirs'. It's an old Irish hymn, versified by a modern Irish poet – Eleanor Hull. Here it is:

> It were my soul's desire
> To see the face of God;
> It were my soul's desire
> To rest in his abode.
>
> It were my soul's desire
> A spirit free from gloom,
> It were my soul's desire
> New life beyond the doom.
>
> It were my soul's desire
> To study zealously;
> This, too, my soul's desire,
> A clear rule set for me.
>
> Grant, Lord, my soul's desire,
> Deep waves of cleansing sighs,
> Grant, Lord, my soul's desire,
> From earthly cares to rise.
>
> It were my soul's desire
> To shun the doom of hell;
> Yet more my soul's desire
> Within his house to dwell.
>
> It were my soul's desire
> To imitate my King,
> It were my soul's desire
> His endless praise to sing.

It were my soul's desire
When heaven's gate is won,
To find my soul's desire,
Clear shining like the sun.

This still my soul's desire
Whatever life afford,
To gain my soul's desire
And see thy face, O Lord.
                    Amen.

The archbishop wrote of that particular hymn, 'It takes us to the heart of prayer and the core of faith. The vision of God will be granted to the clear-eyed, the pure in heart, who will see Him as He is. It involves looking in the right direction, facing up to Him with penitence and courage.'

I said just now that we need to turn our memories into thankfulness, wonder, intercession and penitence, but that all of these need to be remembered within God's love. I've talked about 'gathering up the fragments'. But some of those fragments will be what I will call 'spiritual rocks' . . . things we've gradually proved we can rely on: in which we now have unshakeable faith and trust. These rocks will of course be very few, but they'll be like gold – maybe gold dust rather than gold bars. In fact my gold bar is the love of God. You can take away everything else; but I shall always, I hope, see everything in the light of God's love. That is, of course, a dangerous claim, and even to make it raises another subject: the problem of pain and suffering and evil – especially for the elderly. But if Christ could say, 'My God, my God why hast thou forsaken me?' sometimes we shall have to say that. (Though it is important to note that Christ in his cry of dereliction still called his Father '*My* God'.)

I recently visited a friend of mine – a priest of almost exactly my age – in a hospice in Oxford for those suffering from Alzheimer's disease. Although he was marvellously cared for, the sight of so many ending their days in this way did raise acute questions for faith in the wise and loving Creator and Redeemer. It raised questions, also, as to the 'Spiritual Care' of such elderly people and, no doubt, it raised questions for those who care for all the elderly.

201

At this point I want to come at the question of the spiritual care of the elderly from another angle. I've found myself reading what I wrote about holiness some years ago for a dictionary of spirituality and asking myself: are there some parts of what I've written which should be labelled 'Not for the elderly'? I wouldn't myself know how to separate the subject of spirituality from the subject of holiness. Writing this chapter has made me ask whether what I said about holiness years ago I would say now – now that I'm 78. And does what I believed then have anything in particular to say to those who have the care of the elderly?

Well, this is what I wrote some time ago, revised several times following publication of the original. Ask yourself as you read it, does this subject change in old age, and, if so, how?

> The holy lies at the heart of every religion – and emanates from its heart. Lying at its heart, it has always an element of mystery and the unknown, that sometimes knocks us back and sometimes draws us on. Something in us recognises its transcendent and abiding value. It may evoke from us our best works of art and it may strike us dumb. It shattered Isaiah with a sense of his own sinfulness and the sinfulness of his nation; but the vision of the holy which he saw first in the temple, in the holy of holies, he saw ultimately filling all the earth as well as the heavens. It drew him, and called him, and empowered him as a servant of the holy.
>
> This sense of consecration – of individuals, nations, places and times – is the stuff of religion – but not just of religion. It speaks, for instance, of the truth about our human nature at its depth. But though it is something which is compelling, it can also be ignored and, indeed, betrayed. It can be betrayed by being ignored, or presumed upon, or merely enjoyed in a top surface way as 'religion'.
>
> Israel learnt that the call to the holy has also a very personal content: to do justly, to love mercy and to walk humbly with God.
>
> Holiness in the Bible reaches its perfection in Jesus, as self-giving love. He consecrates himself, and we behold his glory in his coming amongst us as one who serves; in his washing his disciples' feet; as one who prays; and, supremely, in his laying down his life for his friends.

The ancient phrase 'holy things for holy people' speaks of the Holy Communion as the vehicle of the renewal of the holiness of the Christian community – and of the Holy Bible and prayer – all having their part in our growth in holiness, and into the Communion of saints: the holy people.

The Christian idea of the holy has very little in common with a system of taboos. In the Old Testament the holy is often forbidden ground: the God you must not look at. But the coming of Jesus radically altered that. He is the revelation of him whose 'new best name is love': the revelation of the holy in a manger; a carpenter's son; crucified as a criminal. He was born and died not on days which were holy but on days which were made holy by the way he lived and died on them. He did not live in 'the holy land' but in a land that was made holy by the way he lived there. It was from the raw material of the everyday and ordinary that he fashioned his holiness. And for ever after, for the Christian, wherever we are, whoever we are, whatever the time and the day, that moment presents us, in our decisions and responsibilities, with the raw material out of which the holy has to be fashioned in response to God.

The holy for the Christian is therefore never simply the Church, the chapel, the shrine, the sanctuary, the place set apart that a few can penetrate but which is taboo for others. It is never simply the holy day. (As George Herbert wrote: 'Seven whole days, not one in seven, I will praise thee.) It is never simply the holy man or woman – the sacred ministry as distinct from everyone in their ministry. The place, time, and person set apart have their function as resources for our holiness, lived primarily in the world; but they are rarely to be thought of as the place of holiness – and so on.

It follows that most people have to work out their holiness through their marriage rather than through celibacy; through what happens when those we love are taken away from us; through the ordinary decisions at work and home that life throws up; in race relations and relations with those in different sorts of need, and with the people, literally, next door.

Holiness requires daily application. But if it requires us to 'work out our own salvation with fear and trembling', it requires us even more to remember and rely upon 'God who works in you, inspiring the will and the deed' – the God who is both creator and redeemer, the God of love.

Well, I wonder how you related that brief 'essay' on spirituality and holiness to the spirituality and spiritual care of the elderly? Again I shall be very interested to hear. Let me say it provoked some odd thoughts in me.

Jesus died when he was 33. He escaped old age. I wonder how he would have handled it? How would he handle it in my frame – so to speak. He 'tasted death for every man', it's said. Did he also taste old age?

Holiness means relating the past, present and future to God. Do I still need to deal with the past? Does that impede my facing the present and the future?

The death and resurrection of Jesus was followed by the gift of the Spirit; and the fruit of the Spirit is love, joy, peace, patience (not least with ourselves), kindness, goodness, fidelity, gentleness and self-control. That's what I need now. And the first of those gifts is love. It's the love of God and God's love that enables all the other 'harvest of the Spirit'.

There are just two things I want to say to you briefly before I finish. The first is that I write as a Christian priest, but I can never now speak in, say, a hospital or a school, without being aware that we are now one world of many faiths, and without therefore wanting to hear what representatives of other faiths have to say on the same subject.

Secondly, I want to say something very personal. Let me confess to you that what I have personally found surprising about old age is the element of surprise itself. Nobody warned me what it was like suddenly to have a stroke and to have one's capacities so changed. That happened to me and I've been very lucky and very blessed with my GP and my local hospital. Suddenly people start saying to you, 'You really must now learn to say NO' (while they still of course press you to give addresses on The Spiritual Care of the Elderly!). And no one warns you that you will be surrounded by friends who, like you, are suddenly being incapacitated. You discover, alas, a new form of busyness: visiting so many of your friends and contemporaries in their sickness, and attending their funerals and memorial services, which you wouldn't miss for the world.

204

I just never anticipated the number and volume of messages I would receive day after day. People ring up and say: 'Did you know that so and so has been taken into St Thomas's!' That's what being elderly means!

I have included in this book a chapter on Lancelot Andrewes. He wrote a marvellous prayer for those who are growing old to use at the end of the day – which I think can suitably draw what I have written to a close:

> Gotten past the day,
>   I give Thee thanks, O Lord.
> The evening draweth nigh:
>   make it bright.
>
> There is an evening, as of the day,
>   so also of life:
> The evening of life is old age:
>   old age hath overtaken me:
>   make it bright.
>
> Abide with me, O Lord,
>   for even now it is towards evening with me,
>   and the day is far spent.
>
> Let thy strength be perfected
>   in my weakness.

Acknowledgements

Most of the material in this book is based on essays I have written for various publications and lectures I have been asked to deliver. I would like to acknowledge the following:

St James's Church, Piccadilly for 'The house of my friends'.

The University of Newcastle for 'A working faith'.

Westminster Abbey for 'Eric Symes Abbott: a portrait'.

St Stephen's Rochester Row for 'A celebration of 150 years: St Stephen's Rochester Row'.

The BBC for 'Better to hear a good sermon twice than a bad sermon once'.

The *Church Quarterly* for 'A view from the South Bank'.

The Diocese of Winchester for 'Lancelot Andrewes'.

The Sydney Smith Association for 'Sydney Smith'.

Portsmouth Diocese for 'Father Dolling'.

Westminster Abbey for 'Charles Gore: the preacher'.

The Clergy and People of Stepney for 'Trevor Huddleston: from a biographer's chair'.

Westminster Abbey for 'Spirituality, Shakespeare and royalty'.

Southampton University Hospital's Trust for 'The spiritual care of the elderly'.

Index of names